A FISH HAS NO WORD FOR WATER

A PUNK HOMELESS SAN FRANCISCO MEMOIR

VIOLET BLUE

DIGITA
PUBLICATIONS

ISBN: 978-0-9862266-7-0 (e-book)

Cover design: Quirky Circe Book Design, quirkycirce.com.au, front cover by Violet Blue®

Cover photograph: Violet Blue®

Title font: "HACKED" use under Creative Commons CC-BY 4.0 with credit to designer David Libeau.

Interior design, formatting by Quirky Circe Book Design, quirkycirce.com.au. Editing services by jamegangcreative.com

Published in the United States by Digita Publications, Digitapub.com, inquiries to sales@digitapub.com (U.S.).

TABLE OF CONTENTS

NOTE TO READERS

The stories and events in this book are true. To protect the privacy of those living and dead, names have been changed, locations have been shifted, and identifying descriptors have been altered. In select circumstances, real people have been combined into one character. Exhaustive steps were taken to fact-check events, people, and locations, including the author's engagement of services by Striker Pierce Investigations.

Research included interviews and consultation with sources within the San Francisco Police Department, Stanford University, former employees of ArgoSystems, and merchants at businesses on Haight and Castro Streets.

INTRODUCTION

There are reasons for San Francisco's homeless crisis, but no one remembers what they are.

My mother was a hacker and Stanford engineering graduate. When I was a little girl, she worked as a radio signal jammer for a US government contractor in Silicon Valley. She was single, so she picked up a second job: negotiating the import and sale of cocaine from South America into the San Francisco Bay Area. My mother was a very popular techie and she took me to all the parties. Her clients made sure I had all the games and computer equipment others only dreamed of. I spent my days as a ten-year-old cutting and packaging large amounts of coke and watching my mother and her tech-elite companions unravel, until someone got shot and then everything fell apart.

I began junior high school fresh out of federal witness protection. By my freshman year of high school, I was homeless and alone on the streets of San Francisco.

The "war on drugs" was fought here, on home soil. I am one of its many orphans.

San Francisco once had a different name, but no one remembers it. Memories here are fragile. That's partly because we have always had a fairly transient population, but also because history gets algorithmically rewarded by whoever thinks those who suffered are whom deserved it most.

The problem is the architects of the future who have

rapidly changed this shining city have no memories of San Francisco. And that's a bigger problem when you need to figure out the difference between what you've been told, and what's actually happening.

* * *

While finishing this book, I visited an old friend; over the past decade, her and I worked together at local news outlets that include the *San Francisco Chronicle*. We were catching up over drinks in her fog-wrapped Outer Sunset apartment. I told her that coming out as formerly homeless in a city dominated by naive and newly wealthy tech workers is turning out to be really awful. Everyone has a story or opinion to test on me, usually to justify their revulsion.

She starts telling me a story. Recently she sat at a community table in a neighborhood cafe with her husband. A man walked in, came over to their table, and sat down, as if joining them. She described him saying, "Tall white dude. The skin on his face... it had this uneven darkening, like sun and dirt."

I immediately saw what she meant in my mind, I remember it from being homeless, from the soup kitchen lines of my childhood in Upper Haight. I see it now on men standing by the freeway onramp tent encampments.

I nod, saying: "His face was ruddy."

"Yes." She continued explaining the man's appearance: Big uncontrolled beard, but also, the smell. She described it as unwashed, as: "BO and pee." I'm all too familiar with that acrid, stomach-churning combination. I try not to let myself remember it too clearly, but I also wonder where she's going with this story.

I asked, "So, what did you do?"

"The waitress came over," she said. I expected her to say the uninvited guest was then asked to leave, and whatever consequence came after that. Instead, my friend said, "She asked him if he wanted his usual seltzer water."

I blinked, uncomprehending. Was this some kind of punchline?

My friend gave me a sharp look. "Violet," she said. "It was Jack."

As in, the then-CEO of Twitter.

Once upon a time, everyone in the world knew that San Francisco was where you escaped to be free. Hippies, anarchists, beatniks, eccentric scientists, sexual revolutionaries, LGBTQIA+ people, sex workers, AIDS crisis heroes, and thousands of others escaping persecution and abuse flocked to San Francisco seeking sanctuary.

I lived through my city's multi-decade legacy epidemic of homelessness. It wasn't romantic. It wasn't what you're getting when a frat boy app developer tells you he was homeless for a while because he needed to figure himself out. I wasn't homeless to take advantage of progressive politics or the illusion of free and generous services, or our weather, and no one panhandled all day to get in a nice car and go home. Yet the myths persist. For homeless punk kids like me, the revered pastime of running away in American fables hung over our heads like a cloud and choked people's perceptions of us like a noxious gas.

I knew the Haight had been through tens of thousands of runaway kids by the time I ended up there. The year of the famous Be-In, 1967, was when San Francisco drowned in runaways and the homeless, the family-less. The real ones. Not people from upper middle class families trying to "find" themselves -- or just "get laid" in a city synonymous with sexual freedom. Although there were plenty of those, and the many Charles Mansons who preyed on them.

The runaways that came to San Francisco weren't living an American myth of plucky adventurism. They were children and young adults who were running *from* something equally as much as they hoped to run *to* something. Decades before I was born, they streamed into the Haight daily, fleeing violent parents and communities, discrimination, sexual abuse, assault, stalking, and worse. The only youth runaway shelter in the Haight, Huckleberry House, was ceaselessly full to capacity from the day it opened its doors in the 1960s.

The point is, San Francisco's homeless epidemic has been happening for over fifty years. It was shocked to life like a folklore monster when the city's Japanese population was rounded up and put into camps then had few homes to return to in 1946. This was compounded by segregation and SF's brutal redlining practices. The second world war drew tens of thousands of Black industrial workers into the Bay Area for decent paying jobs in Richmond and the Hunter's Point Naval Shipyard. Yet because of segregation, everyone had jobs but nowhere to live. San Francisco went from around 5,000 Black residents in 1940 to over 43,000 by 1950, all forced to squeeze into a couple of neighborhoods.

Still, the Fillmore district became famous for its crown jewels: music, dance clubs, and jazz -- one of America's greatest artistic achievements, surpassing expressionism and inspiring surrealism. Everyone came here to be part of it: Charlie Parker, John Coltrane, Miles Davis, Dizzy Gillespie,

Billie Holiday, and many more. In our exuberant Queen Annes and stately Victorians, for fifteen years San Francisco's Black population flourished under the banner of "The Harlem of the West." Until the city of San Francisco, our city, destroyed it.

The head of San Francisco's Redevelopment Agency, Justin Herman, led the charge for "urban renewal" -- while on the ground everyone knew that "blight" was just another word for Black. Greedy politicians and real estate magnates -- usually one and the same in San Francisco -- were helped along by racist reporting in local papers that were all too happy to run hyped, strategic stories about Black crime. By the time Herman's public housing towers went up in the late 1960s, 883 businesses had been closed, as many as 30,000 residents had been displaced, and 2,500 of our beautiful Victorians were bulldozed.

At this point of writing this introduction for you, a car horn blared outside my apartment in the Castro. I looked out my Victorian's drafty, cracked and crumbling window and saw into the car. It was a parked Uber, sitting with its driver inside, the engine off.

The first time I realized an Uber or Lyft driver was sleeping in their car outside my flat, it was after a few hours of fretting that I was being stalked. I got used to it. I figured he fell asleep and hit the horn by accident, and I go back to my writing. The horn blared again, then once more, right after that, so I got up to look out the window again.

I spot a water bottle in the driver's hand. I think, ah, he must be having lunch. By the time I got back to my laptop, the horn jolted me yet again. I think, come on dude, and go look one more time.

I see him cradling an infant in his lap. Smiling, bouncing,

holding a bottle. I watch as another Uber pulls up, parks, and the mother gets out. She took the baby back to her car, settling in as he drove off.

* * *

San Francisco is home to 75 billionaires and over 8,000 homeless people, over 70% of whom are from San Francisco. For every person who gets housed in this city, my hometown, there are three newly homeless people. And the city's billionaires and millionaires from Lyft, Stripe, Y Combinator, Square, and yes, even Jack at Twitter, all poured money into campaigns opposing wealthy-business taxes to fund homeless services.

If you fly into San Francisco at night, you might look out the window. It looks like you've been coughed out of a puff of mist over a handful of diamonds glimmering in the ebony palm of an outstretched hand. A city of artful and glittering futurism becomes evident in spires you see taking shape as you near, hemmed in on three sides by water so dark it seems to absorb light.

If you see the glowing ruby arches of Golden Gate Bridge at that moment, lasering across the bay's black mouth, I promise you will catch your breath. It is as beautiful as the towers shimmering toward the cosmos, as much a sign of the wondrous technologies made manifest as this city promises.

Coming in, you see San Francisco's fog-softened grid of streets; they seem to melt down over hills, sliding to pool in valleys, seeking escape into the sea. You fly over SOMA coffee shops where once were sweatshops, where pristine, crystal-clean tech buildings tower over block-long lines for shelter beds. Above Chinatown, the oldest outside Asia, you glide above streets once wet with the blood of fortune-seekers, timelessly street lit by swaying paper lanterns. Castro from the sky is a chock-a-block of Victorians like a colorful quilt of names, next to Haight-Ashbury, our creepy tie-dyed Summer of Love hunting grounds for serial killers.

Gemstone streetlights are divided by crime noir shadows, the air is punctuated by moaning nighttime foghorns. You're high above San Francisco's symbolism of sin, its art deco pyramid defiant in the shade of cyberpunk towers, the birthplace of new technologies, and the afterthought of their effects. Below you is an occult jewel on the edge of a continent, glowing through tufts of fog.

Yet San Francisco is a cat asleep. Her whiskers twitch, little feet run along dreamland paths. Muscles ripple beneath concrete. This is constantly going on, geologically speaking, under San Francisco all the time.

Here, one of the largest natural harbors on the planet is where seven different fault lines converge. Ruling them all is the San Andreas fault, which chains Los Angeles to San Francisco, slamming to an end at the Mendocino Triple Junction off the coast of Northern California. This is the meeting place for three of earth's continuously drifting tectonic plates. Unlike other faults, San Andreas is so polished-stone smooth from earthquakes that the only kind of quakes it can really have any more are large ones.

Just beneath the surface, Transamerica Pyramid stands atop a shipwreck. This is surrounded by any number of subterranean schooners paved over for our futuristic downtown skyline. Nearby, a fresh natural spring burbles up from the UN Plaza, and it so surprised construction workers at the time that they made it into the fountain you can see there now. Across the thoroughfare of Market Street,

Salesforce Tower sits atop marshland filled with land and refuse, just like the Marina District across town. Both Sunset and Richmond districts were built on shifty sand dunes.

Maybe building here was foolish. Or maybe it was no less a risk than being ourselves anywhere else.

This is one of the most seismically active regions on earth. It is one of the reasons why the people of San Francisco who have any memory of San Francisco at all, constantly live in a state of disaster preparedness. Once, in 1906, nearly the entire city was homeless. Citizens who lost their homes in the quake lived in the city's parks. Until developers forced them to go be homeless somewhere else.

The United Nations has declared San Francisco's homeless crisis a "violation of human rights." Sleeping in Buena Vista Park at thirteen, circled by mansions and soaring views of the Golden Gate, I wondered how it could be possible we starved in the dirt while the most fantastic technologies fueled the heart of a shining future being made all around us.

Now I wonder how it can be so much worse.

Violet Blue,
December 2022

1

CONSCIOUSNESS HIT me like a cold-water slap. My heart punched panic against my chest and a hospital room took shape around me. A white ceiling framed by curtains the color of a robin's egg swam into focus. A busy city intersection blurred from memory's reach.

The room was quiet. I didn't know how I got here. I moved my hands, my feet. Sore. Squeezed my upper thighs to test for signs of violation. Not sore. Pinpricks of panic cooled along my spine. I heard a murmur of nurses grow near my door, then fade along the hospital's hallway traffic route.

I forced myself to take deep breaths, push the panic further down. A long plastic tube ended with a needle taped to my arm. I marveled at the creepy miracle of a needle in the crook of my arm. If I bent my arm, I wondered, would it stab through my skin?

Outside my room an elevator dinged comings and goings, punctuated with metal clanks and the industrial thrum of wheeled beds and chairs along hard floors. Patients whisked to destinations somewhere within the building's antiseptic warrens. My room was a closed container within these sounds. A place I hoped time and noise could stay suspended for as long as I could stay hidden in the hospital's machinery.

A nurse opened the door, stopped to appraise me. Her smile sparked wattage in large, heavy-lidded brown eyes, unlocked a pleasant map of warm creases in ebony skin.

"Hey tiger, I am glad to see you awake," she ran the curtains back to reveal an empty chair, a dark TV. She checked my IV, worked the bed's controls to ease me into a sitting position. "Now what can you tell me about how you got here?"

Moving hurt my neck and head, it all felt overbalanced. "I--" my voice cracked. My throat felt lined with emery board.

"Here sweetie," she put a straw to my lips.

It helped. "Thank you," I said. Her name tag read "Combs."

"I don't know how I got here. I have ... I think ..." I shook my head and immediately felt nauseous. My memory offered only pictures out of context, like someone's photographs found on the sidewalk. Double-parked cars along Divisadero Street. Smells of gasoline, vomit. An SFPD squad car. The sensation of being strapped to a board, unable to breathe.

The nurse must've seen my face turning green; I felt like I needed to throw up. She sat on the edge of the hospital bed and took my cold hand in hers, so warm. She was someone's mom. Someone lucky. "You've been in an accident," she said. "You have a concussion. I'm going to tell you what we know about the accident, but first I have to ask you a few questions."

She asked my name, my age, the names of my parents, my address and telephone number. Trick questions. But Nurse Combs didn't know that.

My name was on my hospital bracelet so I couldn't fake a cover story and slip out. Mom would be mad about that. Thinking about it made my head throb with what I would come to call The Headache. My new unwanted passenger.

I stumbled over remembering my address and phone number. Nurse Combs took it in stride. I remembered my mother's new identity, her new name, but didn't know her new birth date. I was pretty sure mom never told me.

My mother's rules of interacting with outsiders were muscle-memory: never pause, always have a cover story, keep it consistent, don't draw attention. I had no problem remembering all this, or that I'd never been told an answer I could believe about who my father was. And that my mother was a coke dealer on the run from a cartel she double-crossed, a former Stanford-grad engineer who kept her ties to Silicon Valley's tech cognoscenti.

My mother. Before she was queen of Silicon Valley's 1980s party scene, she'd been a radio signal jammer for the US government, an executive engineer for Valley contractors. Then, boom. Mom went from top-dog coke distributor to the equivalent of a middle manager after coordinating the largest coke bust in San Francisco's history. She told me she went to the feds after witnessing an execution-style murder. After that, we were in witness protection with new names, a new location -- but she kept her coke habit and dragged us both back into her old life. We'd been on the run ever since. Phone numbers and addresses weren't worth remembering for long.

Nurse Combs gently explained that thirteen-year-old me had been in an accident while riding what was believed to be a stolen Vespa without a license. I was going to school when I crashed it. Abraham Lincoln High. It was a long way from where I'd stayed the night with one of mom's friends, the woman who owned the scooter and loaned it to me for the trek from Geary Street.

The nurse told me I was run off the road while making a

turn. It happened all the time with scooters, Nurse Combs reassured me. An ambulance just happened to be driving by. They saw the whole thing. I went over the scooter headfirst and somersaulted to the road, landing on my neck and shoulder. "You got scraped up pretty good," she said. "Those tiger stripes'll go away though, don't worry."

Bits and pieces of the accident flashed in my head while she described it. I remembered some, but not all.

That was two days ago, she said.

Two days ago? My skin cascaded with goosebumps, hot pinpricks rolling up my back and down my arms. I kept my face blank, but swallowing my fear somehow added a layer of unbelievable discomfort to my neck, back, and head. Hiding my feelings was my art. I was so much better at it than mom, though she never missed an opportunity to tell me I learned it from her.

Now I was in a bed at Sutter Hospital. "This is where Dianne Feinstein convalesces when she gets her surgeries," Nurse Combs said. "She's got a giant suite all the way up on the top floor."

The nurse asked if I had a history of seizures. I had immediately seized when I landed on the street. No, I told her. She told me the concussion would give me short-term memory problems that would take time to come back. I would need to work on remembering things, she said, especially the last three months. Nurse Combs said it was remarkable that all I had was a concussion. With a wry smile she added, "It's your lucky day."

"Sure feels like it," I said. It came out as a croak. I looked from the tube in my arm to the IV stand. "I have to pee. How do I ...?"

"I gotcha honey. We'll take it slow." She helped me up and

over, step by aching step to the bathroom, steering me in like a rudderless ship. I felt nauseous, swimmy.

The nurse waited outside as I took stock of myself in the mirror. My short, dishwater-blonde bob had a new feature in the form of a giant scab where forehead met hairline. A chunk of hair was missing. I reached to touch it; raising my right arm triggered the discovery of new abrasions along my left shoulder blade, rippled tight pain along my skin up the back of my neck. My flesh there was hot and hard. I worried about my memory, where it began and ended. It felt like I was back in my skin now, whereas before I'd been floating somewhere up above my life.

I threw up water into the sink.

Nurse Combs eased me back to bed, helped me sip ice water, told me nausea was normal. My mother, she explained, was supposed to visit me this morning but something had come up.

Witness my surprise face. Drug addicts were exemplary at having useless superpowers, but chief among those was manufacturing crisis. All the little things mom never intended to teach me had so much to do with surviving her bullshit.

They expected my mother later that evening, she said. I had no answer, no reaction, there was nothing to say either way. She might not come at all, and that was normal. I had a lifetime of data to compare to. Like spending hours outside whatever school I was in as it got dark waiting for her to pick me up. I snapped out of my thoughts in time to see gears clicking in the nurse's head. Not much was going to get past Nurse Combs. That was good; I liked smart people. "Okay sweetie you just rest now," she said.

I eventually fell back asleep with the TV on very, very low.

Except for The Headache, I felt better the next day. There was a window in my room with a light well, and the muted grey of a foggy sky above felt reassuring.

In between talking to a doctor and the nurses, being moved around for tests, and being told that my mother still hadn't shown up, I started creating memory exercises for myself. If my memory was on the line, or sprained like a muscle, I had to remember as much as possible.

I decided to start with one current fact about my life and carefully trace, in as much detail as possible, how that fact came to be. I began with where my mother and I were living right now.

This was a pretty yellow house on the corner of an Upper Sunset hill owned by the Yang family. They were in China. Their belongings filled the house; jade green living room with a view to the ocean, bookshelves of tomes on topics like Chinese face reading, a tiny kitchen crammed with jars of rank-smelling herbs and strange vitamin pills. We'd been living in the house for nine months. It was the longest we'd stayed in one place.

We rented a room from their daughter Donna Yang, who eschewed her surname. She went by Donna Wild, her modeling name. She was a hard, high-cheeked, beautiful woman who enhanced her unusual height by always wearing tall black leather boots and kept her shiny black hair long.

I concentrated on remembering Donna. Unlike most of my mother's contacts, she wasn't an engineer, programmer, or microchip executive. She was a former limousine chauffeur in Los Angeles; the LA Lakers had been one of her clients. It always disappointed me how beguiled engineers like my mother were by the merest whiff of fame. When her and my mother went out looking for men to party with, at hotel bars or on the Silicon Valley house-party coke circuit, the first thing Donna usually mentioned was that she once posed for Playboy. Sometimes Donna and mom would take men back to their bedrooms and leave me alone in the living room with one of the guys they brought home, a total stranger. I only did what I was expected to do once. After that, on those nights I made sure to be somewhere else, like the night before my accident.

My mother met Donna while working together at a car dealership on Van Ness. Mom and I had been on the run in hotels, motels, and rented rooms, with shifting identities, as far back as I could remember. Right now, anyway. I'd have to circle back to that.

I thought about the Yang's house. Sutro Tower loomed above, directly facing our front door, the radio tower's red prongs always disappearing up into grey cottony mist. The house had a little patch of dead lawn. Its hedges were once in the shapes of animals but had grown scrubby from neglect. I imagined Donna's parents must've cared for the yard. You could still see a bunny next to the front door if you squinted.

My mother and I slept in the main house, shared a room with two twin beds. Donna lived downstairs in a mini-apartment where the two women smoked glass pipes together. They'd call me downstairs and put me to work. With a lighter I cooked baking soda, cocaine, and water until the little rocks were ready for them to smoke. I was always invited to join them. When lit, the smell of it was somewhere between burnt plastic and something sour; the acrid end of something foul and chemical.

I declined every time, but sat cross-legged on Donna's

king-sized waterbed and watched them get high. Next to the gurgling bed was Donna's special issue of Playboy. In it, she posed in a Native American themed pictorial, nude in a colorful feathered headdress, on horseback. I remembered saying to Donna, "I thought you were Chinese." She told me, "It's what they wanted me to wear."

We didn't have many possessions. I hazily recalled fighting with my mother over things she would take from me, like clothes, jewelry, or money from my purse. The cinnamon colored cloisonné earrings I loved, bought at a candle shop in the Haight, which went missing and then turned up on the nightstand next to her bed after a long night -- and how she made me cry for accusing her of taking them. The accusation was proof I didn't really love her, and it's not like I earned the earrings anyway, she said.

I remembered our location and circumstances just fine, though a confusing feeling of wrongness permeated every corner of it. The next step in my memory exercise was to turn the pages backward: How did we get there? My mind rolled back to the previous place we rented.

I came to an abrupt halt before cataloging and describing the images to myself.

My lack of memory wasn't a problem. I had a strong, bad feeling that I was remembering way more than I had ever remembered before. It was as if until that moment I had only ever remembered the surface of my memories. Pictures in need of captions.

There was a further, remarkable thing about these memories. I couldn't remember how anything felt. The emotions attached to the memories, whatever they'd been, were flat where there should've been feeling. Rationally, I knew I should've been angry or scared about what was happening at home. Was I upset before? I felt outrage at myself because if I hadn't been upset, I thought, I should be.

I remembered the doctor saying this might be part of my concussion. Emotional distance. In a way it didn't matter. Because however I felt about all of it before, I knew how I felt now.

I was trapped in a nightmare.

2

I SAT up in my hospital bed to meet eyes with a scowling nurse. It was almost time for me to leave. This nurse was blonde. Not the nice nurse. Her frown was most certainly a permanent feature. Her uniform looked like it somehow shrunk in between the time she put it on, and now. I clung to a false hope that this was the true source of her discomfort.

She asked, "Is your mother coming to pick you up?"

"Yes," I said

"You live nearby?"

"Yes."

"Is she on the way now?"

Maybe. "Yes," I guessed.

I know this interrogation is happening because soon she'll have to walk me down the grey smudgy hall into a bed-sized metal elevator and down to the lobby. She does not want this responsibility.

It's time for me to leave the hospital and my mother never came. My mother will most likely show up. I believe this because leaving me here might draw attention from authorities. Later I will learn that my mother stopped existing years ago, and there was no longer any way to prove I was her child. I was no longer legally related to anyone, and neither was she. I don't think either of us knew this. For now, we both believed she had to come get me.

One thing I knew, reliably: she was always late. I was stalling for time, as usual.

I wore the clothes from my accident. It was all I had.

Except for my belt. The paramedics had to cut off my belt. Earlier that morning, Nurse Combs told me about the belt when she brought my clothes. "I hope it wasn't your favorite," she said, and I smiled. It was.

My jeans, t-shirt, and jacket were ripped and streaked with dirt, spots of dried brown blood here and there. Nurse Combs didn't say anything when I picked little rocks out of my shirt before I put it on. Then she said, "You okay to go for a walk before your momma comes? Want to go see Feinstein's room?"

"Sure. Let's go see how the other half recuperates."

She laughed, an infectious rumble. I still had The Headache but being with Nurse Combs pushed the pain back a bit. I wished she had the same effect on light and sounds. The doctor warned me about this part of the concussion. I instantly wished for a way to turn everything down as we walked from my room to the elevator. Its ding hit me like an aural funny bone strike.

While we rode to the hospital's top floor she said, "You're lucky they brought you here."

"I'm glad I'm not at General, that's for sure. I hear they play Keystone Cops when rival gang members come in after they shoot each other up."

"That they do," she nodded.

SF General Hospital sat on the border between two gangs, the Norteños and the Sureños, who sometimes shot and stabbed each other in a park two blocks from the hospital. SF General also had its own live-in mental ward, a terrifyingly creepy, large brick annex nestled in a decrepit plot of sickly trees along Potrero Avenue. In school we passed around a story about three kids who'd supposedly stolen a tank of what they thought was nitrous, dragging it to the trees to get high. Each one took a hit from a tank of nitrogen, dying on the dark hillside.

"No, you could've been sent to Zion," she said. Mount Zion Hospital was a mile from where we stood. "You don't have insurance," she continued. That was news to me. "It's a good hospital, but they turn people away. When the Zebra Killers shot Tania Smith, she was right out front. Admittance made bystanders wait while they called an ambulance because she didn't have insurance. Ambulance took her to General."

I'd heard about that. Tania Smith died. I guess I was being told I was lucky, but it was some pretty dark kind of pep talk, if that's what this was. I decided I really liked Nurse Combs.

"But then I wouldn't be getting cheered up by you," I smiled.

She gave me that great laugh again. "Okay, okay, now check out this room." She swung open a door into a hospital room that was more like a studio apartment.

The amount of bright natural light in it almost brought me to my knees. Giant windows swept from left to right, wrapped around one corner of the building to make two walls almost entirely glass. A small private bathroom tucked into the corner. A couch, coffee table, and a table with chairs created two sitting areas. One large bed was positioned with a view of the San Francisco Bay. The unoccupied space in the room alone was practically big enough to park two cars.

"Oh my god," was all I could say.

"This is how the other half live when they're getting facelifts," she said. "Wanna sit?"

"Yeah. This view ... can we get room service?"

"You buying?"

"There's probably enough in the couch cushions," I grinned.

We sat together at the end of the bed. "So, this is Feinstein's room," I said. "I don't know much about her except she became Mayor after Moscone and Harvey Milk were killed."

"She found their bodies in City Hall," Nurse Combs explained, looking at the view. "She was a debutante who ran for mayor but didn't win, sat on the Board of Supervisors for ten years. Not a lot of friends in this neighborhood, not at first anyway."

"Why?"

"She refused to march in the Pride parade and vetoed domestic partner legislation. Harvey Milk didn't like her, that's for sure. She spent an awful lot of time shutting down gay bathhouses and porn shops, but that could've been more about real estate money."

I'd never put that together, but she was probably right. Politics here boiled down to corrupt land battles where property developers traded nepotistic favors with politicians, all dressed up in whatever colonialism was fashionable for the era. "Was she anti-gay?"

"Not after her friends started dying from AIDS, and all of a sudden, she was Mayor of a city abandoned by the federal government to die because it hates gays." That was one thing that united most San Franciscans; when faced with the public health crisis of AIDS, the government used anti-gay prejudice to leave us dying in the streets by the thousands. In response, we took care of each other.

I looked out at the view from Feinstein's swank hospital recovery bed, then down at my torn clothes. My eyes drifted back to that magnificent view, and I wondered if my drug addict mom would come pick me up from the hospital at all.

We sat together in silence, drinking it in. The view was unbelievable. Below us was Lower Haight's Duboce Park, locally nicknamed Dog Doo Park. It looked strangely angled from above, like the last slice of pie left in a pan with its tip missing. When lavishly ornamented buildings sprung up around the park area in 1911, it was a homeless camp of working-class San Franciscans made destitute by the 1906 earthquake.

I'd seen old pictures of that camp, a derelict collection of stables, tents, and shacks. It looked like a terrible place to live, a rock and garbage-strewn mess. Along with learning about our state flower (the California Poppy, we were warned in school, was illegal to pick) the rocks in Duboce Park were Serpentine, our state rock. It was a greenish, slippery looking rock formed from tectonic pressure. It was fitting because everything here was about earthquakes, upheaval. You could see Serpentine in the park's steps, from when the area's residents prettied up the park with an early-century makeover in the theme of "pleasure gardens."

My eyes tripped along the Victorians, Edwardians, and Queen Anne properties surrounding the park with their turrets, rounded bay windows, sunburst detailing, spindles, ornamental tiles, and "witch's cap" peaks. I wanted to someday live in a house with a "witch's cap," just because of the name at least, but not those. The ornate and stately beauty of the buildings belied the neighborhood's poverty and neglect within. It was rough down there, right under Feinstein's suite.

Everything here is a clash, I thought, looking out across our whitecap-dusted Pacific Ocean inlet -- I could see across the

San Francisco Bay to Oakland. This is a place of uncomfortable contrasts. Where homeless workers get run out to make way for pleasure gardens, where a blood-soaked gold rush saw smugglers and slaves making alliances, where the wealthy recline in glossy recovery boudoirs above an impoverished Black neighborhood full of heroin shooting galleries. It all clashed like the wind and sea I could see on the horizon. If you fall in that water, it'll kill you.

Back at my own hospital bed later that afternoon, I struggled to smile at the new nurse. She looked at me like I was a sheet she didn't want to fold. I was someone else's sheet.

Then my mom walked in.

When people first met my mother, they always thought she was amazing. For her beauty, her feminine business attire, and how much she just instantly liked you, put you at ease; she was quick and bright. Her charisma reeled people into her orbit, entranced. But most amazing of all were her performances. She offered the world a new one every time.

This time it was The Overtaxed Mother.

In the doorway of my hospital room, she seemed diminutive. Soon she'd fill the room. Undeniably Portuguese in the way women of Portugal are beautiful and handsome in their angled prettiness, her slightly olive skin glowed, her hazel eyes were compelling. Light makeup, soft taupe lipstick, giant tan purse. She still dressed like she was an executive at ArgoSystems or Interglobal, the Silicon Valley government contracting firms she once worked at. Black suit jacket, silky white blouse, mid-length chocolate skirt, sheer nylons that came in plastic eggs at the supermarket, and shiny high heels. She wore her dark hair big with curls and bangs; her style ideal remained Jennifer

Beale in *Flashdance*, but she looked more like Sigourney Weaver in *Ghostbusters*.

My mother spotted the nurse in her peripheral vision and a switch flicked on, a barely perceptible shift in body language; now she was rushed with a shade of burdened. Up went the volume in a pantomime of harriedness. My mother pulled her purse up on her shoulder and jingled the keys in her hand like she'd just pulled them from the ignition. It was showtime. She came in quickly. Everything in motion.

"Hey kiddo," she said breezily, smiling, like she hadn't been absent while I sat in the hospital for days.

"Hey."

"You ready to go home yet?" As if she'd been waiting for me. God, she sounded so loud.

My mother shot the nurse a conspiratorial smirk as I eased up out of the bed, jingled her keys. "Can you believe this? Kid borrows a scooter and wrecks it. We're lucky she didn't break anything." She'd sized up the room and its contents the second she walked in. The annoyed nurse and the Overtaxed Mother could bond over a shared problem. Me.

After reliving my own memories in a sort of quiet disbelief for the past few days, I watched her performance like a stagehand who knew how the tricks were rigged. My mother believed that you never know when you might need to con or manipulate someone, so she just did it to everyone, all the time. Controlling the room meant bonding with whoever had higher status. Like when she called me "kid." It was conspicuous to me when she did this, because she only always ever treated me as an adult and kept me in the company of adults, from as far back as I can remember.

Another mom-trick was using her keys for punctuation or

distraction. They were her second-favorite prop. I was her number one.

"Could've been so much worse," the nurse admonished me. I looked at her. I should've expected that. Some people are always waiting for that moment where they can "get" someone.

"I don't even want to think about that," my mother told the nurse. "I'm just glad she's in one piece after this little stunt."

Now the nurse appraised me like I'd gotten a concussion just to get attention. "There's nothing wrong with MUNI," she scolded.

"I guess you drive to work," I shot back.

"Hey," my mother barked. The elevated noise was like a slap. "What's the matter with you?" She wiped her nose with a tissue kept crumpled in her palm. My memory hiccupped at that tic, and I suddenly remembered when that big purse always had nasal spray in it, until a doctor told her the separation between her nostrils had begun to dissolve. Mom sure loved that Afrin.

I was supposed to fall in with mom's role now. Play a "kid," say something conciliatory. I was supporting cast. My job was to provide authenticity for her performances. Now I was silent. I wasn't being petulant, I just wasn't sure where the roles began and ended anymore. Who they were for.

This unsettled her. That's not how things went. I let the silence stretch. "Aw, c'mere kid." She gave me a brisk hug. I guessed that the heels made her 5'5" -- one inch taller than me. Her smell of chain-smoked Marlboro 100's -- the gold box -- made The Headache twitch, flex. I imagined The Headache as a slippery grey mollusk that had taken residence inside my skull.

I put my few belongings into a plastic hospital bag while my mother chatted up the nurse; about being on just a short break from work, and she's on her feet all day too, working at the car lot selling cars, and does the nurse have a car? Everything was back to upbeat, hurried. Mom wanted to leave quickly. We rushed through the process of checking me out of the hospital. She talked about her daughter like I was someplace far away. I was.

The hospital was nestled up in the side of one of San Francisco's copious hills. All the building's exits and entrances were in its bowl of a parking area, which required driving uphill to exit where Divisadero became Castro Street, lined with pretty Victorians and Edwardians. The bowl was freezing and windy but thankfully in shadows. It was a sunny day; there was no cool blanket of light-dampening fog. I winced at the light's assault and fought the urge to ask my mother if she had extra sunglasses. Even though we walked to the garage alone, she was still calling me "kid." This meant she wanted to remind me of my place in the relationship.

"Well kid, you really made some bills. But look. Jan let me drive the Cabriolet to pick you up. What do you say to that, kiddo?"

Jan was the manager of the Volkswagen dealership where she worked. He was a big Black man with a great laugh. My mother sold coke to him, in addition to all the people who worked there, and she would occasionally tell me about giving him "head." Jan's girlfriend was a young white blonde, a rich SF State college girl named Cassie who also loved cocaine, and whose Vespa I had borrowed and crashed. Lately I'd been staying in Cassie's apartment more than the room I shared with mom in the Sunset.

I was troubled to realize I couldn't remember how long I'd been staying at Cassie's.

I needed to remember as much as I could. To be vigilant about exercising my memory, no matter how much replaying those movies in my head seemed like someone else's nightmare. Or how much it bothered me that I didn't know if it bothered me before now, because it should have. Maybe in the past I had simply become a routine of autonomic responses which allowed me to separate myself from what was happening to me. Partitioning my feelings from my experiences like files in a hard drive.

I also had a new fear. I was my mother's apprentice in everything, from soldering broken electronics to weighing and packaging coke. I could size up a room, spot trouble, lead a conversation, and employ practical paranoia better than she could. She taught me how to be female; to equate sexual desirability with self-worth; to accommodate boundary pushers. While I reworked my feelings about my memories as her daughter, and the things she taught me to accept, I decided right then that had to question it. I needed to be on guard for signs that my mind might twist toward some genetic predisposition for ... becoming her.

I paused before getting in the brand-new white convertible. "Do you have any extra sunglasses?"

I didn't want to anger her because shouting topped my new list of greatest fears. Along with being bathed in bright light while driving in San Francisco traffic.

"Remember what they said about light and noises." I said it as non-confrontationally as I could. "The doctor said it's going to hurt my head for a little while."

"What's the point of a fucking convertible if you can't put the top down?"

Ah, okay. I was past her sympathy now. She kept going. "This is the first thing you say to me? Don't you talk to me like that. Jan did this as a favor for me. Cassie's Vespa is in the shop because of you. Who do you think pays for that? You owe me. Get in the car."

She did a toot of coke before starting the convertible, the obvious excuse being that I was stressing her out. Then she started putting the car's top down and my passenger, The Headache, screamed.

Out of the chilly parking bowl, up and left onto Castro Street; her shifting, acceleration, and stops were those of someone trying to speed race in daytime city traffic. I braced an elbow against the bright white door and cupped my forehead to shade my eyes. She smoked while she drove, flicking her ash up into the passing air. We crested the hill and coasted down again, bringing the Castro neighborhood into view. We'd never lived in this neighborhood, but I had so many feelings about it.

As my friends and I were just starting our teens the Castro had lost most of its population to AIDS. It looked and felt empty. The neighborhood was like a furious, beating heart in the exact physical center of San Francisco, unearthly, at once mournful and protective of itself, and very angry. I could relate.

"What, you're not going to talk to me now?"

"My head really hurts," I said.

"I'm so tired of being wrong with you. Everything I do is wrong."

I could feel her downward spiral happening, like the ambient temperature was dropping off a cliff. I'd run through all potential exits long ago. Asking what I did got me berated for knowing exactly what I did. Calm logic got my word choices picked apart, proof that I was wrong about some little thing I phrased incorrectly, therefore I was wrong about everything. If I started crying and begged her to stop, she would tell me to stop crying or she would give me a reason to cry -- the ultimate threat. My memory flashed; me, curled up on a carpeted floor, crying, asking her to please stop yelling at me. I felt ashamed at myself, angry.

"Please mom, I don't want to fight."

"Then maybe you shouldn't pick fights. Start with 'I'm sorry.' You have no idea what I've gone through for you today."

"I'm sorry."

"Don't push your luck."

My mother turned right on Market Street. The Castro Theatre's vintage red and white sign stuck up like a faded flag in the distance, sunlight making the marquis matte, opposite its nighttime neon voluptuousness. A beautiful white 1922 Beaux-Arts bank made the opposite corner at Market and Castro into a curve. The bank's wide, bleached round face at Harvey Milk Plaza was reflected across the street in the floor- to-ceiling glass of the ancient bar, Twin Peaks, the mirror image a curvy, teasing twin. The bank had curious customers outside this morning. Its porch was peppered with a lineup of black-clad punks; I could see arcs of red mohawk fins, spiky hair and metal-studded jackets. Like a flock of crazy birds had landed.

The punks were hanging out in Harvey Milk Plaza, a MUNI metro underground entrance with planters and benches. I wondered if that was where my punk friend from school, Joe, hung out. It seemed like a pretty punk place to hang out because Harvey Milk was dead, but more so because he was killed for scaring the city's homophobes, pissing off the cops just by existing. Punk seemed aligned with the "Silence = Death" flyers and stickers we saw dotted around the city on lampposts, telling us that anger was power, and that when you see someone being hurt, you speak out. Yell if you have to.

What drew me to punks at school was that they weren't afraid to be angry. They didn't seem afraid to let the world know that they were going through shit, and that the state of things made them mad. It seemed to me that society really didn't want girls to think they were allowed to be angry. Same for my Black, Mexican, and Asian friends. Gay people, too, if the reactions to AIDS protestors meant anything -- and it did, to us.

I knew punk was old by the time I got to it, the music of people's parents, as old as disco. I hated nostalgia. Yet I started to love bands like Bad Brains, not just because they had great music but because their music was defiance, part of a movement, a call to cultural exploration. I didn't look punk, but its culture pulled me like a magnet because it encouraged people to see what was happening to other people, how everything is connected to politics, power, money. Punk encouraged you to be part of the world.

It was the opposite of life on the run with my mother, who kept us isolated and tightly controlled my contact with the outside world. Punk was also the seductive opposite of popular culture, which seemed designed to reward conformity in everything: gender roles, racial discrimination, nuclear families, social status, all of it. It suggested that there was a way to take back power over my own life. It was like the lightbulb that went on in my head so many years ago when my mother showed me that when the digital alarm clock was broken, I could open it up and fix it myself.

I knew Harvey Milk fought for gay rights right on the same spot the punks were loitering and smoking, we all knew it, even if our parents avoided the neighborhood. I wondered if that's why they were hanging out there. None of us were around for the White Night Riots, but that bit of city history was still the source of graffiti I'd see around the neighborhood that read, "VISUALIZE BURNING POLICE CARS."

My mother drove too fast up Market's steep hill, carving its curves. She looked tired. I wondered if she even knew anything about Harvey Milk. Contrary to my mother's rules, I'd made friends at school. Among my friends we talked about those murders in City Hall like scary campfire stories when we smoked in McCoppin Park near school, or hung around the Little Theater reading plays. It made us so mad that no one understood how important he was. How shook we were about Harvey Milk, even though it was a long time ago.

I went over what I knew to test my memory. I remembered a lot. A former San Francisco cop, Dan White, murdered Supervisor Milk and Mayor Moscone because Milk was gay and Moscone was for gay rights. White shot the mayor twice in his office, then straddled him, put the gun against Moscone's temple, and fired two more times. White found Milk in a nearby office, unleashed a tirade of verbal abuse (which we all guessed was about him being gay), shot Milk in the stomach, the chest, in his back as he spun around, and again into his head as he went down. After all that, Dan White sat on Milk as he died and methodically shot him in the head.

Joe, our friend circle's history buff, told us that when news of the killings reached the Hall of Justice on Bryant Street, cheering to match a football game's winning touchdown could be heard outside, and the the cops sang "Danny Boy" on the police radio all that night. Our cops were well-known for hating the Mayor and Supervisor for passing a gay rights ordinance for the city. My friends and I had decided homophobic people were psychos. And that our cops were, too.

White was treated like royalty in jail. Joe said he was delivered homemade meals and take-out food personally by SFPD officers. White got a famously, unbelievably light sentence. When the sentencing was announced, a peaceful protest and vigil (which began at what would later become Harvey Milk Plaza) turned into the White Night Riots. Police cars were flipped, set on fire, and full-scale riots hammered the city. The SFPD retaliated the next night by smashing up the Castro and beating its residents. It had been open season on the city's undesirables ever since.

I thought about all this on the ride back to where my mother and I were staying, that there was this whole real world right here that my mother didn't care to know about. Her Silicon Valley engineer friends and coke clients partied on blithely, talking about revolutionizing the world with microchips and programs, deliberately looking the other way.

Thinking about it made my head hurt more. The drive up over Twin Peaks into the Sunset District was a kaleidoscope smear of light, sound, and pain. With my eyes closed, I kept in my head an image of the punks at Harvey Milk Plaza, and held onto all the rage and sorrow of the Castro.

3

I SPENT the next few days keeping to myself in the Yang's empty house while Donna and my mother worked and partied as usual. I avoided them. Having a concussion was a magic excuse to get me out of their party zone; from having to cook drugs or be entertaining to whatever guys they brought home.

Problem was, I ran out of books to read. The kitchen's pungent Chinese herbs were getting to me, I felt like I could smell them in every room. Worse, the things I got myself to remember while sitting in the Yang's living room made me want to crawl out of my own skin and leave it there on the couch for someone else to find.

The Yang house was on a Sunset district hillside facing the sea. Once, it was loved. There had been care taken in its butter yellow paint job and white-and-orange trim that emphasized its unique 1930s fairytale design. It wasn't one of the Depression-era, cookie-cutter row houses that unified the neighborhood's look and reminded you how fast the sand dunes were paved to house worker families. The Yang's home looked like something out of Hansel and Gretel, with its castle-like turret, portholes, bay window, and a unique entryway to an upstairs front door. You entered on the top floor and descended into the home's interior as it sloped down the hill. Donna lived on her own in a bottom floor studio.

I didn't know how long the Yangs had been in China, but the yard and its hedges and bushes, once carefully sculpted animal shapes, could've been brought back. It wasn't too late. Donna didn't water it and didn't care. I guess we weren't supposed to, either. Outside a window from the room I shared with my mother was the bunny-hedge, lost in its own growth, the creature's shape distorted by neglect.

I tried going for walks through the Sunset's seemingly endlessly foggy, row-house suburban spread.

The Sunset was a quiet district whose center was nowhere to be found. It was mostly populated by working-class Irish, with pockets of Chinese and Vietnamese families just to improve the quality of the food. There was nothing to do within any short walking distance except eat pork buns from any of the neighborhood's metal-counter, Chinese dumpling dives or buy cheap plastic kitchen utensils and waving cat statues at cramped, overstocked dollar stores. Those stores were magical to me. I'd wander into the back and find their tiny altars burning sweet smoky incense over slips of paper marked in Chinese characters. I would've bought something if my money didn't magically evaporate from the wallet I kept in a dresser drawer. I knew who was taking it.

I'd already spent an afternoon finding the Bank of America famous for being robbed by Patty Hearst. One of the most famous bank robberies of the century was only six blocks from our house, so that was neat. I knew that what the Symbionese Liberation Army did to Patty Hearst was awful and that she was later pardoned. Still, I thought the crime photos of her dressed in all black like a French artist and toting an M-1 carbine were cool. The bank itself was boring. It seriously lacked a statue of "Tania" with her rifle and beret, robbing the rich to feed the poor. I thought there should be one in every bank.

I wanted to go for a run, but The Headache had strong

opinions about it. Besides, I noticed that when I ran along the streets behind Sutro Tower, men driving by in cars would sometimes slow down and try to talk to me. I was in no condition to outrun anyone if things got weird up there.

Anyway, there was a new reason I was glad mom wasn't around. I had been exercising my memory. I was quietly freaking out. There were things that happened to me I really didn't understand.

They say memory is subjective, which makes you think that remembering things is some kind of freewheeling fantasy wish list for negative or positive reflections of the self. Maybe that was true for some people. But not for me. Not anymore, if that's what it had been before. I felt like a replicant in *Blade Runner* that had secretly hacked her own governor module. I was reviewing my past objectively, feeling suddenly free to decide how I felt about it.

Back before everything fell apart, my mother kept philosophy and Eastern spiritualism books laying around the house, which taught me that we create our own realities. I knew the stories we tell ourselves about our past can be our ways out of hell, or, if they are flawed by vanity or mental health conditions, they are the prisons in which we suffer. I also read books about lucid dreaming when I was younger, and the subconscious was interesting to me. I wasn't afraid of it like most people; I didn't believe it was uncontrollable. My conclusion was that if you could control your dreams, that was handy if you had a nightmare. But if you controlled it too much, you might miss something cool or helpful your subconscious was trying to tell you. So, I decided the best way to review the movie of my life was to give up control of the narrative: To not decide what I was going to see before the film began.

I imagined my memories existing somewhere in the dark of my brain like strings of unlit Christmas lights. My plan was to examine one little bulb at a time as I untangled the lines. No deciding how it looked, I thought, until I saw the entire string as one, with as many lights on as possible. I hoped that a collection all lit up together as a whole would illuminate that corner of my life. Later I would realize this was my quest for context.

I sat in the Yang's sunken living room. The kitchen and living room were a time capsule of a Chinese family that had seemingly teleported away in an instant, leaving framed photos of smiling family members, lap blankets folded and waiting at sitting spots, and an apothecary's worth of herbs, jars, strange pills, and teas filling kitchen cupboards and shelves in archaeological layers. Like the Sunset District surrounding it, the house was as quiet as the past. Sutro Tower loomed nearby, its red tines overhead like a strange forgotten kitchen implement, transmitting its invisible radio waves throughout the city's nervous system. A smell of medicinal herbs and dried fungus permeated the air.

I focused on the bay window's view over the row houses to a Pacific Ocean muted by fog.

Grey sea, grey sky, no horizon. I started with our present: living in the Yang's house. I worked my way back through the places that came before. There were so many. I couldn't remember all the names of the other people we'd lived with, addresses, or the numbers of motel rooms. When I got back as far as I could, I was pretty sure there were more faerie lights lit up in my head than ever before. I started to wonder, feeling slightly like I was having an out-of-body experience, if what people said about repressed memories was true.

Tracking our locations showed a lifetime on the run. Half

of it was spent moving; apartments, house rentals, suicide motels, and furnished rooms in houses like the one we were in now. No one at school ever knew. The other half was me staying for days, weeks, and sometimes months at a time, away from my mother at other people's houses, going back ... as far as I could remember. She sent me away a lot. For long periods of time. Always with adults, like the giant house in Sunnyvale full of engineers where I'd watch them do acid and read their stacks of *Heavy Metal* magazines. They'd take me to school; bring home the latest Atari games from work to keep me occupied.

The earliest place I could remember us living was a different family home in the Sunset. My mother was married to a man I called daddy, until one day mom was driving to the bank and told me she was changing her name, and I could change my name too, and that I could have my real father's name if I wanted. Or any name. That was how she told me, just like that, that he wasn't really my father. Like my real father was a secret. I think I was around five.

I thought about the man who wasn't my father. His name drifted up to the top of my memory. Dennis. He communicated with shouts, open handed slaps, and occasionally, fists. Usually in the kitchen. I could remember the sounds of his yelling and her crying; the wet slaps of hitting and the grunts and groans my mother made when struck. Clatter of utensils on the floor, ricochet of pans on the stove, shoes hissing for purchase on linoleum. I remember having a really bad black eye, a bruise that traveled across my face, making it look like I wore a bandit's eye-mask.

I remembered this: sitting at the kitchen table waiting for dinner and watching Dennis push and hit my mother, angry and exasperated, until he grabbed her by the hair and lowered her to her knees. Hair pulled tight around her red, wet face. He put a big, shiny knife to her throat. I couldn't remember what he said. But her small voice was loud, so loud to me, when everything stilled and she said to him, knife at her throat: "God is watching you."

Oh no, no no no, I thought, sitting on the Yang's green couch. Repulsed, I recoiled that I had called that man "daddy." Until she told me the truth. This was just one memory. Entire light strings, connected, blinked on in my head faster than I could process it all. As a single mother, she'd landed on her feet after him. Later as an adult, I'd find out she worked in Silicon Valley doing government contracting -- overseeing signal jamming and projects at the Diablo Canyon nuclear plant -- for a stretch of years. But on the Yang's couch, I remembered her taking me to work and how I'd visit the engineers working in a space the size of an airplane hangar. In my mind's eye I could see the giant, long cables along "the floor," and rows of workbenches at which I'd sit and play with a soldering iron to make little curly-tailed mice out of the liquified metal.

Everyone loved my mother. She was magnetic. A leader, a female engineering executive with her own office and secretary in Silicon Valley. She had friends who looked up to her, and who gave her daughter gifts from their workplaces; computers, devices, and video games.

Boyfriends came and went. Cocaine came to stay. She sent me away a lot. When I was home, she had nervous breakdowns in the middle of the night and told me she saw UFOs outside her bedroom window, coming to abduct her.

One day she panicked. She told me she was raped at gunpoint, by a kindly old man I'd once met with her on the day she had a briefcase full of money, a man who had bodyguards. She told me she saw someone killed. I don't know if any of that was true; it was the same time as the hallucinations about malevolent spaceships hovering over our apartment.

She took me with her to the DEA offices. My mother turned over all her friends in exchange for a new identity, a new life for us. That's what she'd told me. Months later, after she betrayed everyone and we'd lost everything in what the newspapers called the Bay Area's largest cocaine bust, the coke and the old boyfriends were back. I remembered mom showing me the article in the *San Francisco Chronicle*. "That's me," she said, pointing at the newsprint. Her name wasn't in the article, but other people's were.

I felt like I was sinking in the Yang's sunken living room. No, it was more like vertigo. I saw myself standing at the top of a cliff at Ocean Beach, somewhere off in the grey distance from where I stared out the window. Then I imagined myself down on the wet, heavy sand, enveloped by mist. Walking into the bone-chilling water, pushing me back, pulling me in. The way ice-cold water makes you hurt inside. I hoped that before this moment I had known what I was going through. That the feelings I had about it were anger, boundaries, defiance. For the hundredth time I really hoped that I did not ever think any of this was okay.

These truths about my mother, about my life, were terrible. Not being able to remember if I'd just gone along with it like nothing was wrong, this was agonizing. What I could be certain of was my mother's role in it.

I decided that I could live without being able to forgive my mother. But being unable to forgive myself would kill me. The trick, I decided, was going to be figuring out how to live with these truths and not let them destroy me.

Here was one of these truths: So many lights came on as I sat there, remembering everything so fast, and in so much detail. That scene in the kitchen wasn't the last I saw of Dennis. I felt its realization crawl up out of my stomach to sit on my chest, pressing my breaths shallow.

My mother always sent me away somewhere for the entire summer when school was out. Like sending me off to stay with the engineers, the acid-tripping Sunnyvale hippies.

For two summers in a row, she sent me to stay at a house in the Los Gatos foothills, in the woods. With "Uncle Dennis." The same man who put a knife to her throat.

I couldn't believe I hadn't put this all together until now. The first time was when I was nine. Uncle Dennis had a girlfriend then, named Anne, and a daughter from another relationship who was around my age. Jennifer. At night he would drink and get angry, violent. The second summer I was sent to stay there the girlfriend was absent, but the daughter remained. There were holes in the walls of his house right where you'd imagine someone's head would be if they were sitting on the couch. The wicker rocking chair, Anne's chair, had a hole through it where her head might've rested. Wicker fronds ringed the hole out the chair's back; I'd run my hand over them and felt them prickle my palm.

In the evenings Dennis would get on the phone, drink heavily, and yell about Anne. He'd slam things for emphasis, like drawers and doors. Jennifer and I would sneak out of the house as quietly as possible and hide from him in the woods, amid shadows in redwood trees. Whispering to each other in the darkness of the forest, we compared stories about Dennis's beatings of our mothers. We watched the house. Waited. We returned only after we were sure he had passed out.

I held myself very still on the Yang's couch and stared out the window. Fog crept toward me from the sea, slowly consuming houses and streets. When I thought about my mother coming home later, all I could think was that she'd been carrying these truths around with her this whole time. Truths so appalling they risked sacrificing her humanity.

But for her, nothing had changed. While I had changed completely. I was back on the edge of a cliff. I was back at the sea, walking into the waves. The concussion was forcing me to be aware of what I was going through. Had I ever been aware? I thought, help me.

Please someone help me.

There was no one to help me, I thought. Except me.

I wasn't supposed to be back in school for another week, but I decided right then I didn't want to be in the house when my mother came home. I left the Yang's forlorn dollhouse at a little past one o'clock. I thought *I see you, bunny* as I walked past the hedge and made the trek to Lincoln High.

Unlike most of the kids at school, I lived near enough to Abraham Lincoln High School that the travel time was the same whether I walked or took the bus. At the thought of actually going inside Lincoln's main building, The Headache squirmed in my skull like it had been poked. The bell. The shoulder-to-shoulder pushing and yelling. The bats with which security staff would strike our lockers like correctional officers -- BAM! -- after the bell rang to hustle everyone into their classrooms.

Our high school was not a place of harmony. When Lincoln was opened in 1940 the neighborhood was middle-class white families. Racial equality was a bell yet to toll for the school systems of the United States. Schools in San Francisco were segregated until the law told them not to be, and even then, like other major US cities, the city dragged its heels through a mire of protesting parental groups and the muck of organized, racist, letter-writing clergy who opposed the mixing of races. Learning about that was so alien; I couldn't imagine life without all my friends.

Busing began in San Francisco in the seventies, but the old busing patterns were why Lincoln had become, in my time, an almost all-Black and Asian school conspicuously in the middle of a historically Irish neighborhood. San Francisco's so-called "horseshoe plan" for bussing took kids from Black-only housing projects into schools far from their homes. This was actually how school busing in San Francisco backfired in a uniquely racist way. It effectively re-segregated Black kids into unfamiliar, often hostile neighborhoods. Most kids at my school came from historically redlined neighborhoods in Bayview and Western Addition.

You can probably guess how that worked out between a couple thousand young adults flipping out on hormones trapped in the middle of a mostly white neighborhood. Lincoln wasn't a high school. It was an aggrieved weather system.

Most of the fights happened at McCoppin Square Park, a block away from school property. That's where the punks and other cigarette-smoking kids hung out. The rejects. My friends. Me.

That's where I was headed.

4

WITH EVERY STEP I hated The Headache more than ever. I hated the as-yet-to-be-determined debt my mother would demand of me from my accident. I'd pay for it one way or another. I especially hated how I was starting to see myself now, like an animal faced with chewing off its paw to escape a trap.

More lights came on in my head as I trekked along the wide, treeless sidewalks of the Avenues and its flat-faced, Depression Era row houses. My memories were bubbling up whether I wanted them or not. All I could do was keep going. I walked to school and remembered the time my mother got a man shot.

It was the 1980's and San Francisco was flooding itself, the Bay Area, and Silicon Valley, with cocaine.

Drugs were always central to the Bay Area's underground economy, but coke began to take over for pot, heroin, and acid in the mid-1970s. Many tech hippies like my mom had decided that unlike heroin, coke was a "soft" drug and accepted it into their lives like they had with pot.

By the middle of the eighties, tons of the stuff was flown, trucked, and boated into San Francisco. Smugglers packed it into suitcases and hollowed-out electronics in brick form, which is how it would enter our house. I spent many days with my mother grinding rocks into powder and weighing it on giant scales on our kitchen table, where my mother would also cut it with baby laxative to increase her profits. I folded the little paper bindles and prided myself on the quality of my neatness, and the colored paper I'd use to make them prettier. The people who helped us at the table and those who carried and sold them for mom were fans of my work.

My mother lost her job at ArgoSystems. As humiliation is death for an engineer, she put her energy and intelligence into being a full-time coke dealer to Silicon Valley's computer and tech barons. She suddenly had within reach the kind of lifestyle she could only dream of with the money and access that came from supplying the tech class with its "marching powder."

My mother grew more paranoid. The parties and houses we went to got more posh. As the only child around always-hyper adults, the tech toys they provided to keep me busy became even more futuristic. I wasn't permitted friends my age because kids talked and parents asked questions. I had every device, home gaming console and game available, and no one to play them with.

My mother was always in demand. She flew to Las Vegas, Miami, and Peru -- from which she brought back a stone pipe carved to resemble an Inca god, its stem a massive penis. She had flamboyant coke accessories, like a gold "straw" and a "bullet" on a necklace. She slept on our couch during the day unless she had a boyfriend over. They were almost always computer guys who gave me new tech toys to win me over, to keep me busy. The electronics station at the kitchen table where she taught me how to solder transformed into an assembly line with two-pan coke scales and various paraphernalia.

And then one night she cracked. I found her in her bedroom alone, crying and saying she was scared, and talking about lights in the sky. They had come for her, she told me while pointing to the stars outside her window. She was adamant they would be back. I told her it would be okay. I was a child, but I was already an adult. I was quite aware that something was really wrong with my mother.

In the following week, she told me she'd made a deal with the police and everything was going to get better. She took me on one of her trips to the DEA's office to meet a man who would be keeping an eye on me. Everyone called him "TK" he told me.

"Like telekinesis?" I asked him. Yes, he said. Kind of like that.

One night she told me TK was going to stay at home and watch movies with me while she was out. There would be other people outside too, she said. TK dressed casually in jeans, and I remember really liking him. I knew the boxy bulge under his blue windbreaker was a gun. I had seen plenty of guns. TK never took his jacket off. We watched midnight horror movies on the couch for a few nights in a row, eating bagels or pizza for dinner and drinking cream soda (all my favorite things). One night while we were watching some *Creature Features* classic, TK told me to "lay on the floor and don't move." He'd seen someone at the window watching us.

Up close the carpet looked like clouds when they turn into thunderheads. While playing back this memory I couldn't remember if I was afraid, but I remember what the carpet looked like. Fuzzy corkscrews of cumulus, a narrow range of elevations, smells of dry dust and musty old spills, blue light of a forgotten TV horror film casting little moving shadows. I heard yelling outside, and then thunder and more noise. It was a gunshot, I knew that. I couldn't believe how loud the shot had been. I remember wondering why the sheer sound of the shot didn't break the window.

My mother's boyfriend Don had been going out of his mind with paranoia, theirs being a coke-fueled romance. She hadn't told him anything; she'd just stopped seeing him. So, he came sneaking around the house at night. When he saw me on the couch with the DEA agent, paranoia became jealousy. Convinced my mother was cheating, he prowled and decided to confront the man in her house. He had never been more wrong about anything in his life.

That night my mother had gotten very dressed up before going out. Her hair was perfect, she had on makeup, a skirt, and high heels. Underneath a red silk button-up blouse she wore a microphone.

She took a taxi to the city's most opulent hotel (at the time). It had soaring glass elevators, graduated Art Deco interior, with a space-age round bar and steak restaurant at the top that slowly turned as the wealthy dined and drank. After meeting her coke colleagues at the bar for a drink, they went to meet more people in a hotel suite.

While a man got shot in front of our apartment, my mother went into the suite to meet her friends and contacts. They examined suitcases of coke and suitcases of money. She was then invited into an adjacent suite to sample the blow. Once she'd entered the second suite, she later told me, there were loud bangs as agents rammed open the door in the room she'd just left. The people waiting for her in the second suite removed her from the hotel as if she were under arrest. All of her friends and colleagues were apprehended in what was described as the largest San Francisco coke bust in history. Newspapers reported collecting firearms and precious gems. Some of the apprehended would face life sentences.

Days later, she showed me newspaper articles about it.

My mother told me her deal with the cops was to "get out." She'd bargained for money, a new identity, and to be relocated. She said it was all for me. To make her 'little girl' safe.

Yet what struck me was that she never really bargained for anything to protect her child -- me. I remember getting the impression that she'd had some say in where we were relocated, and Santa Cruz wasn't, to my mind, a safe enough distance away. And it seemed to me in retrospect that we could probably be found through my school records. I didn't yet know what happens when the feds change someone's identity, that they scrub every trace of you. I didn't know that was the night my mother ceased to exist.

There was no remorse for the gunshot I hid from while face-down on our shag rug, or for violently uprooting my entire life. (Again.) It was as if there was no child she was trying to protect that night, after all. I was the excuse, yet outside the event itself I simply ceased to be.

That night was probably one of the most honest things my mother did, in a way, while it was also still a lie. Like so many other things.

We left San Francisco that night. Like her cokehead boyfriend, she hadn't told me what was happening, either. Our belongings were packed up and sent to a rental house she'd picked out for us by the beach. She spent the next few months establishing ID for her new identity. She told me in a beachside kitchen one sunny day that she'd sliced open her fingers while in line at the DMV to change her fingerprints.

It didn't take her long to find a new coke connection. Soon we were on the move, a lot, and back in San Francisco. Our belongings just ... disappeared.

As I walked up to my high school I wondered where all my stuff went. I used to have so many books. I was so angry.

I stopped at the intersection of 24th and Quintana in front of Lincoln High. What about your past, ugly building? I wondered what this place looked like when the lily-white student body was cracked open by desegregation. My school sat primly atop an intersection with clear views of the Golden Gate Bridge, Sutro Tower, windswept trees, and the Sunset's iconic cookie-cutter houses. I wondered if this picturesque setting had been the scene of yelling and spitting, like I'd seen in old photos of racists. I hated those cardigan-wearing assholes and their parents for creating them, and the ones who sabotaged generations to come by sneakily trying to keep segregation alive.

I transferred my hate to the walk past Lincoln to McCoppin Square Park.

In my mind McCoppin was "The Trail" -- that place where all the misfit toys of every school went to smoke. I'd seen plenty of schools, so I'd seen many versions of The Trail. Every Junior High, Middle School, and High School had one.

There were various constants about whatever version a school had of The Trail. It was often exactly that: A dirt trail along some trees tucked out of sight from school grounds. Clove cigarettes were popular, cigarettes too, and occasionally someone would have pot. Its population was always comprised of metal heads, punks, drama geeks, toughies, dirtbags, goths, and occasional nice girls who wanted to be "bad."

Lincoln's only version of The Trail wasn't McCoppin, though that was where I went to find Joe hanging out with some friends. Not far from Joe's group were four cheerleaders puffing clove smoke. Three giant Black girls that I'd somehow managed to convince not to beat the shit out of me over the fact of my existence, and a blonde, white cheerleader I sort of ended up fighting anyway.

When I'd started at Lincoln, the three big cheerleaders cornered me every lunch hour and after school. But for some reason I'd just kept chatting to them, kept talking my blah-blah-blah at them, until they finally got tired of me after a few days.

Then the other one, blonde Ashley Bailey, challenged me to a fight on the football field when no one else was around. No punches were thrown. She just kind of crouched down and ran at me as hard as she could, like a football player.

Ashley was a long way coming like that, no surprises about her plan to knock me down, and I could've stepped aside. Instead, I didn't, and hopped up a little when she made impact to latch onto her and bring us both down. Three years of martial arts classes before the drug bust taught me to do this, and how to land without getting the wind knocked out of me. The field was mushy, soaked, wet. We rolled, grappled, pinned, and crammed mud into each other's faces and hair in the slop at the goal-end of the field.

We did this until we were tired, filthy, and bone-deep cold.

Then she said, "let's go clean up." We went to the girls' locker room. While we cleaned rocks out of our ears, she told me she learned to fight from her brothers. Hers was a giant Irish family with five kids, and very Catholic, she told me, and that her mom frequently said she wished Ashley had been a boy.

I could've told her everything there was to know about mothers who wished their daughters didn't exist. But I didn't

41

say anything. I didn't think we were friends. It was the strangest fight I'd ever been in.

I wanted nothing to do with the cheerleaders eyeing me through a cloud of smoke on the playground when I got there. Those girls were psychos.

5

THE PARK'S loamy soil was soft underfoot, encouraging the unevenness of our teenage postures. Tobacco and clove smoke hesitated in clouds around us, hiding the Pacific Ocean's usual salty scent threading through trees. A continual hum of city traffic from 19th Avenue purred from blocks away. Bird chirps halted at the shriek of a seagull, then returned as if annoyed by the interruption. Kids clustered in tribes around McCoppin, watching each other and talking, as they'd done there for generations.

Joe saw me walking over. He smiled. No one else did.

Tina Chan, the drama geek, just stared at me. So did Aiden, a mohawked punk. Same for Mara Doyle, another blonde Irish girl. Did they make the Irish girls in factories out here in the Avenues somewhere? John stared at me too, though the feeling was mutual because I didn't know quite what John Gone was in general, except he was a sort of Satanic looking punk of some kind. Pale skin, the beginnings of a sinister black goatee, black leather jacket, everything black. Weird, but sweet.

It was one of those moments when everyone's gawping at you and you wonder if you have a head wound, except I realized in that moment I actually did have a head wound, so I smiled.

Joe never smiled, so it had to be the head wound.

Joe was intimidating. He wasn't any taller than me. He made up for it with a long-angled face and skinny front teeth, all of which reminded me of a friendly rat. If a pale, blue-eyed rat shaved his eyebrows off, wore his hair in short black spikes on top, stuck safety pins in his nose, lip, or ears (depending on the weather I guess) and stomped around in combat boots. At fifteen, Joe was quietly smarter about history than anyone I'd ever met. He could beat anyone at trivia games, especially with war stuff.

Plus, like I said, he never smiled.

"Oh no," he deadpanned when I got to the group. "Your trendy haircut."

I couldn't believe it. Joe was being funny.

"At least mine's not an ass brush," I gave back, teasing about his short, wide mohawk. I'd recently learned that this is what punks called newbies' hair when they first got a mohawk, but hadn't grown enough hair to make it tall yet. It showed a lack of commitment.

I didn't have time to enjoy everyone's laughing at my joke because Joe was trying to stick his thumb on the oval scab along my forehead's wrecked hairline. I dodged him poorly, laughing for the first time in ... a long time, even though my skull felt like it was made of lead. "Stop it!" I laughed, and Joe said he'd stop it when I got a real haircut.

When we calmed down, Tina offered me a cigarette and asked what happened.

Fall weather had brought a chill to the playground. We stood in our circle of kids who smoke, that ritual assembly, and I did something I had never done with anyone. I told them the truth about my life.

It was a distilled replay of my memory's pageant of nightmares. First the accident, then the remembering. Mom and I were supposed to disappear but instead we were hiding in plain sight, on the run mostly. My role at home cooking drugs. Being left alone with scary dudes.

"Oh my god," Tina kept saying, in between drags on a cigarette and flips of her shiny black bob. She had this way of emphasizing the "g" and "d" that drew people up short with its feeling, made you pay attention. Tina once taught me how to read Shakespeare in drama class. When she told me to read the lines out loud, they suddenly made sense. Some things came in focus only when expressed. Still, it sometimes sounded like she was saying "cod" but her eyes told me she was freaked out, worried.

"I think I need a place to crash for a little bit," I told the group.

It was Friday. Tina said she'd ask her mom and dad, but that it could probably only be for the weekend. Her parents were older and only spoke Chinese. Tina translated their world.

"That's cool," I said. "Thanks."

I looked around. Joe shrugged, his too-big Derby jacket curtseying around him like an igloo. "There's no way," he told me. "I'm never even there anyway." I knew something was up with his dad, a combat vet, but I didn't know what. "There's a squat in Lower Haight," he added.

"A squat?"

I imagined kids crouched in the bottom of a decrepit Victorian. Squatting. I figured that a squat meant people stayed there, but I was too intimidated to ask Joe stupid questions. I filed the squat away in my mind for later investigation.

"Yeah," Joe added. "No hippies allowed, so it's not fucked up."

Aiden coughed the word, "*Crusties*." There were clearly opinions about this.

"You should come hang out," Joe said. "We can fix your hair."

I smiled. "Thanks dick, that's really nice of you."

John said, smiling: "You know I live in a fucking trailer or I'd say okay." John had never told us why he lived in a trailer by himself behind an apartment building, and I didn't know if teachers at school called him John Gone. I didn't care. What people wanted to be called was who they were. It was usually more who they were than whatever identity curse was put on them at birth.

Aiden just shook his head, which I expected. He rarely spoke. Aiden's mohawk was brown, his natural hair color. I knew nothing about him except he was tough, quiet, the oldest among us at 16, he always wore a trench coat, and he would always give me cigarettes or gum if he had extra.

I looked at Mara just as she said, "I can't." And there was something, for a second. A ripple on the surface like a tentacle uncoiling at the dark bottom of a tide pool.

Mara and I had cut class a few times to smoke pot I pinched from my mother's stash. We'd walk up Quintana to the hill, sit, and hollow out cigarettes. Carefully repack them with little bits of weed so if anyone noticed us, they'd just see two girls smoking cigarettes.

With Mara, pot made me laugh at the dumbest things. Once we took turns laying our heads on each other's stomachs and trying not to laugh, our heads bouncing and making us laugh harder. We spaced out looking at the Sunset's domino rows of houses below us, trying to imagine the windswept sand dunes as they used to be. Her brother was a cute muscly skater, and Mara was ridiculously pretty, and it made sense in that lucky way of Mexican Irish families. I tried not to take it personally that he had no interest in girls.

One year later Mara found me panhandling in Upper Haight. She asked if I needed a place to stay for a few days; she was living with her grandmother now with her brother. The courts had placed them there.

After her grandma was asleep, we stole a bottle of wine and accidentally broke the neck trying to get it open in the dark of her gran's garage. We shared the wine from a single cup anyway, and kept our voices low, the lights out so we wouldn't get caught. She told me what happened, a few weeks after the day she didn't offer me a place to stay.

"I drank and ate everything in the medicine cabinet and under the sink," Mara explained. "I ate every pill, I drank rubbing alcohol, I swallowed everything." As she raced to oblivion trying to die, her father was outside the locked bathroom door punching her brother's face to a pulp; he'd intervened on their father kicking Mara in the back while she lay on the floor. "He fucked me. He fucked us both. No one knew." The way she said it was blunt. So matter of fact. That night I slept next to her in a little twin bed with my arm around her.

In that split second on the playground, I could tell Mara wanted to help, but couldn't. "It's okay," I told her.

I wanted to say more but Ashley Bailey was glaring at me through her forest of violent cheerleaders. Whatever was trying to heal in my head wouldn't be improved by another weirdo wrestling match. I had to leave. I said as much and everyone took turns hugging me, like someone had died and they were sorry, so sorry.

I walked home thinking about how we were all friends but didn't really know anything about each other. We were the ones who could pretend to be normal but had to lie or bow out when everyone else started talking about their normal lives. We always find each other, a circle where no one asks questions, where together we can breathe for a minute. Our lives were secretly as unstable as the fault lines we walked on.

The overgrown hedge bunny stood sentinel back at the Yang's house, its paint flaking like skin. My mother waited in the living room.

"I want you to apologize, young lady." She was in her work clothes but I couldn't tell if she was coming or going. Always a button-down blouse and skirt. Ready to clock in at the Valley defense job she didn't have anymore, ready to jam the enemy's communications. Very "before the bust." She wiped her nose. Her eyes radiated fury. She waited for my response.

I didn't know what I'd done wrong. It didn't matter; I could tell by the way gravity grew heavier, pulled everything toward her like a black hole. I could feel it approach sometimes, like the whole room would downshift in her head. That quick temperature drop.

Once it was that she saw me move a piece of furniture by sliding it, nearly -- but not quite -- scratching the floor of a rental we were in. This infraction turned into a rage session that ended with me on the floor crying, saying I was sorry, and trying to convince her that I still loved her. Another time I'd asked if she could take a turn at doing dishes instead of me. One bad day I saw her wearing my earrings and said I wished she'd asked me before taking them. The tricky thing for me was, sometimes these things wouldn't trip her switch. I could never predict it, except she only did it when we were alone. Of my mother's performances, this one was always just for me.

The script was a timeworn re-run. It was How Could You Hurt Me Like This.

There was only one way through it, and that was down, down, down into her dark cyclical arguments. She prided herself on moments when she felt she'd verbally outmaneuvered me. I was quarry, and she put all the brilliance of her engineer's mind into running me down. But the drugs, and maybe life, had made her crazy. And crazy cancels smart every time.

I just let it run its course. The dark storm came in and blew back out again. My crime this time was that I went to school without telling her I was feeling better. She needed me here, she was having people over later. And then, she left. My head pounded from the yelling, but I didn't cry, I didn't even crack a feeling. That made me feel stronger. I went upstairs to lie down.

The party came home at night. I stayed in the bedroom. I read until I was sleepy and tucked myself in.

Eventually the voices and music downstairs depleted to a trickle of sound; my mother and a man. The talking stopped. Then the noises began. They were like the old noises, the beating noises, but they also sounded like fucking. My heart pounded, I swear I could feel it hitting the front of my chest. My hands shook.

Wet slaps and groans echoed up the stairs, and more thumps, until finally I heard my mother say, "No. Stop!" The sounds continued, and I heard her saying no, no, no. I wanted to scream. My hands sweat wetly into the blanket and sheet balled in my fists. I wanted to yell STOP! but what would happen then? I backed into the corner of the bed where it met the wall. I could still hear them. *Stop it*, I thought. *Please.*

Then it stopped.

I heard someone coming up the stairs. It sounded like heavy steps, but maybe mom was hurt. Should I get up and see if she's okay? I stayed in the corner as floorboards creaked under the Yang's hallway carpeting, snitching out every step. They came down the hallway. The steps stopped outside the bedroom door.

I waited. One breath. Two. I was breathing as quietly as I could. It was like when I was a little kid and woke up afraid there might be a vampire from Salem's Lot in my room, and if I was perfectly quiet it wouldn't know I was there, and it would go get someone else. There wasn't enough air. It felt like I was suffocating in open space, just waiting like that.

Mom would've come in by now.

The house was quiet. The floorboards sounded the footsteps away, back down the hall. I was trapped. Then there was an earthquake.

The wall slammed like a bus hit the house. Jewelry on the dresser jangled, the lamp next to me rattled. I felt my consciousness jerk like a fish, my mind tried to latch onto what was real. That first few seconds of an earthquake where your awareness double-checks that it isn't a dream; yes everything around you is moving, and your training kicks in. In school, constant earthquake drills had us practice racing to a doorway or bracing under our desks. Earthquakes were just part of life in San Francisco. No one puts a bookshelf above the bed unless they want to wake up with a dictionary-shaped dent in their forehead. Earthquakes are as normal here as the fog and the sea, and if you're not practiced around either, you die.

It wasn't an earthquake: It was a door. Whoever was in

the house had opened a door in the hallway and slammed it shut.

He was checking doors. And he was pissed. I knew he was going to check all the doors.

We didn't have many belongings in this bedroom. But one of them, I knew, was my mom's Beretta 70 semi-automatic.

The gun was in its original aging box under her bed, Spanish writing along its papery sides. She'd bought it in Mexico. I slipped out of bed and crawled silently on my hands and knees. I took the heavy pistol out and crawled back into my bed. I sat. I waited.

I saw myself from above, sitting in a little bed, scrunched up in the corner, in my t-shirt and sleep shorts, on top of a hill, on top of a fault line wishing that there had just been an earthquake. Thinking that this city had been built on top of a violent fault lying in wait to buck and twist. On the other side of this hill, Market Street's ribbon of nighttime diamonds waited for the whip-crack of an invisible hand. And a whip-crack had happened, not once but many times, sometimes so bad that people were crushed into pulp under building rubble, or burned to death in earthquake fires.

Yet people still built on top of the fault. They made more weak buildings on top of the death, they doomed the future with faulty design and corrupt real estate deals, and still lived here. Our city with all its terrible planning was a wonder of the world, where the amazements of technology were becoming everyday, a spider-spun nest of fools and dreamers atop shifting tectonic plates.

Why would anyone live on a fault line? I heard the bedroom doorknob twist.

Because this fault line is my home, I thought as I raised the Beretta. I was born here.

I held the gun with both hands, and my hands did not shake.

In the open doorway I saw a man lit in silhouette. Looking at me, illuminated in a sliver of light. I could smell what he did to my mother on the draft he let in. His hand rested on the doorknob. Then he closed the door, and he creaked away down the stairs.

I stayed on my bed with the gun, just in case.

Eventually I heard him leave. My mother had left, too. I was alone in the house.

My hands started shaking as I packed a bag.

6

THE PURSE WAS LAYING on a sidewalk in front of a bank on Haight Street. We walked around the corner to squat over it in someone's doorway on Cole. Our plan was to keep just the cash, then lost-and-found the bag in a store saying someone left it.

Behind us, the tired squeal of MUNI bus brakes charted their passage, in between the rattle of Luxor Cab engines, and the unintelligible mutter from SF city tour buses as they passed us. A human caravan of homeless hippies, grimy faced with enormous backpacks, Grateful Dead shirts, and a mangy, exhausted Labrador padded by in the direction of Golden Gate Park, avoiding our eye contact. The Haight on any other day.

I had joined a multi-decade legacy of youth homelessness, and the kids, in my case, punks, who were Haight runaways. It wasn't romantic. It wasn't what you're getting when a frat boy tells you he was homeless for a while because he needed to figure himself out. Yet the myths persist, and it came clear to me pretty fast among my new tribe that most everyone had the wrong idea about what was going on with us.

"Stop! Don't stick your hand in the bag!"

I froze. "What?"

"Needles," Rogue said.

You mean AIDS, I thought. But I didn't need to say it. We both knew. Every kid in San Francisco knew. Rogue's perpetually cocked eyebrow joined the other one on her brow, up high in alarm. She was right. I felt stupid. I was learning.

More to the point, I was hungry.

"Flip it and dump it out, quick," Rogue prompted. She shielded our work from passers-by with her body, but she was neither large nor inconspicuous. There weren't many Black punks in the city. If her short, red-tinted mohawk and nose ring weren't memorable enough, her jacket and messenger bag blared words like FEAR, The Dicks, "Mommy's Little Monster," and FANG in buttons and hand-scrawled paint.

After slipping out of the Yang's dilapidated family home, I practically ran to Tina's house. The Chan family let me stay for a week. I went to school with Tina every day and used breaks, lunch time, and after school loitering at the playground for networking. To find the next place to stay. I'd found a few. I wanted to stay in school more than anything, but eating and sleeping were stiff competition.

Besides the obvious benefits of getting people to buy me lunch or give me their sandwiches, I thought school could keep the heat off me. If I didn't turn up missing from classes, they'd have no reason to call my mom. I didn't think she'd come looking for me at school because that would bring unwanted attention -- to her. But I was extra careful to stay away from the after school pick-up areas after the last bell, just in case.

Tina felt bad when I had to leave. She took me to meet her secret boyfriend Seth, the lead singer of a band living in a South of Market warehouse. People crashed at Seth's warehouse all the time and it was "totally cool," Tina explained on our bus ride. "No one will bug you about your mom or anything."

Seth sang in a cover band that made money getting booked for boat weddings on the Bay and sad school proms in Burlingame. The guys were playing a cover of "Stray Cat Strut" when we walked in. The warehouse was a maze of poor, unfinished construction, found furniture, band flyers, milk crates as tables and lamp stands, and a stage they'd built in the back room for band practice and house parties. It stank of sour beer. Band girlfriends and random hangers-on drank beer in cans, applauding weakly after songs.

Tina's boyfriend was twenty-three. Tina was fifteen, so that really bugged me. Seth was short, charismatic, and had giant brown eyes with long black lashes that held Tina captivated. Especially when he sang to her, and she'd dance, glowing, her glossy black bob swinging like curtains from under her vintage porkpie hat.

When we said goodbye Tina pressed a blank notebook into my hands. To help with my memories, she explained. If there was a next time where I woke up and had to remember who I was, she told me, I wouldn't be feeling along a string of lights in the dark willing each one to turn back on. She left me in a dump, but I knew she cared.

She was right; no one at the warehouse noticed when I just started sleeping on one of their couches. One person noticed me, though. On my second night at the warehouse their lead guitarist put his arm around me when I stood in the filthy kitchen doing their festering dishes. Kevin was twenty-eight, had a girlfriend who wasn't around, but said he'd keep me warm in his bed. I spent my fourteenth birthday trying to sleep on a couch they found on the street, worrying Kevin would come downstairs, the rank smell of beer in the cushions permeating my clothes, carrying with me into the next day at school. I didn't tell anyone it was my birthday.

Instead of going to school one morning, I went to the Castro. My stomach hurt. I was sure I was so hungry it was eating itself. Harvey Milk Plaza was buzzing with people going to work. There were a few punks sitting on the planters, and one of them called out to me. "Hey. Got any spare change?"

I didn't hear her because I was lost in my head. My nightmare was supposed to be over. All I needed to do was finish school so I could get a job. Have a life. Before starting high school, I'd spent hours picking out college subjects and classes, trying on ideas about what cool career I'd have. Psychology. Anthropology. Art.

I couldn't get warm even though I'd walked all the way from SOMA. I was repeating words in my head. It's not fair. It's not fair. I tried. I tried.

"Please pardon the interruption," one of the punks announced, suddenly in front of me and going down on one knee, hand outstretched. I snapped back into frame. He'd said it with a silly, over-pronounced affect. He looked to be around sixteen, tall and gangly, with sparkling brown eyes and a giant red mohawk that waved at the world like a crazy fin. His jeans and jean jacket were ripped and covered in safety pins, paint, and ink that yelled at the world about Angry Samoans and Circle Jerks. The way he fluttered his eyelashes at me, he looked like a goofball, his steep chin angled like a grinning shovel.

"Or not!" He jumped up and resumed his seat among the punks, wrapping his arm around a scowly, mohawked Black girl. They had matching nose rings. Her mohawk had the same red in it.

"I'm looking for Joe," I managed. The girl relaxed.

A scar-faced boy in black leather and spikes smiled from

behind curly black mohawk bangs and said, "You can call me Joe if you want to!"

"Oooo, things is hotting up," grinned a younger boy with bleach-blonde hair flopping like puppy ears beneath a dirty black Motorhead baseball cap. His high voice had a practiced roughness, like he was trying to seem tougher and older for his age, which I'd find out later was twelve. A serious, round-faced boy next to him in a leather jacket laughed quietly, shaking his head and looking off in the distance like he couldn't believe he was sitting with these people.

"Nooo, Jimmy," red mohawk sighed, emphasizing vowels like an exasperated parent, shaking his head theatrically. "Don't you make me pull this car over, fella!"

"I'm Joe," said a boy sitting on the girl's other side. He wore a tatty fake leopard coat, his lips glowing with bright pink lipstick. Huge blue eyes glittered through black raccoon rings of slept-in eyeliner. His voice dropped an octave in a bad British accent, "But I'm not the Joe you're looking for."

Jimmy smiled at me sweetly, and it was a little scary. Scars split his eyebrow and chin, lighter brown against his tea-with-milk skin, accent marks for sharp cheekbones. He wore combat boots, a black leather jacket splashed with red paint over a muscled frame, and wore a skull belt buckle to complete a threatening picture. He looked like a murderous hair model.

"I'm Jimmy," he said, extending his hand. Red mohawk rolled his eyes. I smiled, but didn't take his hand. The girl came to my rescue. "There's room over here if you want to hang out and see if other Joe shows up."

She said her name was Rogue while moving her bag to make a space, the glamorous one scooted over, and that's how I came to sit on the Magic Bench.

It wasn't really a bench. The long concrete planter was situated directly outside the subway station's main entrance.

"Prime real estate for spare changing," Rogue explained. She said the "bench" was magic because sometimes people here were so nice that amazing things happened. "Like people giving you $5 bills, or buying you a sandwich from Rossi's."

Leaving the magic bench happened when cops came or when the Stop AIDS Project set up a table to save some lives in the plaza. Or, if the panhandling might be better somewhere else, like in the Haight.

The boy next to Rogue -- he of the red mohawk -- stood to theatrically bow and give me his name. "Greetings to you! I am Zeke, or Mrs. Rogue if you like." He grinned an expanse of big teeth.

My "hello" came out in a giggle.

Rogue offered me a cigarette. "So," she said. "Whassup?"

A few hours later we migrated to the corner of Haight and Ashbury. The panhandling is better there during the day because of all the tourists, I was told.

"And for girls there's no pressure for sex work," Rogue added. "You go spare-changing in the Mission, SOMA, or Polk Street and that's the only way to make it. Up here," she swept an arm at the intersection, "you can get more for selling drugs, but no one tells you that you have to fuck for cash in order to even be in the neighborhood."

This was far and away from the world my mother demanded me to be in. For my new friends, punk was about building different values than the ones making everyone around us miserable. Individuating your experience, and respecting the experience of other people -- as long as they respected yours.

"You gotta decide your rules right away." Rogue directed that statement at me. Her tone was serious. "And you can never, ever break them."

That afternoon she used the same tone of voice when we saw the abandoned bag on the corner of Haight and Belvedere. "Don't run. Just walk like normal."

In a doorway on the 600 block of Cole, we looted a tourist's purse. Rogue and I were almost literally on what used to be Charles Manson's doorstep.

Unlike the Castro, the Haight was a neighborhood I already knew pretty well. Its reputation as home for the Summer of Love baffled me, but that myth brought the tourists. They took souvenir photos at the corner of Haight and Ashbury, their fingers in "peace" signs, and bought big round plastic purple sunglasses from the drag queen and "stripperwear" stores.

The 1960s were so long ago that for us kids it might as well have been the 1940s. Yet it was the fake way people remembered the hippie times in San Francisco that cranked up our cynicism. More evidence that people remembered what they wanted to. For them, it was a fabled time of enchantment for San Francisco, where there were "Human Be-Ins" and people danced naked in the park during festivals celebrating the freeing of the spirit.

That's what was sold here. According to postcards, tour guides, TV documentaries, and movies about the era, San Francisco in the 60s was wave after wave of enlightening music, rallies against injustice, shining sun, magical awakenings, and the hippie spirit of caring. There were beads and flowers, and countercultural icons urging people to open their minds. Everyone in the world knew that San Francisco was where you escaped to be free. Hippies, anarchists, sexual revolutionaries, LGBTQ, and thousands of people -- mostly kids -- swarmed San Francisco seeking sanctuary.

The revered pastime of running away in American lore hung over our heads like a cloud, choked the Haight like a noxious gas. During "Summer of Love" time, it was illegal to run away from home. But even then it was touted in books, film, newspapers, and TV of the time as a quaint rite of passage. The vision of the smiling young white boy with a stick and sack over his shoulder, off to his adventure of becoming a man. The enduring fantasy of those with a nice home and a future to return to, after gamely throwing themselves at life just to see what happens. The fable that good people are rewarded, despite the fact that from day one on the streets it was pretty clear that the people with rewards already had them to begin with. And were seldom good people.

I knew the Haight we were in had been through tens of thousands of runaway kids by the time I ended up there. The year of the famous Be-In, 1967, was when San Francisco drowned in runaways and the homeless, the family-less. The real ones. Not people from upper middle class families trying to "find" themselves -- or just "get laid" in a city synonymous with sexual freedom. There were plenty of those. But many runaways sought the sexual freedom and expression represented by San Francisco, in hopes of finding people like themselves and to escape persecution.

The runaways that came to San Francisco weren't living an American myth of plucky adventurism. They were children and young adults who were running *from* something equally as much as they hoped to run *to* something. Decades before I was born, they streamed into the Haight daily, fleeing violent parents and communities, discrimination, sexual abuse, assault, stalking, and worse. The only youth runaway shelter in the Haight, Huckleberry House, was ceaselessly full to capacity from the day it opened its doors in the 1960s. My new friends brought me up to speed on why shelters like that weren't an option for me. No room at the inn.

The key to survival was, as Rogue and her friends told me, to seem invisible to the serial killers, cops, rapists, and creeps. Because where there are runaways, there follow those who prey on them. Rogue warned me about parents looking for their "lost" kids. Not all of them were actually anyone's parents, and even the real ones just wanted to drag someone back home for more beatings, or worse. Some homeless and junkies on the streets with us, even among the groups of normally tight-knit and protective punks, would "sell" runaways. They'd rat you out to your abusive stepdad or some Charlie Manson for twenty bucks. It was despicable, and something we all had to look out for.

The Haight was where men with destructive black thoughts came for eternal summer. Everyone knew what Charles Manson did -- drugging runaway hippie girls, abusing them until the end -- because it was common. Talk to anyone: There were so many Mansons in the Haight. He blended in here. The Haight was a place of violence, fear, suffering, and desperation from the start. Everyone here knew the Summer of Love was a sham.

There were men who saw us as a consequence-free outlet for violence or abuse, and there were the addicts, often one and the same. By the 1970s it was estimated that fifteen percent of the veterans who returned from Vietnam and landed in San Francisco were heroin addicts. Many sought solace and a steady drug pipeline in the Haight. Life in the neighborhood was violent and desperate, made crazier by the next wave of drugs: cocaine, crack, speed, and PCP -- evidenced in spikes of overdoses endured by overwhelmed staff at the Haight-Ashbury Free Clinic. The police struggled with grisly, sometimes unspeakable drug murders in the neighborhood.

The epicenter of peace and love was for us a place of guns where life was cheap and the police had closed down the nearby Park Station -- abandoning the neighborhood to consume itself. Next door, the AIDS crisis played out over the hill in the Castro. Both neighborhoods were broken fables with people dying in the street. Still, the tourists came.

Due to its history, the Haight I was in had become one part street urchin ecosystem and one part mental hospital for violent offenders. It was a tourist destination dotted with dusty vintage clothing stores, bars, cafes, and head shops that sold drug paraphernalia and incense with names like "peace." Its residents were UCSF students, old hippies and various communities like punks, gay people, vintage lifestylers, artists, and writers. Despite its dangers, there was a vibrancy and intersection of subcultures that made it pulse with vitality.

Yet the Haight's history stalked its streets. Walk down its stained sidewalk, among its stale, moldering Summer of Love paint jobs and you could feel it. It was not a place children should be, and yet there we were, the newest generation of a multi-decade homeless epidemic. It was crazy to me that while all this had been going on in the Haight, the epicenter of high- tech research and development had been architecting the future in semiconductors, microchips, and software in companies like Lockheed and Apple while we starved in its shadow. Begging for spare change, we talked and thought about all of this, often.

Looking around at tourists stepping over panhandling kids, and ranting, bearded homeless men exuding auras of violence, I believed that the Haight had always been this way.

Haight was not "Summer in the City." It was never summer in the city here. It was fucking cold. Painful pit of my empty stomach cold. Stealing money from someone's purse cold. A hundred Victorians in my bones raking the fog like knife blades held upward. That kind of cold.

7

ROGUE and I dumped out the purse we found in Upper Haight only to find it held no wallet. All we stole was a collection of things someone would miss. We left it there. For Charlie Manson, we joked.

We walked along Haight back to where Jimmy, Zeke, and Big Shaun and Little Shaun waited. I kept my eyes on the sidewalk, a mosaic of mystery stains, occasional chalk drawings of peace signs and other hippie crap. I hoped to spot dropped change, a bus pass, anything of value. I noticed Rogue's low-slung, boy-like stride, and I matched it. It was somehow a way of walking that said, "don't fuck with me."

She said, "You know, we're all set for the zombie apocalypse."

That surprised me and I laughed saying, "For real. Everyone'll be freaking out, but we'll be all, huh, more zombies. Aim for the head."

She was nodding. "More zombies, totally! But we'll know, like, how to survive. Or if there's a nuclear war."

"Me too," I said. "We're so ready. I used to keep a survival kit under my bed when I was a little kid, for when the bombs fell."

"What was in it?" she asked.

"Just … everything. Ketchup packets, plastic forks from takeout food, creamers from Denny's." Thinking about my old survival kit made me wonder what happened to it when my mother and I were put into witness protection.

Rogue did a little skip while we walked. "Zombies ain't

gonna get our brains, but we're still gonna need your ketchup for our fries! Oh man, I want some fries right now so bad."

"Me too," I said. "We'd be rad zombie hunters though."

"Fuck yeah! And we'd have our pick of all the mansions because all the rich people would be dead or too scared to deal."

I knew Rogue had to be a horror fan like me. The films were about survival. And gallows humor, which is also about survival. I asked her, "What's your favorite horror movie?"

"Man ... I dunno. I like 'em all. *Evil Dead 2?*"

I hadn't seen that one. "Have you seen *Alien?*"

"Ripley!" she yelled. "Fuck yeah. The ones with chicks kicking ass are the best ones. I hate the ones where the girl is weak or doesn't fight, or has to get raped or some shit."

"I know!" I said. "How come the girls have to be the victim all the time? It's stupid."

"Hollywood just doesn't know any girls like us, that's why. Fuck 'em!"

We felt big and bold walking up to the gang, proud, despite that we'd bombed on getting food money.

"That's okay," Zeke said when we told him we got to the purse too late. He wrapped his long skinny arms around Rogue, and her smile was so warm. "Look at all our pretty hair, no one can resist us! I can feel it."

I worried about my hair, and as if on cue, Joe found us like that. He was accompanied by a harsh-faced punk girl named Jenn. I wasn't being mean thinking that about her face; her angles evoked a John Waters film casting decision. Joe looked relieved to see me. He gave me a huge bear hug that lifted me off the ground, then set me down to put his forehead to mine and said, "I wasn't worried about you."

It took me a minute to understand before I said, "Thank you." I even smiled a little.

The afternoon went by while we asked strangers for money or food. We all spread out to divvy up the street for better chances of getting spare change or leftovers from people leaving restaurants and cafes. I was a little woozy from hunger, so I sat on the sidewalk outside a bookstore with Big Shaun and Little Shaun.

The Haight went about its day around us. Japanese tourists in fanny packs and shorts eyed us cautiously, stepping past quickly in their struggle to find the Haight's attractions. Shop workers on break said hi to us, their facial piercings glinting sunlight, each heading back to vintage clothing stores, head shops, skate shops, bookstores, and bric-a-brac stores hawking "I heart SF" postcards.

The more I sat on Haight's sidewalk, the more I learned. Both Shauns seemed to enjoy explaining everything to me. It wasn't the summer, Big Shaun instructed in his stoner monotone, but fall was still a pretty good time of year to panhandle. Tourists were thin on the ground but there was still change to be had because the college students were back.

Little Shaun was excited to be knowledgeable, opening up to me like a tour guide for Haight homelessness when he rattled off a laundry list of tips for staying safe. Stay away from the crazy homeless adults, he told me. They were wet brain alkies, psycho vets, speed freaks, and pedos. Don't have anything to do with the hippie kids, the white boys and girls with dreadlocks who pretended to be homeless while using their parent's Gold Cards. They were called "Trustafarians" -- rich white kids who pretended to be poor, often appropriating Rastafarian or other Black cultures, or were [Grateful] "Deadheads." (These later morphed into loathsome

Burning Man "burners.") There was a punk version of these proto-hippie jerks, derisively called "Crusties." Trustafarians, Deadheads, and Crusties shoplifted but didn't need to, pissed off Haight shop owners and residents with drum circles, left piles of trash, and did open drug sales on the sidewalk. They'd rip you off, I was told, and worse, much worse if they got a chance.

Around us flowed a society of people with cars, jobs, homes, families, music and TV, fashion and nightlife, passing through on their way to shop, consume, to fit in. We begged them for quarters and food.

Just when you thought the Haight is all razor wire smiles and cold sidewalk, it surprised with a burst of color and life: we stopped to smile at a girl with bright pink hair in a vinyl coat as she hurried past, carrying overstuffed shopping bags on her way to sell vintage clothes, the smell of mothballs trailing her. The Haight had a strong underground fashion scene. There was something about its style you couldn't see anywhere else.

The bookstore didn't mind us sitting out front. The store was close to a Mexican restaurant; our goal was to score enough for one of their giant burritos, which could last a person a whole day or feed two people. They cost nearly four dollars. But since they were often too much for one person to eat, the restaurant's patrons usually came out with leftovers. I spotted a man coming out of the restaurant with a styrofoam box. His blue Patagonia jacket swished as he walked. I asked if he could "spare any leftovers."

He came over, appraising me. "You don't look homeless."

I didn't look homeless... Didn't I? What did I look like? My mind quickly indexed my appearance. White girl, short. Dirty Vans on my feet. Worn black jeans, a t-shirt over a long john top, under an Army jacket. I was trying so hard to keep my clothes clean. I had a straggly, growing-out, dirty blonde bob that I tried to keep tucked behind my ears to hide a little chunk of bald space -- the bit missing from my hairline above my eye from the accident. Patagonia's hair had gel in it.

I didn't know what I was supposed to look like to deserve his leftovers. But I took so long thinking about this that after a minute he said, "Yeah, I thought so."

He started to walk away but stopped in front of the boys. Little Shaun's poker face was like a shut door. "Here," he said, handing the box to Little Shaun. "Don't share it with her," he nodded in my direction.

I would soon encounter more versions of the man in the Patagonia jacket than I could count. At first, the viciousness of adults toward us shocked me. He was a normal person. To him, we were trash. Others would tell me to go home, to get a job, take a shower, get a life, to fuck off -- or, to fuck them.

With me, Mr. Patagonia sensed an opportunity to do right by a certain set of principles, a mission that was warped and executed with vigor. He was no doubt this way in the rest of his life to varying degrees, and in ways that relished wounding others with excitement of purpose. We saw the raw truth of him, because to him we were disposable. I came to learn that people show you who they really are when they believe they can behave without consequence.

Little Shaun took the box and gave the guy a nod. When Patagonia-guy was out of earshot, Little Shaun thrust the container at me while exhaling "Doooooousshhh."

Giggling, I said, "Are you sure?"

He thrust his chin up at me and went back to scanning the street like a little tough guy. "Nah, s'cool. We've almost got enough to split a burrito anyway."

"Thanks," I was still incredulous. "Fuck, man. That dude has no idea what's going on with me."

"Well, you're out here, you're public fuckin' property now," Big Shaun told me. "And you're a girl so they're already gonna be mad about how much they think they own you."

"Shit." I never thought about it like that, but he was right.

"There are definitely types and you just stay away from them," Little Shaun added. "Like him, people just waiting for their chance to get somebody."

"We know who all the regular assholes are though," Big Shaun added.

It was true: News traveled among us up and down the street like inmates passing secrets in jail. We watched everything, we saw everyone. Your good days, your bad ones.

Within a few hours I learned that the crazy hippie lady who owned the craft shop would call the cops on you if you panhandle out front. She mistreated her employees, too. The guys at the Blue Front Cafe would let you use the bathroom if they knew you, and if you don't take too long. They were grumpy but they cared about the Haight. You could hang out in the comic store and they'd let you read comics and 'zines if you were polite about it, careful not to damage the paper.

Sometimes at the end of the night, guys at the pizza slice place gave us slices too old to sell because one time a deadhead tried to steal their tip jar and Jimmy caught him, and returned their tips. After he'd thrown the hippie face-first into a parked car. Because, that's Jimmy. He was also the reason the skinheads seldom fucked with us. Jimmy scared them, Big Shaun told me, because "Jimmy fights like he's got nothing to lose."

When it got dark, Jimmy offered to walk me to the band's warehouse. It was on the way to his sleeping spot in SOMA. With me he was warm, considerate. He said his spot was a place he could crash sometimes, but apologized that one of the conditions of sleeping there was that he couldn't bring anyone.

"It's okay," I said, thinking I didn't want to hurt his feelings by saying I probably didn't think of him the way he might be thinking of me.

We stood in front of the warehouse while I finished explaining the scene I was dealing with there. A bunch of older dudes with high school girlfriends. Smelly couches. The older guy, Kevin, who wanted to fuck me. Sleeping with one eye open, as it were.

After a moment Jimmy said, "I can make him leave you alone."

His features had changed so slightly; the upward pull of a smile around his eyes seconds ago was gone, flattening his expression into cold stone. It was a quiet violence, and I realized how dangerous Jimmy was. He was serious. I thanked him and explained that no, something like that would get me kicked out for sure, and then Jimmy smiled his goofy, disarming smile and said, "Oh! Duh, sorry."

We hugged and said goodbye. I slipped into the warehouse. One of their lackluster parties was in full swing. Music, a beer bong, but no Tina Chan. I was exhausted. I blended in like I'd been there all night, waited until everyone left. Cleared a spot on a couch, got my aching feet up, and finally slept.

I woke up in a freezing, quiet party husk. In reality, their warehouse was technically uninhabitable. The band had built out its interior themselves; they treated the space like daddy would someday come finish it and mommy would magically appear to clean it. The shower was a pipe and nozzle fastened to a wall. It projected water over wooden pallets atop a concrete floor with a drain in it. Its walls were part plywood, part plastic tarps, and all mold. The guys all had plastic slip-on sandals they wore when showering, but I didn't have that luxury. The hot water felt so good that morning I didn't care.

I dressed and walked out to find a girl sitting on the couch I'd just slept on. Waiting for me.

"I don't think we've met," she said. "I'm Kevin's girlfriend, Sarah."

Ah, so the creeper did have a girlfriend after all. Sarah looked to be in her twenties. Her long brown hair topped a curvy physique straining to escape an outfit straight out of a John Hughes film. A green cummerbund bisected her white asymmetrical top, layered over pleated turquoise cargo pants. An ensemble for a girl who was into boy bands.

Her round face was set in concern mode. Apparently, they'd all had a discussion about me. Well, that's just great.

Sarah said that when she brought me up, Kevin was shocked to discover my age. Now, she explained, it was time for me to go home. It was for the best. Sarah was genuinely concerned about my mother's feelings. "She loves you," Sarah said to no one but herself. "You're her baby and she must be worried sick about you."

I complimented her outfit when I left. "God bless," she said.

I went from the warehouse to the Magic Bench, spotting my friends assembled there. I took in the neighborhood ebb and flow as I walked up to Harvey Milk Plaza. The Castro Theatre's coolly shadowed entrance yawned its empty morning mouth into the sunlight, ticket booth a vacant promise of a later showtime. I heard a gently murmured "excuse me" from a tree-trunk of beard and man heading to work in sport coat and khakis, threading past a slow-moving pair of thin fellows out for a walk. A slow-strolling Twiggy-of-a-man passed them in tight jeans, zip-jacket, glittered scarf, enormous sunglasses, and an elbow planted at his hip as if to accuse the world of being too messy with each step. It was the Castro warming itself up for another day.

Along the planter my friends were in varying stages of just-awake, mohawks were at rumpled angles. An intermittent hum and a smell of dusty metal exhaled from trains below while I told Rogue, Zeke, Jimmy, Joe, and Aiden that I'd just been kicked out of the warehouse. I hadn't seen Aiden since my last visit to school and he looked and smelled like he'd been sleeping rough. As in, outside. We hugged when we saw each other.

Zeke joked, "I can't believe she brought God into it! She left out the Lord Jesus!"

Rogue's eyeroll sprung Zeke off the bench and into a Jesus-on-the-cross pose. In his best Southern accent Zeke belted out, "JEY-sus is a BIS-cuit!"

Rogue cackled. Her laugh was crazy, infectious. Zeke pivoted to face Rogue and started walking toward her like a zombie, moaning "Let him sop you uuuup!"

Rogue bolted off the bench past him and ran into Harvey Milk's own MUNI station while Zeke chased her, swerving around an old man on a cane.

The old guy tottered. He regained his balance as Jimmy hopped up to help him, asking: "Do you need to sit down?"

"If you guys don't mind," he said. Softly, with a real Southern accent. He added, "I'm Terry." We made space on the concrete and he eased his frail frame onto the bench.

Jimmy asked if Terry went to Cafe Mimic. "No," Terry said. "Where is it?"

"What is it, is more the question," Jimmy said. He explained the Cafe happened in a warehouse on Natoma Street four days a week and was run by a couple who lived there, Frank and Joey. "It's not a real cafe in the strict sense of legality," Jimmy smiled, "but we serve coffee and tea, and bread things, and Frank makes killer chili."

Jimmy said Zeke worked there two out of the four days, and Joey was "like a manager," organizing art shows and sometimes music in the back room. Jimmy helped care for their gigantic Akita, a dog named Duchess.

Terry sat with us, somehow becoming part of our group, asking about the different band names scrawled on jeans and jackets. We resumed asking for spare change, people argued about bands (old punk was better than new punk, which apparently was for Berkeley and LA posers), and I wrote in my journal. For me, even doing nothing meant I had to be doing something.

"Read me!" Jimmy said, interrupting me.

"What?" I had no idea what he meant. Jimmy repeated with a smile, "Read me!"

Zeke had returned with Rogue riding piggyback. "Jimmy can't read," Rogue said, sliding down to stand and stick her hand in Zeke's back pocket.

"I'm dicks-lexic," Jimmy winked to Terry, our new elder statesman. Terry smiled and shook his head, looking at Jimmy in an oh-you-kids way. He got the hang of Jimmy just fine.

Jimmy wanted me to read something to him. "Maybe later," I said.

I was trying to write a poem. I was angry at Sarah, but not

for kicking me out. For presuming that my life was anything like hers, with a mother and a home to go back to. I also wondered if my mom was okay. I'd been doing mental gymnastics to prevent remembering the sounds she made in the living room with that guy.

Rogue asked me, "Do you play D and D?"

"No, is it fun?"

Everyone got really excited. I didn't understand why, but I was excited, too. "I'll teach you at the cafe," she said.

"We gotta get you some dice though," Rogue added. "There's a place on Divisadero, we'll figure it out."

Terry didn't ask us personal questions. He just hung out with us, smiled, listened, and laughed at Zeke's theatrics for passing strangers. Jimmy and Terry chatted amiably, and I overheard their exchange while I was trying to think of words to write.

Terry wasn't old. Terry was 30. Younger than my mother.

I looked up from my journal. Now I noticed the patches of pink skin on his ear, slight discolorations on his neck. Terry looked like he weighed less than me. When you're young you think everyone is really old. I realized my mistake. There were a lot of old guys with canes in the Castro, but like Terry, they weren't old. They were dying.

Everyone here knew what the federal government was doing by ignoring the AIDS crisis. And no one outside San Francisco seemed to care because it was gay people. There was no justifiable excuse. It made me furious.

Terry announced that he had to get up and go, he was on his way to a doctor's appointment. Jimmy offered to walk him up the stairs to the bus stop on Castro, and I got up at the same time to hit up the plaza's pay phone.

I needed to make a call.

8

I PAUSED at the pay phone and noticed how the morning commute emptied the neighborhood. It was eerily still. I could hear the drumbeat hiss of a barkeep sweeping last night's cigarette butts from sidewalk to street. "Stop AIDS" flyers on poles tick-ticking in a salty breeze drawn seemingly by gravity from Twin Peaks. Brakes of MUNI buses squealed in the morning air while Market Street's river of cars purred downhill toward shoreline skyscrapers in the distance.

I called the number at my mom's work. I wasn't sure if I was going to leave a message or not. It didn't matter. When I asked for her, they said she quit last week.

Shit. Really? I dialed Donna's number.

"Hey kid," she hissed taking a drag on a cigarette. Great, now she was calling me a child, too. "You guys moved out."

I couldn't believe what I was hearing. My mother ... left? I felt like I was in two places at once, my body down in the Castro and my consciousness floating up, looking down, watching myself get smaller and smaller.

I needed to stay in my body. I fought my way back down. Stay present, I reminded myself. Quit freaking out and focus.

"Kid, you still there?"

"Yeah, I'm here," I managed. "When ... where did she go?"

"She said she was moving in with Charles."

A few stumbled questions later and Donna told me that Charles was the guy, that guy, the one who searched the house for me, though Donna didn't know that. The guy that

I'm pretty sure raped and beat my mother, and came looking for me next. That one.

I could almost hear my brain struggling to process this.

My mother was smart. By her estimate, the smartest person in the room at all times. *But the thing was,* I thought, *I'd only missed two, maybe three days of school since I left home.* If she really wanted to find me, she could've. What if ... she had found me, and told me she was planning to move? Would I say, "Wow I'm so happy for you. Congratulations on moving in together. It's magic when you meet the right person."

"You guys need to come get your shit," Donna exhaled another puff. "Those boxes in the garage. And I want my keys back."

I played along and made a plan with Donna to come over that night and get our stuff and hand over the keys, full well knowing I couldn't do it. I didn't know what else to do.

Also, there were boxes?

I told my friends I'd meet them back at the Magic Bench later. I set out for the Sunset District.

Donna had let it slip that she was leaving for work after our call, so by the time I got there the house was empty. I went straight to the kitchen and made a sandwich. I was so hungry I had to remind myself to chew. Stuffing my face with baloney and cheese on white bread while I walked through the house, I peeked into our room and sure enough, it was empty. Any stuff I left behind was gone. I beelined for the garage.

There was a huge stack of boxes with my mother's name on each of them. It was as if the truths my mother wouldn't tell me might be in them. I had to know what was in those boxes.

I tore into box after box. Clothes. Dishes. Mom's albums:

The Beatles, Rolling Stones, Bee Gees. Total crap. A lamp, a macrame plant holder, books. I'd read these as a child: *Cosmos, Be Here Now, Johnny Got His Gun.* Sheets. Framed prints of my mother's photography, the Golden Gate Bridge.

The last box I opened wasn't the last of the boxes, it was just the box where I stopped.

I sliced packing tape and pulled open its cardboard leaves. Under layers of paper was an American flag. It was folded in a very special way, a tight triangle. On top of it was a dog tag and two photographs of the same man.

The back of one photo, a small black and white, was labeled with the same name as the dog tag.

The other photo was a color Polaroid of the same man reclining on a weird, black-fur chaise lounge. A leopard skin was draped across the seat beneath him. On a table to his right was its skull.

The smell of the leopard's dry skin and hair came to me in a rush, a combination of animal musk and dried parchment. That skin and skull used to be in our house when I was a child. I remembered the texture of its fur all the way down to its tail, soft and thick, its eyeholes, its nose black and hard. I stared at the photo. Was that my father?

I needed answers. Only one woman could give them to me. I stashed both photos and the dog tag into my bag. I closed the boxes.

Then I got the hell out of there.

Everyone was at the Magic Bench when I got back.

"There's a show tonight," Zeke said, in his best over-pronounced sing-song voice. I shot him a confused look. "Would you like to attend a punk rock musical event?"

I had no idea where I was going to sleep that night. My mouth opened. "Yes!" Jimmy interrupted, "She says yes!"

77

"They won't let you in looking like that," Little Joe told me. Smiling, he started pulling messy little makeup pots, pencils, and tubes of color out of his crazily packed shoulder bag. I had a quick image of him pulling impossible things out of it like a magician; a hairdryer, a horse, a submarine. I suppressed a giggle. "It's a punk house party in the Mission," said Little Joe. He patted the seat next to him. "Sit, sit."

Once my green eyes were rimmed and smeared with black, I never wanted them to look any other way. Jimmy wouldn't stop staring at me. "What color do you want your lips," Little Joe asked, gently dusting my cheeks with white. Our faces were so close.

"Blue," I said quietly. "Blue."

"Okay Miss Blue," he smiled.

Little Joe did makeup for anyone who wanted it, like Harvey Milk Plaza was our own personal salon. Everyone with a mohawk sprayed it up with Aqua Net, hissed from a big metal can, like spray paint. I imagined us there like the wild parrots that roamed San Francisco yelling at the sky, with our medley of hair colors, and ripped up clothing that screwed with gender concepts while saying "don't touch." Birds on a line along the planters. Asking people for change, inviting them to conversation.

We were decked out by dusk and took to the street with our long-legged, swinging tough-guy strides, with our heads up enjoying the stares all the way to Valencia Street.

The party was in the basement of a decrepit Edwardian-style apartment building, in a huge room dimly lit, hazed with smoke. The Mission District was changing and you could see it around the room. All the white kids partying in a poor immigrant neighborhood rich with its own history. Lingering in groups along the walls were punks, some goths, metalheads, new wavers, and assorted rockers in boots and band t-shirts.

The room had a soundtrack of its own even before any music began. In that low-ceilinged, dim space was a steady murmur of conversation, punctuated by the clink of bottles being pulled from grocery bags, or the staccato stomp of a can being crushed underfoot. Boxes of beer and empties littered the floor along the walls. At the back of the building was the "stage" -- not a stage at all, just the area where the band was plugging everything in. It was a makeshift punk club in a Mission Street basement, warming up for a night of noise in the San Francisco underground.

I noticed the way Zeke and Rogue scanned the room, silently noting the presence of skinheads to each other in the way couples can silently communicate danger. I followed their lead as we found a spot to call our own, along a side wall and away from the violent racists. When the first punk band started, Rogue looped her arm through mine and hauled me out into the middle of the room where people started to slam dance. Arm in arm we skipped in circles like two little kids, whirling and bashing into everyone who did their best to bounce off us.

There was a secret I kept from my mother before this. There were times when I would sneak away on my own, and I would go to the beach. Whichever beach was nearest whatever awful motel or rental flop we were in. And I would swim. In the Pacific. Ignoring signs warning of dangers, I'd go into the freezing ocean alone, whenever I could escape. Past the line of wave breaks I could float peacefully on my back and make angels in the water. I've been slammed breathless by shorepound, pulled out by riptides, giggled hysterically gasping for breath as I swam parallel and boggled at how far down the coast I ended up. And that night on Rogue's arm, I felt the shock and exhilaration of diving under a massive wave just as it's breaking.

We ricocheted off strangers who crashed onto the next person, human projectiles glancing off one another endlessly. If someone fell, someone else pulled them up. We couldn't stop grinning. Each smash felt like letting go, bodies slamming into mine making me feel harder, tougher, alive, and part of something. It hurt, and I knew I was alive because I hurt. At that moment, I thought that trauma only exposes who you have always been. The singer screamed, Rogue and I screamed, and we spun harder, erupting in fury and joy in a place where we had no future.

We left the fray and tagged Jimmy and Zeke to go in; we'd watch the stuff and drink beer while the guys went slamming. Rogue and I cracked open our cans, toasted, and bobbed our heads and looked around. Joe was in the pit, a violent merry-go-round of flailing bodies in the center of the room. Little Joe was smoking and chatting up a goth boy. Big Shaun and Little Shaun were hanging out with Jenn, Joe's friend with the harsh face. I spotted Aiden and John Gone, waving hi. They waved back.

A hand waved right in my face. I jerked my head back.

Two skinhead girls stood in front of me.

They looked like bald bookends. Dressed identically, each had green flight "bomber" jackets, white shirts, red suspenders, Ben Davis work pants that had never seen a day of work, and oxblood red Doc Marten boots on feet that had never walked a mile in anyone else's shoes. Both had what Rogue would tell me later was called a "Bash cut" -- a style of haircut named after some skinhead asshole. It had little fringes at the front, I guess so people could tell that

Tweedledum was the blonde one, and Tweedledumber was the brunette.

"You kicked her," Tweedledum shouted at me, indicating her friend.

"Oh well," shouted Rogue.

Both skinheads snapped to attention at Rogue, moving forward. I stepped between them just as Rogue stepped forward, bumping me in the back, which had the cool effect of making my chin go up like I was a tough guy. Hey, I meant to do that.

"I'm sorry," I yelled in their faces. A smile tugged at the corner of my mouth, and it felt wicked just how much I didn't mean it.

"What's up, girls?" It was Jenn, Joe's friend. She put an arm around me, grinning like a maniac at the skins and said, "Can I play too?"

"Yeah, you're fuckin' sorry," the brunette skinhead yelled at me, turning away from us. Both skins stomped off, over to where their male counterparts huddled over a twelve-pack of beer.

Jenn looked at Rogue and I. "Did I ruin it? I thought we were gonna beat those bitches."

Rogue shook her head and popped open a new beer, chugging it with a vengeance. "We're good, thanks though," I said.

Jenn seemed okay with that, but something lingered in the air that said it wasn't. A need. Like she wanted to show us something inside her, something glittery and violent that would make us like her.

We left when Jimmy got too drunk. Zeke, Rogue and I convinced him it was time to go. Rogue said they were sleeping in a spot that night and I could join them. It was only okay to stay there on certain nights, and I had to keep it a secret and not take anyone else there.

I asked, "Is it far?"

"Set a course for Our Lady of Safeway," Zeke announced, using the nickname of a church that was on, well, Church Street, across from Safeway. Its nickname came from all the AA people who went to the church for their meetings, he explained.

We walked to a parking lot behind Kinko's, a 24-hour copy and print store. It was one of their sleeping spots; a wedge-shaped building in a mish-mash of old and new San Francisco business construction at the corner of Market and Duboce. Across the street was Safeway's dully lit parking lot and a recycling center that was a sketchy hub of homeless activity.

Zeke and Rogue left Jimmy and I alone behind Kinko's while they went to go get the ladder. Jimmy swayed and smiled at me, and I couldn't help but smile back. The longer Rogue and Zeke were away, the more I guessed they were having a quickie. Jimmy leaned clumsily toward me as if he was coming in for a kiss and I stepped aside. "Jimmy, later," I said, thinking maybe when you're sober, but also maybe not.

Jimmy said, "But," and then said, "I'm sorry. I mean it, I'm sorry." Jimmy looked like he felt way worse than the situation called for. There was something else here. A rock some river was flowing around.

Zeke and Rogue walked up. "Are you getting sweet on my girl," teased Rogue. She put an arm around me.

"I'm just..." Jimmy started, but didn't finish.

Zeke said, "You're just climbing this ladder veeery carefully, right Jim-Jam?"

"Always bring the ladder up after you," Zeke told me

once we were on the roof and the guys had hauled it up. We started to make a bed from a stack of painter's tarps but were interrupted by a noise on the roof behind us. There was a skylight, and someone was in it. The hatch creaked open.

A guy in a Kinko's uniform popped out. He said, "Okay, just making sure it's you. Seriously though, try to be quiet." He looked at me, and even in the dark I recognized the mad grin of someone doing amphetamines on the job. "Come on down if you want any free copies!" The hatch slammed shut behind him.

Jimmy crawled under a blue tarp and opened his leather jacket, motioning for me to come in. I went in and put my back against his stomach. Rogue wormed in as my little spoon, and Zeke snuggled up into her: Rogue's lanky "little spoon."

We curled around each other like kittens under the tarp and slept.

9

WHEN SARAH the skinhead's right fist connected with my left cheek I remember thinking very clearly that all I wanted today was for something to go right.

Yep, another Sarah. Made of the same condescending, empathy-deficient water and molecules as the other Sarah, who recently evicted me from her loser musician boyfriend's stinky couch.

My brain was managing new inventory with lots of duplicates. Two Joes and now two awful Sarahs. It was getting hard to believe parents of our generation had any originality whatsoever.

The side of my head exploded in stars, whitening out my field of vision. I stumbled a step backward on the sidewalk in front of Cha Cha Cha's, doing my own little dance to stay upright. A solo cha-cha in front of the restaurant's window at Haight and Steiner. The establishment was a trendy upscale spot in the dangerous, walk-on-the-wild-side Haight where fine diners guzzled sangria with a side of food on the table to keep up appearances.

I knew that technically, time wasn't slowing down. It was just my brain's prefrontal cortex lighting up like a Christmas tree to gather as much information as possible. A little hitch between breaths in slo-mo while my system simultaneously slammed adrenaline into a network already jacked from Sarah's pursuit. Moments before, I'd been sitting with Big and Little Shaun in front of the I-Beam, a gay punk club across the street, appealing to the generosity of late-night drunks for spare change.

To my surprise, I didn't go down from the punch.

I really didn't see that punch coming. You could say she threw a decent sucker-punch. But I gave her low scores on follow-through. I gripped Sarah's windmilling arm at the bicep of her green bomber jacket with my left hand and yanked her the rest of the way off balance. I could see her eyes were wide and way too bright. She was wired.

A small crowd of punks and club-goers gathered around us on the sidewalk. I thought I could hear yelling. Sarah stumbled forward, and I surprised myself again by not punching her back. It would have been a really ideal opportunity, perfect really.

But I'd had it with Sarah in a wholly different way.

I also knew that this was a point of no return for me.

It's not that I'd colossally fucked up by standing up to the skinhead girls the other night at the house party. I mean, it was tempting to go that route, blaming myself for making a big mistake by standing up to them. This is what you get for being brave. This is what you get for being a smart-ass, my mother would say.

After the confrontation at the party, Rogue, Jimmy, and Zeke filled me in. The skinheads had been around for years, with most of them coming into the city from Sacramento, Santa Cruz, Los Angeles, and gross little 'burbs like Bakersfield.

According to Rogue, there were three main skinhead houses in town. One was an apartment in the Tenderloin, another in the Haight, and a squat somewhere around the South Beach neighborhood. They grouped up mostly on weekends, stomping their stupid Nazi duck-walks up and down the Haight-Ashbury. They drank at the top of Buena Vista park -- that was their spot. That location made sense, Zeke said, because that was the Temple of Saturn and the park's gutters were lined with tombstones.

Okay, that was unexpected. I laughed, "What are you even talking about?"

"It's true!" Rogue said. She was clearly on board with this theory.

"The gutters are lined with old tombstones, I swear it," Zeke added. "And the ancient Atlantean city of Tlamco put their temple of death at the top of the hill where the skinheads hang out. That's the Temple of Saturn. How can that be a coincidence?" He saw my face. "What? They're soulless, so they're attracted to death."

I looked from Jimmy to Rogue and back to Zeke again. "The Atlanteans had temples in all of San Francisco's parks," Zeke continued in his best documentary narrator voice. "Alamo Square Park is the Temple of Venus. Right where the Painted Ladies are! See, it all makes sense."

Zeke went back to explaining the skinheads. They had a uniform. Doc Marten boots laced in a specific way (straight across), thin suspenders, jeans cuffed above their boots, and flight jackets. Many had tattoos and they all had shaved heads. The girls had fringe bangs at the very front, or all around the edges in what they called a "Bash cut." Their cult was racism and Hitler, they claimed to be working class, but most lived off their parents, they picked unfair fights, and ruined things just because they could.

How could people buy into this narrow-minded shit, I wondered. Maybe we punks were feral, but skinheads were vicious -- with the luxury of society backing them up. Hurting other people just to pretend they could survive pain.

Earlier that day, Rogue, Zeke, Jimmy and I had just missed the window for free Salvation Army sandwiches. It was a long, hungry walk from the Mission back to Haight. Rogue and I split off from the guys to see if we could get leftovers by the Blue Front Cafe.

Sarah and two of her skinhead clones came by a couple times while Rogue and I panhandled. They flicked lit cigarettes at us and spat on the sidewalk where we sat. When the coast was clear, I used a nearby pay phone to call Donna, keeping an eye on Rogue because I didn't like the idea of three skinheads finding her alone. But I wanted to find out where my mom moved to. There was no answer.

So, I was already having a bad day when Sarah found me later that night. I'd been abandoned by my mother again, spit on, had lit cigarettes flicked at me, and was either ignored or insulted all day by people I asked for food. Sarah the skinhead found me in front of the I-Beam and called me things -- things related to Rogue. Sarah was a vicious child obsessed with the idea that my friend's Blackness only existed to staunch the bleeding-out of her Category-5 insecurity.

Which is why, after Sarah sucker-punched me, instead of punching her back I put all my weight behind an open handed slap. I aimed my point of contact for the other side of her head, which should give you an idea for how hard I hit her. I was done with her racist bullshit.

I watched Sarah twist as she fell, and later I wondered if I should feel bad about the fact that I just stood for a second enjoying her go down. I thought about telling her to stay down. It would be a really good idea. Then I felt someone grab me hard by the shoulders and spin me around. His whole look was classic Less

Than Zero, like coke parties by the pool. Oh, I knew this breed of tech jock. His linen suit was a dead giveaway that he was slumming it in the Haight -- at Cha Cha Cha's.

"I'm sick of you little scumbags," he roared in my face as he gripped my shoulders. Yeah, I was getting the impression that guys like him found poor punk girls like me really upsetting. Spit flecked onto my face; the Summer of Love was all around us.

"You fucking trash!" He threw me into the restaurant's blue brick wall. At that moment, I really didn't understand why everyone thought wealth was a validation of goodness. As the air went out of my lungs, I realized his suit was white, he was wearing all white, and right as the back of my head connected with the brick I thought, *You've got to be fucking kidding me.*

All the lights in the world flickered. My feet hit the ground as he turned to help Sarah. I recovered and sprinted into the dark neighborhood of Victorians climbing the hill behind us.

I spent the last of my change to take the 33 bus to the Castro. The driver looked at me like he'd just found me under his bus, not boarding it. *Please,* I thought, *please just let someone nice be at the Magic Bench.* All I wanted was to see one friendly face.

Exiting the bus, I could see from the top of Harvey Milk's steps that no one was at the bench. Tears welled up; each blink of my left eye was hot, tight, and starting to get painful. Note to self: don't forget that everyone is right-handed. Block left, block left.

"Hey!"

It was Jimmy. He ran up the sidewalk from where he'd

been standing in front of a leather bar on Castro. "Hey, hey, hey," he said as he got closer.

Jimmy's face hardened. "Who did this to you." It wasn't a question. It was a pronouncement.

"I .. I just ... Fuck!" I started crying. I was more frustrated than anything. Jimmy put his arms out, pulling me into a hug. He smelled like alcohol and sweat, but also leather jacket and familiar skin. I flinched my way into it. Oh, tomorrow was going to suck.

"I just want a beer," I wiped my nose on my sleeve. "They're gone, I just want a beer," I told him. I wasn't even hungry anymore.

Jimmy took over and made a plan. We'd drink beer in Duboce Park, and then Jimmy would stay with me in the Lower Haight squat. Before I found him, he'd already made enough cash hustling at the bars that night to buy me a slice of pizza. I found out I was wrong about being hungry. I ate the pizza so fast I bit my own finger.

Jimmy said, "Wait right here, okay? I'll be right back. Ten minutes."

I watched Jimmy hustle drunks in front of the gay bars. He was a Mexican punk rock James Dean, and he moved like a cat amongst the older men. The doormen posted outside the bars clearly knew him; Jimmy knew how to use his looks. He got some round, smiley, and quite sweet little drunk gentleman to buy him a six-pack. This turned into a five pack after Jimmy and I got on the bus and I put a cool can against my swollen eye. It stung and ached and felt better all at once.

We walked a block to the park and sat on its Serpentine steps, the stone formed from tectonic pressure. I looked up at Dianne Feinstein's hospital room, dark atop the hospital building next to us. Her suite stared out at a view I knew I'd never see again. Being up there felt like it was years ago. We cracked open our beers in the damp, cool air, and I hoped it would be enough to get me drunk.

The squat was an abandoned Victorian three blocks from where we were sitting. There were plenty of those, each a marker of the neighborhood's descent from respectability into squalor. I'd paid attention to local history; I knew the dark windows around us were the result of San Francisco's twisted segregationist history. Lower Haight's nearby housing projects were part of a racist social engineering experiment that served as a constant reminder of World War II, something I knew most other US cities didn't share. Rogue was from those projects, and she didn't like to talk about it. But she was pretty clear on the legacy that got her there. It seemed to me that only white people could afford to ignore history.

The second world war drew tens of thousands of Black industrial workers into the Bay Area for decent paying jobs in Richmond and the Hunter's Point Naval Shipyard. Because of segregation, everyone had jobs but nowhere to live. So, architects pitched grandiose "city within a city" housing designs slated for redlined districts, like the one near where Jimmy and I sat drinking beer in the dark. What the city got instead was barren, concrete barracks style living quarters in five neighborhoods that we all just called "the projects."

San Francisco went from around five thousand Black residents in 1940 to over forty-three thousand by 1950, all forced to squeeze into a couple of neighborhoods. Yet the Fillmore neighborhood became famous for its nightclubs and nightlife, dance, and jazz -- one of America's most important artistic contributions to the world. All the legends came here to be part of it, a celebration of music and hotbed of inspiration including John Coltrane, Chet Baker, Duke Ellington, Miles Davis, Charlie Parker, Billie Holiday, and many others.

In those exquisite Victorians, bop joints, kitchens, record stores, and more, for nearly two decades San Francisco's Black communities prospered, bought homes, grew flourishing businesses, all in "The Harlem of the West." And then, the city of San Francisco destroyed it. The packed, segregated yet thriving neighborhood was considered by city officials as a "slum area" even before the neighborhood's Japanese residents were rounded up and put in camps.

M. Justin Herman, San Francisco's Redevelopment Agency chief, branded the forced removal of 30,000 residents, the shutdown of 883 businesses, the bulldozing of 2,500 beautiful Victorians as "urban renewal." Local papers ran blatantly racist, trumped-up stories about Black crime, conflating it with Herman's campaign against "blight" -- which everyone here knew just meant Black. By the 1960s when Herman's towers and projects went up, politicians and real estate profiteers, indistinguishable from one another at SF City Hall, had profited and moved on.

This pushed a lot of people into Lower Haight, which, through the 1970s and 80s, combined with the dual crisis of unemployment and drug addiction to transform a picturesque working-class San Francisco neighborhood into a violent and desperate twin of Upper Haight. All around where Jimmy and I sat were neglected "painted ladies" carved up into cheap multiple residence flats. Or, they sat vacant and were squatted by homeless people, drug dealers, and junkies. Once lush and ornate houses, they were now a grotesquerie of peeling paint, elaborate mold splotches, and windows covered by blankets or tin foil. The punk squat I'd be sleeping in was one of several that stood abandoned and empty. Some, like the scary-looking Hotel Casa Loma building on Fell Street, were notorious "shooting galleries" for heroin addicts and crackheads. I leaned into Jimmy and let myself feel safe for a minute.

He listened to my story of Sarah and her actual fucking knight in white. Somehow, right then, this invited Jimmy to open up to me. Jimmy was Mexican-American, and from Fremont, or at least he was until he ended up in group homes after his dad strangled his mom. When he told me that, he quickly switched to talking about sexual abuse in group homes, rushing past any discussion of his mom or dad. Two cars racing in opposite directions, confusing witnesses.

"That's where I met Zeke," Jimmy said. "Group home. Nice ones have cameras in the hallways. Never cameras in the bedrooms. It wasn't a nice one. We needed to get him out of there."

I wanted to say something supportive. "He's lucky to have you care about him."

Jimmy said, "He wasn't lucky enough."

10

JIMMY and I drank our beer and watched fog snake through Lower Haight, surrounding streetlights in shifting clusters of cotton wool. Decrepit Victorians and rotting Queen Annes embraced the empty park. We finished our last beers in its nighttime quiet and stillness. I was tipsy, my face was hot and swollen. *Moldy painted ladies, take me in your arms forever, goodnight.*

I could see my cheek bulging in my peripheral vision when we walked to the squat. Jimmy pointed out that the squat was easy to find if you looked for a pair of Converse hanging from a nearby power line. I kept forgetting he couldn't read. The shoes actually indicated where the speed dealers lived, he explained, across the street. They could be relied on to freak out if cops came around. Nature's own early warning system.

The squat looked like any other run-down Lower Haight Victorian. Its power had been shut off, and I was glad Jimmy was there to lead me into its dark interior. People were asleep on the floor and derelict couches in its big downstairs parlor at the left of the entry, framed by once-grand double-doors. One person looked up, exchanged a nod with Jimmy, then shifted back into a sleeping position.

It smelled like wet cigarettes, old sweat, and some kind of organic rot. Creaking stairs took us upstairs. The rooms contained familiar faces in various sleeping configurations. The smell wasn't much better up here, but there were holes in the walls you could see through to the street, and this created a welcome draft. From what I could see, the walls had been spray painted, kicked in, possibly punched, stickered, written on in pen. We settled on the floor near Little Shaun and against a wall that read, STEAL FROM SAFEWAY NOT YOUR HOUSEMATES. Jenn slept in a corner near two other punk girls. Rogue would never come here. The squat was too close to the Lower Haight projects.

We slept until a loud shot and car-crash noise startled us all awake. We gathered around the room's one window to peek outside. The blanket covering it was a stained patchwork quilt, long past disgusting.

A shopping cart full of flattened cans was angled slightly, its progress stopped by a parked car. I remembered we were near the recycling center behind Our Lady of Safeway. In the street was a man laying like he'd just decided to have a little rest, a nap on the comfy blacktop.

We all knew better than to go outside. Or make any noise.

Nothing happened. Aiden was the first to sigh, then wander back to his sleep spot. The last ones remaining at the window were Little Shaun and I. We watched as an ambulance pulled up, in no hurry whatsoever. No lights. No sirens.

"Is he shot?" Little Shaun whispered, "I don't see any blood." The way his face looked in the mottled streetlight, full of wonder and maybe a little fear, reminded me that he was still just a little kid.

Two medics slowly moved the body into the back of the ambulance. "I don't think so," I whispered. "I think he just ... died."

The ambulance drove off, leaving behind a shopping cart under the streetlight. Little Shaun was still at the window when I curled around Jimmy to go to sleep.

The shopping cart was still there in the morning. Jimmy and I got up and went straight to SOMA on a crosstown bus. The name "SOMA" evoked Aldous Huxley's Brave New World pleasure drugs and ancient scriptures of Vedic India. But even SOMA's history was a jagged opposite. The Zodiac Killer sent letters to Hearst's *San Francisco Chronicle* at 5th and Mission; Harvey Milk's murderer, Dan White, was treated like royalty in the jail on Bryant; Jack Kerouac once worked in the rail yards.

Now, former sweatshops, often right next to current sweatshops, populated a run-down neighborhood peppered by methadone clinics, residence hotels packed with drug addicts and mentally unstable veterans, gay sex clubs, industrial artists, musicians, painters, students, and a few performance spaces. Daytime SOMA was all junkies and sweatshops, and SOMA was a concrete wasteland of desperation. At night it was the same, just with nightclubs, warehouse parties, and BDSM hotspots.

We walked along the alleys near Market Street on our way to the cafe, where open drug use, sex work, and violence was the norm. No one wore sandals outside here in warm weather because a stubbed toe would surely get you Hepatitis. Puddles of blood on the sidewalk marked where junkies had found a vein and shot up. Vomit was normal, the reek of urine never abated, and human feces streaked from waist-height to the ground along buildings. One morning, when walking from the band warehouse to go to school, I came across three men sitting chair-style against a building with their pants down, evacuating their bowels. They waved "hi" to me. I waved back.

Oh, and SOMA was also built upon about 60 feet of mud

and landfill. She was slowly sinking. A strong earthquake would be an apocalypse.

Despite all that, within the walls of many SOMA warehouses, there was magic.

The walls of Cafe Mimic, when I first walked in, were lined with gigantic paintings in riotous layered colors, shapes atop shapes of what looked like flowers, hands, and possibly a UFO or two. They filled two of the tall walls inside the warehouse. An open space to my right looked like a cross between a proper cafe and a living room; mismatched tables, chairs, couches, plants, and people. A song by the Violent Femmes filtered in from the back kitchen where a very tall, heavyset older man wearing thick square glasses in a striped apron stood over a stove stirring a giant pot. It smelled like heaven. My mouth watered involuntarily.

"Da-amn," called Zeke from behind the counter in the back right corner, perched on a stool. At the counter's edge a battered tip jar read "Alms for the pour."

"Look at that shiner!" A silver espresso machine squatted behind Zeke, along with shelves of tea, pots, cups, plates, two drip coffee machines, and more. He grinned at me like a loon and said "You're late but ya didn't have ta beat yourself up about it!"

He did this "ta da!" with his hands. My face got red-hot as I tried to ignore everyone else in the room, who I was sure had all stopped whatever they were doing at their tables and couches to look at me.

The aproned man in the kitchen leaned out to say "Jimmy, you are late."

"Jimmy's here?" Another voice from the kitchen. A small, compact fellow with a determined gait and cigarette punctuating the corner of his dark mustache came out, headed our way like a tidy, unsmiling missile. "Jimmy, you were supposed to walk Duchess this morning." He folded his arms and noticed my cheek. Nervous, I focused on the fact that his deep brown eyes were also magnified by his glasses, like the cook's.

"So," he said to Jimmy. "Do we need to worry about the other guy?"

Rogue appeared at my side. "Oh, shit," she said. Jimmy mentioned the skinhead, and Rogue said it again, gently rubbing my arm.

The man with the cigarette touched my elbow, peered at me up-close. He clucked his teeth like I was one of his kids. "Let's go get you cleaned up in the bathroom, honey." He gently led me toward the back of the warehouse.

We got as far as the kitchen doorway when a wall of striped apron blocked us. "Joey, the girls are already in there. Oooh, ow, let me see that."

The cook leaned down to look at me, drying his hands on a towel. If Joey's dark eyes looked big behind his glasses, they took a back seat to this man's magnification. His light brown lashes circled light blue eyes, delicate, like his amber shoulder-length hair.

"Oh for fuck's sake! How long have they been in there?" Joey stormed off into the back trailing puffs of smoke like a little tank engine.

Still peering at my bruise, the cook said "Long eno-ugh." His soft singsong whooshed mint in my face. He smiled. "I'm Frank. And I'm going to make you an ice pack. Now, when was the last time you ate?"

I was so grateful I started to cry. Not sobbing, but I couldn't speak.

"Oh! No, no, no. Come here," Frank straightened up and

pulled me into an apron that was like a circus tent over his belly. I was being hugged by a big, soft tree.

Zeke's red mohawk preceded his goofy smile around the corner and he said, "What are you doing to that poor girl!"

Before I was freed, Joey herded two twin-like punk girls past us like an annoyed goose with goslings. I recognized them from the Magic Bench, Haight, and the squat. "Come on, come on," he motioned at me. "It's back here, on the right." A stage filled a surprisingly large back room.

"Don't rush honey, but don't take forever," Joey's Brooklyn accent weighted every word. "And don't forget to wipe the sink dry when you're done."

I didn't want to spend too long in the bathroom anyway. I barely recognized myself in the mirror. I somehow managed not to get a black eye, but my cheek was puffed up in a rainbow of colors. Plus, I could still see a spot where my hairline was broken from the accident. It was going to be permanent.

When I emerged, Cafe Mimic was bustling. Rogue held court on couches arranged like a cozy nest around a coffee table of books, papers, pens, pencils, and dice. Joe and John Gone listened intently, as did two other new wave-looking guys I didn't know. The punk twins sat off to the side, watching. Both girls had the exact same haircut, just in opposite colors, but weren't exactly twins.

Nearby, an artsy straight couple spoke in low voices to each other over a table of notebooks and teacups. Three guys in jeans and t-shirts sat around a table, reading paperbacks and smoking. Two older men had an animated argument punctuated with laughs and wild gestures. A small girl in flowing skirts with long blonde hair sat alone, sketching in a big newsprint pad, a mountain of cigarette butts piling up in front of her.

Two women at a table near Zeke's barista station were playing cards, or they had been. They could've been older and younger versions of each other. Both were in jeans and white t-shirts, had black leather jackets, and each had their hair close-cropped, like a military cut. Neither wore makeup. Their confidence in the way they sat, held their bodies, was something I had never seen women do. For some reason it made me feel relaxed, like my body's appearance, for once, wasn't how I was going to be judged. They both looked at me. The younger one had bright brown eyes and fat chipmunk cheeks, made impossibly rounder with her grin. She said to me, "Wanna play?"

Her eyes sparkled and she added, "I promise I won't cheat." She wiggled her eyebrows at me. It was downright cheesy.

The older woman smiled at me. She was thin, angled, and her t-shirt sleeves were rolled up. A tattoo of a spiderweb crept up her neck, like the short silver hairs that glittered skyward along her temple. "Alex likes to overcompensate for losing all the time," the older woman said.

"Hey!" Mock horror on Alex's face, looking back and forth between us like she'd been ambushed.

Frank walked slowly out of the kitchen with a bowl of chili and set it at the empty seat at their table. "I see you've already met Alex and Spider."

I decided to go with the flow and took my seat. God, his food smelled so good. Alex pantomimed clapping as I sat, emitting a soft "Yaaayyyy."

Spider's cigarette dangled as she dealt. "You watch me

win until you're done." (Alex said "Hey!") "Then you join us for some three-handed gin. Sound good?"

Their big white coffee cups were stained from hours of use. I had to let them know I wasn't going to be a gin rummy patsy. I couldn't really afford to lose any pennies. "Do I have a choice?"

Alex chimed with a smile, "Nope!"

"Look at that baby-dyke charm," Spider said.

"You comin' up short on charm, old man?" Alex said it to Spider, but winked at me.

Spider effortlessly dealt two hands saying, "Age before beauty wins every time." She told Alex, "You're going to need more pennies."

Alex grinned and scooped up her cards. I wanted to bottle whatever was in Alex that made her so happy. Spider nodded toward my cheek; around her cigarette she said, "You wanna talk about it?"

I tried to explain what happened as best I could through mouthfuls of chili that was so delicious, I could swear the world went from black and white into color as I ate it. With a spoon. I'd been eating with my hands for so long, this felt very different. I had done what I could to prepare and survive, but never thought to pack a spoon. Huh.

Spider and Alex knew exactly who Sarah was. They both seemed to know who everyone was on the streets. They also knew every place I described being in the past 24 hours. Before I could ask how, Alex told me "Spider is like neighborhood watch on a stick. Me, I do needle exchange, so I get to know all the movers and shakers."

Spider said, "Accent on the shakers."

"What does Alex mean by neighborhood watch?" I asked her.

"I just like to keep track of everyone," Spider said. "There are a lot of creeps on the streets, more and more every day. Dangerous ones."

"Like Ivan," Alex interjected.

"Like Ivan," Spider said. "Ivan's a pedo who hangs around Haight and down by Safeway. Homeless, schizo. Blonde, very tan, blue eyes, early thirties. He's always either smiling or telling people what he wants to do to them."

I knew exactly who she was talking about. Holy shit. That guy really scared me. I'd seen him around Haight and Masonic, and by the Safeway recycling center.

"Why are guys like him ... why are there so many of them?" Now that I was on the streets, it really seemed as if San Francisco's streets were like an overpopulated zombie film of mentally unstable homeless people.

Spider looked at me. "Well," she said. "That's a bit complicated."

"Try me," I said. "I want to know."

Spider didn't miss a beat. "Suit yourself. There didn't used to be this many on the streets. When Reagan was elected president, he basically let all the mental patients loose."

She saw the look of disbelief on my face. "No, he really did. He repealed a law that would've kept money going to federal community mental health centers. That wiped out all the services that kept them off the streets, made it so they're either in jail, in a temporary emergency mental ward at SF General, or on the streets."

She paused for a drag off her cigarette, watching me. "But California got the worst of it. He did it here first. Reagan did the same thing on a state level back when he was Governor of California," Spider said.

She continued talking while I forced myself to eat Frank's

chili slowly. I wanted to tip the whole bowl into my face. "When Reagan was governor in the sixties and seventies, he dismantled the public psychiatric hospital system and released our state's mental patients onto the streets." She stubbed out her cigarette, seeming to just notice that I was eating. I didn't care. I was starving, and utterly blown away by what she was telling me.

Reagan, Spider explained, is widely cited as the cause of contemporary homelessness, from his abandonment of federal housing funding to the disastrous changes he made to mental health care in America. But California got the worst of it all.

Spider said, "Reagan passed a California state law abolishing involuntary hospitalization of people experiencing mental health crisis. It also made it so people couldn't be helped if they needed additional care, or if they relapsed. So, basically a whole lot of violent, crazy people with nowhere to go were deinstitutionalized onto our streets."

"That's ... insane." I couldn't think of another word to use, and Alex giggled a deep, coughing laugh. I said, "Why would anyone do that? Where are they supposed to go?'

Spider shrugged, then shook her head. "Like Nixon, Reagan associated psychiatry with Communism."

This concept struck me like the way people used to treat dental problems with leeches. "But California was the canary in the coal mine for deinstitutionalization," she said. "Our streets are the asylums."

Reagan, who was fond of saying America's homeless explosion under his leadership was simply because some people choose to live on the streets. He did it again on a national level in the 1980s. When elected president, he repealed a law that would've kept money going to federal community mental health centers. This wiped out all the services that kept people seriously struggling with mental health off the streets. During the AIDS crisis, at the same time San Francisco was abandoned by the federal government to die, the precursor era to me becoming homeless in San Francisco at thirteen.

I finished my chili in silence as Spider and Alex played gin. They exchanged a comforting, timeworn banter of old friends. I thought that I finally understood why I grew up in a state known for its abundance of serial killers. I realized I was really lucky to have found these people, and this place. And how that bit of knowledge Spider shared with me had changed nothing and everything around me all at once.

11

NIGHT BROUGHT a blanket of stillness over Upper Haight's hillside. Aiden and I moved silently among tightly-packed parked cars. Between Victorian apartment buildings, I saw the black silhouette of a slow-moving raccoon loom like a small hunchback bear, foraging in a small alley's trash bins. I heard a motorcycle whine, muscling its engine in an uphill struggle. There was city din like static in the background, always, but everything was mostly quiet.

Aiden and I had spare-changed along Haight-Ashbury until around midnight. Now we were "carbombing."

It was simple: Walk along parked cars, try car doors to see if they were locked, take stuff if they weren't. Carbombing was good for snatching parking meter change people left in their ashtrays. It surprised me how many people neglected to lock their cars. A lot of them. The first time a car alarm went off, Aiden grabbed my hand and calmly said, "Just walk normal and slow." Then we strolled like a couple who merely happened to be near a car whose alarm was blaring, waking dogs and residents. San Francisco had a strangely sleepy, small-town vibe at night. Perfect for thieves. Perfect for gliding through neighborhood shadows. We zig-zagged across blocks, hopping over fences meant to keep riffraff like us out.

On Page Street I slipped into a white coupe and found a sweater someone forgot behind its passenger seat. I really needed a sweater; it was getting colder out. I got out and pulled the sweater on over my head. Some guy yelled: "Hey!"

I was about to run when Aiden said, "Walk."

I looked back to see a young hippie dude in dirty tie-dye I recognized from the Haight-Ashbury corner. I'd seen him yelling at an even younger, dirty, dreadlocked white girl wearing an enormous backpack with peace signs drawn on it. I'd wondered if their bags were full of all the shit they were trying to leave behind.

The hippie spread his arms wide and smiled, saying: "You know this used to be Janis Joplin's house, man!" Arms outstretched, he walked toward us.

Taking my hand Aiden said. "Who gives a shit." He pulled me with him across the street. Aiden said under his breath, "I fucking hate nostalgia."

We bombed dozens of cars. It was a relief finding enough change to go to Cafe Mimic in the morning and get coffee and food. And probably refills, so I could just sit there in one place for a while. Being homeless was more than a full-time job. That's what those who constantly told me I didn't "look homeless" or to "get my life together" failed to comprehend. (That, and the fact that I was fourteen and not legally able to work in the state of California for another two years, which I'd found out, embarrassingly, when I tried to apply for a job at Buffalo Exchange.) On top of it all, the cops kept us moving. SFPD hated us for having nowhere to go.

At the Cafe, Spider and Alex had filled me in on so much. They told me about Larkin Street Youth Center, way over in the Tenderloin, which had a drop-in center. Alex told me about free food in different locations around town, but their schedules were all over the place and you had to get in line early at all of them or lose out. (And even then, you could wait in line and still lose out.) I convinced one of the Larkin Street staff to get me some food stamps only to discover the "only food" rule made the paper 'money-not-money' useless. I could get a can of beans, but not a can opener or spoon to eat it with. I couldn't buy tampons, toilet paper, aspirin, soap, or shampoo. Just uncooked food. I had nowhere to cook.

Shelter beds required waiting in line just to make a reservation. That's if I wanted to risk theft and molestation (or worse) from the adults in the public shelters.

I had an idea of who would be in those shelters from my Upper Haight soup kitchen experience. I'd lined up in front of the church with a long line of older men with hard, grimy features, in layers of dirty clothing, some wearing hats over greasy smelly hair, each offering his own display of a serious mental health crisis. Some crouched against the building, in a private world that required rocking, glaring, hand gestures, or a glossolalia monologue of anger. The soup kitchen made us pray before they let us eat. For some reason I found that to be the most humiliating part.

No one talked to anyone else in that soup kitchen line. Eye contact was avoided. It was as if we were all in some outdoor otherworld jail, except for a few men here and there who stared violently at me, hoped for eye contact. Ivan was there, the guy Spider and Alex had warned me about. He stood out with his blonde hair and reddish-tan skin, white teeth flashing a nonstop grin and shining blue eyes pinned to my every movement. All I could think about was a recent night when I'd walked by Ivan ranting in the doorway of a closed Haight Street head shop, casually saying he was going to shove a metal rod up my cunt. I didn't react when that happened, but it chilled me to the bone. I felt so much relief to get seated far away from Ivan and not near anyone who smelled sour or rotten.

My survival depended on identifying threats. Some people are, at the moment you cross paths with them, just looking for someone to hurt. And the truth of random street violence is that it's almost always a matter of timing, awareness, and opportunity. Men especially seemed to be always looking for a consequence-free chance to do some extreme venting.

We were always refining our survival strategies, often the hard way. One afternoon I was leaving Larkin Street Youth on my way back to the Castro. The Tenderloin was another rough, depressed San Francisco neighborhood. The area's sex workers of all genders were out and about, attuned to the passing cars; street cool but work-ready. I could practically see the "click" as they decided I was neither threat nor competition. I walked like a punk now; an androgynous glide of sweeping legs, low center of gravity, attention on the ground ahead. That let me pass without hassle any drug dealers hustling for trade, addicts and homeless against buildings and sitting on the sidewalk, scratching, glaring, sometimes yelling at whatever they were seeing. I was good at scanning a crowd while not making eye contact.

A white boy with dreads riding a small bicycle, like a little kid's bike, came into focus more than once. I noticed him spot me, trying for eye contact, so I angled myself to cross the street, to be moving away from him. Minding my business. He raced his bike toward me on the sidewalk, stopped it just short of running into me. I almost tripped. It was then I knew he had "picked" me, and I had to get away.

"Hey girly," he said in a sing-song voice. "Where you going?"

I stepped wide and tried to get around him, keeping my cool. I gave him a nod and continued. "Hey," he backed up his little kid's bike. "C'mere girly," he taunted, smiling. Afterward, there were so many things I wished I'd done instead.

He rammed his bike into my legs from the side. I stumbled; the pain was immediate, I wondered if I'd been cut through my jeans. That's when I saw the bike chain; thick steel links looped around one of his hands. He said, "where you going girly," through a grin of yellow teeth. He was tweaking, hyper on chemicals and arrogance and jubilant with hate in the way that predators with power feel elation.

There were plenty of people around, but no one was looking at what was happening to me. No one would. He swung his bike chain at me, grinning, so I turned heel down the nearest side street to run. My mistake.

He sped up and rammed his bike into me, knocking me to the ground. He ditched the little bike before I could get up, swinging his chain and saying something I vaguely understood anchored around the word "girly." He swung the heavy links in a wide arc toward my face; I scuttled backward in terror. I wasn't fast enough. He came down on top of me with his whole body reeking of sour sweat and pee, pressing the chain to my neck and it hurt, it hurt so bad to have my throat crushed like that. Gulping for air I could hear cars driving by, honking. *Why are they honking*, I thought. Why honk?

I felt gravel grinding into the back of my head. I forced myself to think: I'd been in this position before at martial arts class. In a different life, a million years ago. When I was a little blonde girl in a class of older boys. My sparring brothers in enviable blue belts. This was different than sparring in class. This was when I wasn't supposed to hold back.

It was like doing quick math while my heart screamed in panic. With his hands on the chain at my throat, his balance was at the top of his body, on his hands. This meant I could slip my knee up ... I remembered everything in a rush as my body went through automatic motions. My hands went to his shoulders; my left hand pulled while my right hand pushed, skewing his balance. I brought my right foot under him and planted my left foot on the ground. I twisted him again and pushed my foot up, into him with all my cornered-animal strength.

He launched over me onto his back, just like I'd practiced in class. I heard the chain land nearby, but I was already scratching pavement to get up. I saw that my throw hadn't gone exactly as it was supposed to. I was supposed to have kicked him in the stomach, launched him from the center, but I'd missed. My kick was low. I'd kicked him off of me by his softest part, his crotch.

I got up off the street with little pebbles, and maybe glass, stuck into my palms, tears streaming down my face. I walked over to his chain and picked it up. He was curled in a fetal position in the filthy street. I could hear him wheezing: "You ... bitch ..."

I looked around. Cars just drove on by.

He was crying now, too, and staring to gag. I threw the chain at him. I said something when I did it, and I think it was "Here's your fucking chain," but I can't be sure exactly what came out. Then I made sure nothing had fallen out of my bag, and walked away, still crying. I was determined to walk, head up, not run. I hated myself for crying.

There were men like him everywhere.

Carbombing with Aiden and sleeping in the park felt safer.

We walked to Upper Haight's Buena Vista Park, a dark forest threaded in fog. Nighttime in San Francisco's first, and oldest, public park was beautiful and eerie. Aiden and I picked our way through the chill, footfalls crunching softly on well-worn paths between trees whose branches above looked tangled in cotton wool. In darkness, the enormous trees felt ancient, sentient, engorged with moisture that filled the air with the warm scent of bark.

Buena Vista straddled a hillside between Upper and Lower Haight, demarcating the zones between neighborhoods. Uphill on the south side of Haight Street, its 37-acre forest of redwood, eucalyptus, Cypress, and oak trees virtually absorbed ambient light into the ivy and brush along its footpaths. The open lawn along its northern bottom border sloped onto Haight Street. By day it played host to aggressive druggie hippies and recovery-challenged drug addicts from the nearby four-story Victorian rehab home for adults, Walden House.

Luxurious Victorian mansions circled the park's top half. I imagined their insides of sweeping staircases, fireplaces, incredible views, all their warmth and comfort and possibilities. Like a crush, I knew in my heart those Victorians were more beautiful than the Painted Ladies tourists flocked to in Alamo Square Park. Buena Vista's mansions filled me with wonder and circled the park's strange magic, held it in. As Aiden and I walked into it, the close bubble created by fog made the park and its baroque surroundings darkly gorgeous, like an exquisite sculpture captured in an opaque snow globe.

At night the park divided into turfs. The trees saw it all

and knew everything. Its proximity to the Castro made Buena Vista's forest a select cruising spot for gay men. Junkies slept in the crags and hollows of park forest along its West side, near Walden House and avoided the gay men, as if the cruising area were an invisible border for the park's East side. That's where Aiden and I went. Gay men could never really be safe anywhere, but being around them was safer for us by a magnitude.

I followed Aiden up paths in the dark, some paved, some not. I imagined San Francisco's house and streetlights ribboning away from us in every direction, diluted into mist. Aiden's damp mohawk hung in strings around his face. I was so tired my whole body felt like a bruise while I pushed myself forward, uphill, and still forward some more. My left cheek throbbed continuously.

"Hang on a sec," I said, my voice low. We were near the park's center.

Aiden came to where I crouched over a wide, long drainage gutter along the paved path.

I could clearly see the word "Died" inscribed in the flat, white stone.

"Zeke was right," I was incredulous. "These are all headstones. Hundreds, there must be hundreds of them," I could see broken marble tiles arranged flat in the gutter trailing out of sight, away from me in both directions. "God," I said, feeling a little creeped out, "there are so many." The park felt anxiously darker, now hemmed in by mansions as if otherwise something would get out.

It didn't help that I had just started reading Fritz Leiber's *Dark Ladies*, which included a terrifying horror story about Corona Heights -- the hill right next to us. I wondered if there was a place in San Francisco where they left the bodies but moved the headstones, like in the film *Poltergeist*.

"Can you take me to the Temple of Saturn?" I asked Aiden.

"Sure," he laughed, "it's kind of on the way."

We hiked to the top of the park. The trees opened into a circular clearing of dead grass, half-mooned in by stone borders that made one side look like a sagging layer cake. *So, this is where the skinheads party*, I thought. *The Death Temple of Tlamco*. I could just barely see the glowing orange Golden Gate Bridge to the north, glittering like a ruby bracelet across the bay inlet's slender wrist. Fog shrouded the view to my right where the hills beyond Berkeley loomed, like Mount Diablo (the Devil's Mountain), across the Bay.

Aiden led me downhill through trees to a barely-there trail along the hillside. We ducked under low-hanging Cypress branches into a small clearing with a blue plastic painter's tarp covering the ground, keeping it dry. Like me, Aiden had left home completely.

He was still a mystery to me, never quite opening up beyond hints of alcoholic parents and "shit-kickings," and not showing romantic interest in anyone, including me. I did have a crush on him, though. Aiden was so handsome he was actually on "punk postcards" sold along Haight Street. It was cold and under our blue tarp we spooned on the hard ground for warmth, and that was enough for me. We were all so tough, and we were all so wounded. I drifted off wondering how we could live this way with the world's newest technologies so near us, the heart of those marvels pulsing and commanding fortunes only miles away in the Valley.

We were startled awake by Alex. "Good morning, kittens!" How was she always so perky?

The bright blue tarp seared my eyes, so I shut them fast. My eyes were still sensitive to light from the concussion. Sun shone through the trees, cooking moisture off trees, chasing fog away. In the redwoods and eucalyptus overhead, I could hear birds chirping, and somewhere off to my right, the scurry of a small creature fleeing. Buena Vista Park had held its wild population close for another night, and another day in the city had begun.

Alex stood at our feet in work pants and boots, bundled in a scarf and jacket against the cold, her rakish bleach-blonde bangs dancing around smiling eyes. The plastic sheet crinkled as Aiden and I sat up, dew rolling off the sides.

Alex rattled a square red plastic bin marked with ominous medical symbols, grinning her cheeky chipmunk smile. "Got any sharps?" She was doing a morning round of needle exchange outreach in the park.

"Nope." Alex lingered to chat while we wiped our eyes, stretched, yawned. "How's business," Aiden joked.

"Too many customers," Alex remarked. "But it's working. People want clean needles. So, you know," she shrugged, "maybe someday less sick people."

I remembered a conversation over cards at the cafe where Alex couldn't remember an issue of the Bay Area Reporter newspaper running without HIV obituaries in every issue. Spider claimed she could.

"Wanna get your ass kicked at gin again?" I could tell Alex was fishing to see if I'd be around the cafe later.

My smile widened. "You can try, loser-bait."

Alex's giggle turned into a cough and then we joked that smoking will kill you, and does anyone have a morning cigarette?

We were up too early to go to the cafe. Aiden and I

stashed the tarp and ambled over the hill to see if the Magic Bench had anything to offer. Thanks to the generosity of Castro morning commuters, we got cheap coffees and split a bagel from Rossi's Deli. Like the Blue Front Deli in Upper Haight, the family that ran Rossi's knew us, and were always kind. Kindness was the hardest thing to find out here. The way San Francisco's family businesses made the rest of the neighborhood into extended families were its shining spots of magic.

Back at the Magic Bench one hour turned into several as we collected more people outside the MUNI underground. Joe turned up, he was skipping school again. He got everyone's attention when he said to me, "I saw Sarah, that skin. You really did a number on her face."

"What?" I was confused.

"Her face is a mess. She's lucky Marina Guy was there to save her." Joe looked at me like he was ... wary of me.

I got the feeling that everyone was impressed, but I was flummoxed. "I don't get it," I said, mostly to myself. Yeah, I slapped Sarah hard, okay maybe satisfyingly hard, but was Joe trying to make me look good, or bad? I felt like it was time for me to exit this weird conversation.

"I'm not sure," I told the group. "But I'm gonna try calling my mom again. After that, let's go to the cafe?"

Everyone agreed. James, a metalhead guy everyone knew but I'd just met, said "Hey, I'll walk that way with you."

James was a long-haired hesher, his heavy metal band affiliations in patches and ink across his worn-in, light blue jean jacket. He had red curly hair, billions of freckles, and a gap in his teeth that was disarming when he smiled. Most of all, he was really nice.

We walked to the pay phone together and I told James, "I don't think Joe's got the right girl."

"I wonder where Joe saw Sarah," James remarked. He added, "Definitely not at the cafe."

We stopped at the pay phone. I frowned. James said "Hey, I gotta go. Can I give you something?"

"Uh ... sure?"

He reached into the front pocket of his jeans and pulled out a scrap of paper. "Use this."

On the paper was a long string of numbers, around twenty, written in ballpoint pen. I took it and asked, "What is it?"

"It's a number you can use to make free phone calls. To anywhere. It's unlimited. Just dial this number in first, then wait for the dial tone," he explained. "Then dial the number you want to call."

I didn't believe it would work. "Where did you get this?"

"You should know, Miss Blue," James said, "that I'm a snitch."

My confusion folded in on itself.

"I'll catch you later," he said, and walked away toward 18th Street, leaving me with my mouth hanging open.

I tried the number. It worked. I'll never need to pay for a phone call again, I thought as Donna's number rang and rang. But does that mean he's a cop? Does everyone know?

No one answered and Donna's voicemail didn't pick up. That was odd. I turned all this over in my head as I walked back to the bench. I stopped near the Plaza stairs.

Ashley Bailey and her psycho cheerleaders from school were standing at the Magic Bench talking to Joe.

Great. Just great.

12

"HEY!" Ashley Bailey shouted at me, walking across Harvey Milk Plaza.

I stayed put in case things were going to get ugly. When Ashley got to me, she said, "What happened to your face?" She looked puzzled.

"I got in a fight," I said, trying to look tough. "Skinhead chick named Sarah."

Ashley gave me a once-over, then said "Here." She wrestled a pen and school notebook out of her bag. Her cheer squad eyed me, unsmiling. They were the same three Black girls I'd barely talked out of beating me up.

Ashley wrote her phone number in the girliest script I'd ever seen on lined paper and said, "Call me and come stay this weekend. You probably can't stay more than that, but call me. Just do it."

If I really was going to call Ashley and stay at her house, I had two more nights to figure out where to sleep. If I could stay at Ashley's, I could take a hot shower. But what did Ashley want from me?

With that, she turned on her sneakered heel and left.

Cheerleaders at the Magic Bench. Ashley being nice to me.

I desperately needed this day to stop being weird.

Everyone was looking at me when I got back to the group. The cute punk boy from New Zealand, Mark, smiled at me, his dimples cutting lines in smooth almond skin.

I looked around. "What?"

Mark faked an American accent saying, "Gimme a P!"

The twins (who weren't twins), named Lisa and Jess, answered in chorus, "P!"

"What does it spell?" Mark was grinning and I was dying inside.

The girls shouted, "Peeeeeeee!"

I burst out laughing with everyone else, even though my face still hurt. Then Aiden and Joe blew my mind by saying two guys from Rogue's D&D game were coming... To pick us up in a car! Getting a ride anywhere felt like an unbelievable luxury now.

"Luxury" was the wrong word for Bozie's baby-poop brown, dented, exhaust-chugging, cracked-windshield beast, an Oldsmobile Delta '88. Bozie pulled up in the bus zone and honked. It sounded like the car was old and just wanted to be left alone. Bozie's bleach-blonde buzz cut reminded me of Billy Zoom, of Billy Idol, and especially Perfect Tommy from *The Adventures of Buckaroo Banzai*. My crush hit like a lightning bolt. Next to him was the other D&D guy, Jay, a very glum-looking brunette goth.

In the back was Jenn, Joe's pushy friend. Jay leaned forward with the front seat and mumbled complaints as we squeezed in, with me going in the car first, squishing up next to Jenn. She looked thinner. Maybe people just seemed bigger when they were picking fights. The guys cranked up the song "Pablo Picasso Was Never Called An Asshole" and Jenn craned her head around to talk into my ear.

"Did you like my little present for ya?" Her smile revealed wide grey teeth.

"What?" I decided this wasn't where I wanted to be sitting ever again. Next to her, that is. Why couldn't I be squished up against Mark?

"I chased that skinhead bitch around the corner while that

asshole dude threw you around. She'll never fuck with you again," Jenn smiled wide, her eyes too bright. She added, "No one will."

"What did you do?" I felt queasy.

"I just put her up against a car and slapped her around a little bit. Okay, a little *lot*," she snort-laughed.

I nodded, not knowing what to say. Jenn smiled and rocked her head to the music, like we were buddies now.

Rogue wasn't surprised when I got to the cafe, pulled her aside, and told her what Jenn had done. "I knew she was a bad scene," Rogue remarked, shaking her head. "Don't you worry, okay?" Rogue hugged me and said, "I miss you."

"I miss you, too. I'm glad you can stay here though."

Jimmy watched us from the kitchen doorway. "What about me?" He looked actually hurt. "Don't you miss me?"

Rogue smiled and said to him, "Awwww, boo-boo face!"

Jimmy waved his hand in front of his face as he said, "Shut up." This was clearly a routine with them.

Still, I went over and hugged him. "I totally miss you too, Jimmy," I said. Zeke made a fake crying face at us. "And you too, Mr. Mohawk!" He grinned.

There was a brief squabble over whether or not I was playing gin with Spider and Alex, or making a character for Rogue's D&D game. Rogue won, of course.

We played for hours, vibrating on sugary coffee refills. Cafe patrons came and went; I lost track of time, my problems with Jenn, and everything else. I was going to need my own dice. It felt good being something else, somewhere else, for a while.

Bozie offered to drop people off in Upper Haight. He was going to a punk show at the I-Beam with Jay. Aiden and a couple of other people came with us. Bozie said he needed gas, but before I could worry about contributing Jay hauled a gas can and rubber tubing out of the Oldsmobile's trunk, grumbling that he was always the one who had to get gas.

"I'll help," I said. I followed Jay down Natoma as he fingered gas flaps searching for a loose cap. Once he found one and started his process, I was pretty sure he was the worst person at siphoning gas I would ever see. He sucked a mouthful of gas out of someone's tank, and spat it everywhere, hurrying to get the tube into the gas can. Jay complained to Bozie when we got back to the car.

"I think I swallowed some," he grumbled. "Why do I always have to do it?"

That night Aiden and I slept in the back of his friend's station wagon parked on Oak Street. We had to be quiet and stay covered up so police wouldn't notice. I woke to morning traffic racing down Oak's four-lane, one-way street as San Franciscans went to work. We spilled out of the car; my bones hurt from sleeping curled up to fit the wagon's hard bed. My arms and legs jerked spasmodically when I unfurled them.

I woke up angry, but not at Aiden. Who thought this was a choice? I hated people who had money but said they were poor, or thought homelessness was a phase where you lived off other people before college, or said it to pretend hardship, and it burned in me in a way that settled and stayed within me, like a secret I would carry inside forever.

"Are you okay?" Aiden asked me.

"Yeah, I'm okay."

He smiled and said, "No you're not."

"Sometimes I just think of what we could do if we had everything they did," I nodded toward the commuter traffic.

He looped his arm in mine and we walked to the street corner. "You know what, though?" he said. "They're asleep at the wheel. They don't know who they are, or what they're going through, and when shit falls apart, because it always falls apart, they'll freak out and crash. Most of 'em only know who they are when they're hurting someone else. Don't be jealous, bunny. Not of them."

From anyone else I would've been pissed that he characterized me as a jealous girl. But the way he put it reminded me we were in this together. I smiled and said, "I *am* a little jealous if they had breakfast though."

We hugged and parted. Everything felt better when I got to the cafe. I got a bowl of Frank's chili and a mocha, extra sprinkles courtesy of Zeke. His tip jar read "Scuse me while I tip this guy."

I wrote in my journal, hoping to turn more lights on in my brain's memory strings. Different people filtered through the cafe, familiar faces and new ones. Rogue was sitting with me when Jenn came in.

Jenn had shaved her head, leaving little fringes at the front.

"Oh no," Rogue said to Jenn from across the room. "Oh no you don't!"

"What? I have a right to be here," Jenn's voice was raising.

"You go, now!" Rogue shot up out of her chair, advancing fast on Jenn. "You gotta go. You get out now, Baldeusa, go on! *Git!*"

Frank appeared in the doorway; Joey came rushing past, cigarette dangling off the edge of his mustache. Joey got to Jenn first, took her elbow and walked her out the door. I heard him saying "I'm sorry honey," while Jenn glared over her shoulder at Rogue, allowing Joey to lead her outside.

Rogue was incredulous. "What. The. Fuck." She plopped down in her chair, hard.

"Why would she do that?" I asked no one in particular, sitting back down. I didn't even realize I'd stood up too.

Joe came over to our table. "You don't know the half of it. Jenn's Jewish."

"Wha-*at*?" I'm no expert, but I think Rogue's voice went up two octaves. "You have got to be shitting me."

"How does that even work, I mean ..." I couldn't continue.

Joe shrugged. "We're not that close so, I dunno." He looked at Zeke, then Rogue. "I'm sorry."

"Yeah, thanks for introducing us to Baldeusa!" Rogue was pretty worked up, but her saying the nickname again made me burst out laughing. "Seriously though," she looked at me, her giggle bubbling up.

Joey came back in, trailing smoke puffs. He was alone. I had to know. "What happened?"

"Well, little miss new identity is on her way to wherever they all go do whatever it is they do. I just said, look, you know this isn't going to work and told her she was smart enough to know why." He puffed his cigarette and crossed his arms. "She knew what she was doing. Anyway, I asked if she had somewhere else to go, and she said she did."

Zeke shook his head, tamping coffee grounds out of the espresso machine's press. "That's the way the Baldeusa bounces," his over-pronunciation making it sound like a narrator's voice. We were laughing, but other cafe patrons had resumed their reading, coffee, quiet conversation.

Rogue stayed in "I can't even" mode until the D&D crew assembled and we got our dice rolling. After the news of Jenn's transformation into Baldeusa was relayed to everyone in the group, it got forgotten by the time we were screwing up our dice rolls. I was still so crushed out on Bozie that if it wasn't for the game, I wouldn't even be able to speak to him.

It was the same kind of awestruck attraction as I had for Little Joe, who was gracing us with his glorious, gorgeous presence in the cafe that day. It didn't matter that Little Joe was gay, I crushed on him hard. I just wanted to be his everything, to spend as much time in his smart, eyelinered, completely beautiful aura as possible.

I loved that he talked to everyone like we were just as beautiful as he was, too. I soaked up and memorized his comebacks. I was convinced that the way he saw the world was how I could learn to be happy: The world was his stage, and we were all his beautiful muses and sexy co-conspirators. How could you not want to live in that world? But I was content with being crushed out on both Bozie and Little Joe quietly inside myself, forever. I was just glad they were in my world now.

I wasn't going to be telling Jimmy any of this, though. I also wasn't going to tell Jimmy that the cute lead singer from the punk band at the house party, Mark, not only had a cool accent, but he was funny, too. Mark scooted up a chair between me and Joe while we (me as an elf, Joe as a dwarf, which he hated) struggled to fight our way through Rogue's Valley of Pain. I knew, as I swirled all of this around in my head and rolled 20-sided dice trying to get past an ice witch, that my hormones were making me insane.

Just one more night until I could stay at Ashley's house, which was weird to think of. It was kind of a challenge that she told me to call her, so I had, and she came through. I would soon meet her Irish Catholic parents and brothers. I wondered if her family were hardcore church-on-Sunday Catholics, or the kind that only absolve their sins with a smidge of confession every now and then. I looked forward to sleeping on something soft. I couldn't figure out what

Ashley wanted from me, and the suspense was kind of killing me.

I ended up in the Lower Haight squat that night. I didn't see anyone I knew when I made my way upstairs and found an open spot on the floor near the Safeway graffiti. I used a trick I learned from Jimmy to stay warm, wrapping a t-shirt over my head and eyes. It trapped heat, kept out light, and hid me from creeping eyes.

I heard someone come in. I peeked through the fabric.

I couldn't believe my bad luck. It was Jenn.

"Hey!" She whisper-yelled, swaying. "Shhhh. Don't tell."

She sounded wasted. I heard her sink to her knees and start moving papers and wrappers to clear a spot. I didn't want her staying here -- no one wanted a skinhead here, we were all clear on that, they were fucked in the head about humans, and they ruined everything because they could. If you let one in that was it, your spot was ruined, it was the skinhead spot now.

I didn't know what to do and she still scared me after what she did to Sarah.

I didn't say anything, didn't move. Please think I'm asleep, please think I'm asleep.

"Hey," she whisper yelled again from her spot on the floor. "Heeeeey."

"What." I wasn't into this.

"Just ..." she sighed, "you're cool, that's all. Thanks for being nice to me. Thank you for letting me ..." There was a long pause. "Stay. Here."

I didn't have a fucking choice, did I?

To my great dismay, Jenn was still next to me when I woke up in the morning. I did not want anyone to come stumbling in here and see me, and think I was with a skinhead. *Goddamnit Jenn. Why did you do it?*

I figured the best thing I could do was sneak out while she was still asleep, as quietly as possible. I warily watched Jenn as I moved in slow-motion to put my t-shirt head wrap into my bag, close the flap, and silently secure the buckle. I wished I'd made a mental note of where the floorboards creaked in here. I kept my eyes on her.

And that was when I knew, I knew, I knew as I came into a kneeling position to put my bag strap over my head, and I looked at Jenn, I *knew*.

I saw a puddle on the filthy carpet next to her mouth, which was open. Her eyes were half-open.

There's a way life radiates off a person or a pet like invisible waves from a space heater, an undercurrent of motion from even the slightest breathing that you maybe can't see but notice when you don't.

Malevolent tingles of shock ran up my arms and down my back; it felt like having a fever in the middle of an ice storm. Jenn was dead. Something was shaking inside me, threatening to break. I sort of fell back on my ass. Sat there in the silence. Alone. How long had I been sleeping next to a dead body?

This wasn't how it was supposed to go. A body. A corpse. *Jenn*, I thought, *her name was Jenn*. I didn't know her last name. I didn't know anything about her. But now she was dead and that was it.

Everything about her story stopped right there in that rotting Victorian. Somewhere she had friends who actually knew her, and parents, or maybe just one parent, who would have to see her not breathing anymore. To identify her. Probably Jewish parents whose hearts would crack open and cry forever and ever that their daughter -- Baldeusa was someone's daughter -- their Jewish daughter was a dead skinhead.

I'd had a plan, not like this. Escape the drug dealers, my mom's violent boyfriends and whoever wanted us dead, escape the older men she left me alone with expecting me to have sex with them. Escape and ... go to school and have a future, and have dinner parties with amazing friends, and be surrounded by artists and art in a giant Victorian mansion in San Francisco, a living fable. A long life that mattered.

My plan was supposed to be a straight line. Get away from danger. Find a place to stay. Get stable. Finish school. A simple, clean, straight line. Now it was a tangle, a mess winding back in on itself.

I don't know how long I sat there alone in the morning's quiet and stillness with Jenn's body.

I didn't know what to do.

I considered being practical and looking for her wallet or whatever to see if ... I don't know, the thought didn't go any further once I realized she had gone out like a light switch using her bag as a pillow. I didn't want to touch the ... her. The idea of touching her, there in the quiet, alone, made me scream inside over and over in a way that blocked out all rational thought, like a speaker being blown out from too much volume.

I had to leave. Jenn wasn't Jenn anymore, I told myself. This was a body, and it would need official or technical people to come get it, and it would also start to decompose, and this room could never be slept in again. A dead body meant the end of this squat, I realized. Congrats Jenn, you were an asshole to the finish. Once the city found the dead body of a young girl in an abandoned Lower Haight squat, this place would get boarded up, for sure.

I stood up, dizzy. The world shimmied and sparks traveled the skin of my arms again. I thought I might be hyperventilating but I wasn't sure. I was in my body, but not in my body. I had to get out of there.

I walked to Haight Street. I used the number James the Snitch gave me and called the police non-emergency number. I knew I was the one ruining the squat, but I just couldn't leave her there. Not like that.

I didn't go to Upper Haight, or the Magic Bench, or the Cafe that day.

I went to Child Protective Services and turned myself in.

13

BY 2:30 my stomach was growling so loud I was sure the case worker sitting behind the desk could hear it.

At least, I thought, *she was a caseworker.* She had her own office. The giant blonde, white lady squeezed into a sweater the color of flat beer and white polyester pants stretched to capacity seemed to be at the top of some food chain at Child Protective Services. She occasionally shook her head, adjusted her sitting position, and absently sipped at a straw protruding from a can of Diet Coke while I pleaded my case.

What I'd learned so far, after walking into the beat-up, monolithic halls of the Human Services Agency of San Francisco (undecorated, I was sure, since the Vietnam war), was that no one actually goes to Child Protective Services. The ancient Black lady at the front desk sincerely didn't know what to do with me when I walked in and told her I was a child who needed protecting. She first looked me over like a fish miraculously walking on land, then eyed me suspiciously, and I sympathized: It's the city. You never know if someone needs help or is running a con, and the truth is probably both. I saw that the only thing expedient about the institution was how fast she resigned herself to the fact that I wasn't going away. Between long rheumy blinks behind thick oval glasses, the front desk grandma explained that the CPS is an institution of intervention and placement.

"Great," I countered. "I need you to intervene and place me somewhere."

"We have a hotline if you'd like to report suspected abuse," she said.

"I'd report myself if I even knew where my mother was. Or my father. Maybe you can find them."

Another blink. She pursed her lips. It was a stand-off. Despite her best efforts to wish me gone, I remained. "Have you tried Larkin Street Youth drop-in center, or the Huckleberry House emergency shelter?" She started rummaging behind her desk for leaflets. "They can help you."

"Huckleberry House is always full. They can help me live on the streets," I said, "but I don't want to be on the streets. I want to go back to school and be a normal person. Can't you put me in a foster home or something? There must be someone who wants to adopt a child. Aren't there, like, lots of them?"

"I think you're a little old for that," she said.

"So, what am I supposed to do? C'mon, there's got to be someone," I pleaded.

So, she did what all people do in her position: She made me someone else's problem. The old woman slowly got up, her back bent like a question mark, and she walked me down a hall that, by her plodding gait, must've seemed like ten miles for her.

That's how I was reluctantly granted an audience with Mrs. Biddle inside the stale chambers of the CPS. On the other side of her metal desk, Mrs. Biddle waited for me to finish my story, or rather, my pitch. I couldn't read her tiny pale eyes, buried in a moonscape of mountainous flesh, but I now knew I needed to sell myself if I was going to get any help.

All I wanted was to go back to school and graduate, I told

her. I explained that my mother had moved and I couldn't find her. That I didn't know any relatives; my grandmother and my mother's half-siblings had disowned her when I was young and I had no idea where they were or how to find them. That I didn't know who my father was. That I'd fled the house in fear. Because I didn't want to get my mom busted, I left out the drug dealing and the cartels, and the whole witness protection thing, and only told Mrs. Biddle my mom's newest name. Not the name she had before. Or before that. It was a careful story, but one anchored in truth.

I was met with silence. "Maybe you can find her," I pushed as Mrs. Biddle chewed on her straw. "I can't. I've tried. I'll write down the last number I have for her, and where she worked last, but it's not much. She didn't even tell my school where she went."

Her face puckered in what I hoped was a frown of concern. "I'll take the information you have. But we don't really do that here."

"What do you mean?" I knew she was going to repeat what I was told at the front desk, but I figured I'd keep trying. "I don't have anywhere to go."

She shifted behind her desk, and I caught the glint off a small gold cross at her neckline. She opened a drawer. "I can give you information about our independent skills programs for young adults, age sixteen and up."

"I'm fourteen."

"We don't deal with homeless issues."

"You're supposed to help kids," I pleaded. "Don't you work with placing kids in homes? Isn't there like, a family you could adopt me to? A family that wants a kid?" I imagined pair of parents, wishing they had a child, or a sitcom family living in a giant Victorian with a herd of mismatched kids they'd taken in, lined up from youngest to oldest. How did people like that find those kids, I wondered. If not at places like this, then where?

She sighed. "You're too old to adopt. Even if you were under 12, we'd still need to have you come in under a report of abuse or neglect. In which case you'd be entered into the foster system. Unless you get arrested and can't be returned home safely. In that case, we'd place you in a group home, or you'd get assigned to a county facility."

I reflexively gripped my bag on my lap. What Jimmy had told me about group homes was fresh in my mind. Guys standing over his bed at night, hierarchies of sexual abuse, no one getting medical treatment they really needed, and a lot of junkies. Something really bad had happened to Zeke. Both of them had run away to be safer. Like me. And there were work camps that were like a group home jail somewhere in Northern California, with a corrupt system of abusive guards. I'd heard about the work camps from Joe, who hadn't actually been in one, but knew people who had. I didn't want to know what any of this would be like for a girl.

The whole place smelled like peeling linoleum and mothballs. I felt too warm. "So, what you're telling me is that I'd have to find my mother and get her busted or get arrested in order for you to help me," I said.

"Watch your tone." The way she said it, I knew I was going to have to fall back on the patois of children to get her to help me.

"Oh my god I'm sorry Mrs. Biddle, I totally didn't mean anything bad! I'm just so scared right now." I wasn't exactly lying.

Mrs. Biddle looked at me with a combination of superiority and a discernible, self-serving pettiness. She was a pure symbol of an adult world that threatened to absorb me and flatten my future.

"I might know a family that could work for you," she conceded. "I need to make a call. They've helped a few girls out."

I couldn't believe it. Why didn't she just say so in the first place, I wondered on my way back to wait in the lobby. But I didn't want to be a failure for not believing in the system. I got peanut butter crackers from a vending machine in the hall that were old and dry to swallow, sticking painfully in my throat while I waited. I wrote in my journal. I read.

Hours later, she lumbered down the hall to collect me.

We drove in her loud, freezing, beige Volkswagen Rabbit to a home on the other side of San Francisco that was the color of wet sidewalk. She told me that this was my only chance, that these were people who were doing her a personal favor. No one else would take me, she assured me. I said I understood. This family, she explained as we walked up a long front walk peppered by dull red steps, occasionally takes in "youth such as yourself." I wasn't sure what that meant. But being in Ingleside, I realized, meant that I could go back to Lincoln High. Even if this family was total boring weirdoes I'd just concentrate on school and studying, then get out. Have a future. Not die alone in a filthy squat.

A small, stout brunette woman with a short masculine haircut opened the door. She wore jeans and a dad sweater. I was immediately thrilled to be living with an older lesbian. "Hi Amy," she warmly greeted Mrs. Biddle. "David," she called over her shoulder. No one acknowledged me. Uh, okay.

We entered a sparsely furnished single-family home. David came in, greeted Mrs. Biddle, and I followed them to sit in a living room directly adjacent to the front door. There were two beige couches, a matching overstuffed chair, and nothing on the walls except a large, rough-hewn, dark brown wooden cross. A girl my age sat on the smaller sofa watching something quiet on an old TV. Her glance told me I was an interloper. She had the kind of bright blue eyes that got actresses cast as witches in horror films.

I was introduced to David, addressed to me as Mr. Cutler. He was short like his wife. A thin ring of trim white hair circled the wide expanse of his shiny head. It matched a bushy mustache that concealed the entirely of his lips. His face creased in a disarming smile, setting a strange firelight in eyes that sparkled like blue ice chips. He wore jeans, cowboy boots, and a black satin starter jacket. Mr. Cutler sat in what was apparently his chair, and Mrs. Cutler seated herself on the same couch as the girl, though not next to her. In the lineup, his wife's dark hair, dark eyes, and compact masculinity was striking. The scene was an anathema to femininity. Or transgression.

The adults talked about getting me back into Lincoln by Monday. I was admonished to do my housework, to "be good," and to follow the Cutler's rules. It seemed to be happening pretty fast. I wondered if there were other girls like me hidden somewhere else in the house, away from the eerie set piece of the living room.

"I will," I said.

"Taylee," Mr. Cutler said to the girl on the couch. "Get our new guest acquainted with her room and the shower so she can clean up for dinner."

Taylee rose, flashing eyes that matched her father's.

Taylee walked ahead of me down the hallway without a word. When we got to a nearly empty room at the end of the hall she said, "This one's yours." The room was furnished with only a bed, dresser, lamp, and another giant wooden crucifix on the wall that reminded me of *The Exorcist*. I followed Taylee down the hall to the bathroom, which I noticed was filthy.

She handed me two towels. "Shampoo, soap, there's toothpaste in the medicine cabinet," she monotoned.

"Why two towels?" I asked.

Her face lit up in a huge smile. Taylee said in a conspiratorial whisper, "You don't wanna touch your face with the same towel that touched your cooze."

I had no idea how to process that. While I stared at her trying to figure out what to say, she left.

I showered and thought about Taylee using the word "cooze." I couldn't wait to tell Rogue; that was some Cletus and Joe Bob shit right there. And why did she think that? It was weird to think that she was grossed out or afraid of one of the most vital and powerful parts of herself. I mean, okay, grossed out, I could kind of understand that sometimes. But to hate or fear your own sex parts? If someone taught her to think that, I mused, it was like some kind of next-level bullying. It was as if when she thought about her pussy, instead of understanding it, she had been reduced to a shrieking, fearful incoherence. A cruelly cultivated hatred of her own body.

I looked down at myself naked in the shower. I felt a powerful urge to tell my body, especially my girl parts, that I loved them. I almost giggled then, and stopped myself. I acknowledged how exhausted I was. I felt incredibly, otherworldly tired, but the hot shower eased the aches and pains of my joints. All I wanted to do was lay down and take

a nap. I was called to dinner before I could finish drying off --
with one towel.

Mrs. Cutler had made the greasiest, most delicious-
looking burgers I'd ever seen, set out at four place settings on
a table that had an unsurprising centerpiece of wood-carved
clasped hands. Mrs. Cutler was also a centerpiece of sorts, a
stern but dutiful servant toiling in the background. There was
a lone cross on the wall bearing down on this room, too.

I was becoming sure I knew where Taylee learned to
believe her own sex organs were nightmarish.

Of the people in this room, it was Mrs. Cutler who
fascinated me. It seemed to me that, like most women, she
had manufactured a sort of empty husk within which her
emotionality was deeply buried, and needed to be, in order
for her to survive as a wife, a mother, and a woman.

Mr. Cutler said we would talk about my new house, then
say grace, and eat dinner. I'd never been at a table where
anyone "said grace" before. I didn't really know what it
meant. Except it appeared I had to pretend to pray before I
could eat, just like at the soup kitchen.

My mom once told me she'd had me baptized, but I had
no idea what that meant. There was no praying in my
childhood, no church, and no religion. My single mom's tech-
hippie house was furnished in a sort-of classic Silicon Valley-
meets-artsy mysticism. As far back as I remembered, the
bookshelves in our living room held tomes on Sufi
spiritualism, books about meditation, and everything ever
written by Ram Dass. I read them all, and especially
remembered *Be Here Now*, the story of a Harvard psychiatrist
who dropped acid, went to India, and adapted Hinduism to
San Francisco values. So, other people trying to make me do

their religion, like with the Cutlers right now, always made me worried.

I got the rundown. They ran a strict house, meals were at set times, and chores were important. Mr. Cutler was a preacher. Mrs. Cutler said he was a "healer of souls." A man people would travel miles to see for "laying hands," faith cures powered by god. As they told me about this, I noticed a framed picture behind Taylee of a kneeling Jesus, supplicating to an invisible light source. Jesus: always coming but never actually showing up.

Thanks to growing up on guard against a highly intelligent drug addict, I had evolved a cautious allergy to people who refused to be accountable for their own actions. Otherwise, concepts like heaven seemed cartoonish (fluffy clouds and harps), vague (some irrational guy with a white beard), and manipulative (be good or you'll never see grandma again). I didn't get it, and I was okay with that. I also didn't believe in ghosts.

We sat around the small circle of their kitchen table; everyone folded their hands and closed their eyes. I copied them. Mr. Cutler white-knuckled his prayer grip and boomed, "In the name of Your Son, Jesus Christ, please Lord bless this food and this child who you have delivered unto us for salvation. Help her with her struggles, cleanse her spirit..." I let my eyes drift slowly back open as he continued. I noticed with a start that Taylee was watching me.

Faker, I thought.

14

MR. CUTLER BEGAN our dinner conversation by telling me his family were Evangelical Christians. I didn't want to ask what that meant, plus I was too busy eating. He said they moved from rural Bakersfield to San Francisco after the death of Mrs. Cutler's aunt, whose house we sat in. Mr. Cutler said that the house had been a sign of divinity calling them to "turn back the night" in San Francisco.

"Daddy's got powers," Taylee said to me.

It was still unclear to me what her father did for work. I wondered what they did with her aunt's stuff because this place felt stark. Somehow simultaneously dirty and un-lived in.

Mr. Cutler ignored his daughter. "The devil is hard at work in this city." He fixed me with his flinty eyes. "We have to be vigilant in this house."

I was pretty sure he had that backwards, but I kept my mouth full. Everywhere I went in the poor neighborhoods of San Francisco, someone was trying to get you into their cult. I learned quickly not to encourage them by asking questions. And I need this safe place to stay, I reminded myself.

"Do you know the tale of Sodom and Gomorrah?" he asked.

Jesus fucking Christ, I thought. I looked to Taylee, hoping she'd say something stupid.

"San Francisco is Sodom!" Taylee quipped.

"Good girl," Mr. Cutler said. He turned to me, "While we all know AIDS is God's punishment on the homosexuals, there was a powerful act of faith by the good leaders of this country to let it run its course."

I fought the urge to flinch backward as if shocked. He was talking about a legacy of presidents refusing to acknowledge the existence of AIDS at the expense of thousands and thousands of dead people, dead Americans. Reagan's press secretary Meeks who, every time a reporter asked about the AIDS crisis, cracked jokes about "fairy tales," because, you know. Gay people. My escape plan's Hail Mary was already curdled, I felt, but I was determined to see it through.

Around the sounds of an ordinary dinner among family; chewing, utensils scraping against plates, the creak of Mr. Cutler's chair, he continued. "The hope we had was it would be contained here."

Mrs. Cutler nodded, chewing. "Leviticus 20:13," she said around a mouthful of food.

"But the city, in her liberal blindness, is fighting to keep these animals alive. We can't let diseased homosexuals spread it to Christ's Americans."

"Imagine if one touched your food," Taylee nodded toward my hamburger.

God, she was such an idiot. Her harebrained father was repeating the same propaganda as Pat Buchanan and his ilk. They'd been on TV blasting the nation (and guiding politicians) with moral rationale justifying the 300,000 people that had been exposed to AIDS by the time we were sitting at that dinner table. In fact, at the time Mr. Cutler's dinnertime sermon to me about "nature's war" was in full rant-mode, twice as many people had died from AIDS in the US than would someday die in 9/11.

I wondered if Mrs. Cutler believed you could get it off a toilet seat. Or a towel.

The funny thing was, I never said to Mr. Cutler, "Hey, tell me all about Satan and the homosexuals." His words were so violent, his belief so sincere, his reasoning so faulty. I'd never seen this in person. While we formed generations of care circles to ease friends and loved ones into death, this guy rallied his family around a shared enemy.

This house was definitely an outpost, but not against the forces of darkness as Mr. and Mrs. Cutler were selling it. It was more like a temple of repression. So far, Mr. Cutler didn't do chores. The existence of women here was bounded and oppressive. I was going to have to self-censor every reaction to make this work, because it was pretty clear that some thoughts and feelings were permitted, and a whole lot of others were forbidden and unclean. *This wasn't the place for a curious mind,* I thought, or especially a girl who liked to ask questions.

There were a lot of real-life things I wasn't going to be able to talk about here, I thought. I giddily realized that playing an elf in Rogue's D&D game was definitely one of them.

Which was too bad, because while I ate and tried to tune him out, Mr. Cutler's fiery crush on Jesus gave me an idea. When we made our role-playing characters, Rogue gave each character an extra handicap of her own making. These were taken from people on the streets, and could manifest during times of character stress, like during a battle.

Joe's dwarf was cursed with a very stinky homeless-guy smell that got better or worse depending on the roll of the dice. My elf would sometimes just start air-drumming like a skitzo. John Gone's gnome was a drug addict and always high on something. Bozie's human character heard voices that argued with him. Sometimes these handicaps could be really bad, like if during a bartering session I started air drumming really violently, or they could be good, like the time Joe's smell became so bad it actually made some orcs crap their pants. As Mr. Cutler talked about how I might want to think about accepting Jesus in me, I realized we needed a religious-nut handicap in the game. It could really work.

I decided to keep my mouth full.

After dinner the Cutlers left me alone to do dishes and then watch TV on the couch with Taylee. I kept quiet so she wouldn't try to talk to me. My brain was all over the place. I felt sweaty, overemotional beneath the surface. I was having a hard time trying not to think about Jenn's body. I definitely didn't want to think about Mr. Cutler's faith. For a man of god, his compassion was a thoroughly extinguished impulse. His religion radically decentered him from the necessary human mechanisms of accountability and empathy. Those who are hated are always more human than those who hate them.

I figured if the Cutlers didn't make me pretend to agree with them other than when it was time to eat, I could try to endure it until I was 16. After that I could get a job, work, and be on my own while finishing school. I mean, there was a refreshing lack of dead bodies in the Cutler's house for me to wake up next to. I excused myself and went to bed early.

I woke up on Sunday in a matted pool of sweat, tangled in my bed's wet sheets with Mrs. Cutler pressing a cool washrag to my forehead.

I had the flu. It had taken me down like a tranquilizer dart. *I can't be sick*, I thought, *I need to go to school tomorrow.*

But I couldn't stay awake.

I floated through ether, watched my mom cover the

backyard of our Mountain View rental with thick plastic to create a greenhouse for her pot plants. In the darkness a UFO came into view, terrifying me, lighting up the sky and spotlighting the ground, looking for us.

I ran along giant cables that spanned the work floor at ArgoSystems. It was Take Your Daughter to Work Day at Interglobal, and my mom's secretary led me into her executive office. Mom doesn't know I'm there, I am a shadow, intangible, a ghost.

I'm scared, there's an evil presence in the house. It's chasing me, and when I turn around it assumes shapes, but it's invisible, and I'm terrified it will enter my body, because that's what it wants to do. I run outside and hide under parked cars while it angrily enters the bodies of other people and rips their flesh apart from the inside out like a horror movie. I can hear them scream and gurgle as it rages out of them, and I hope I can crawl quietly to the next car over, and maybe the next one after that, hoping it won't find me.

I woke to Mrs. Cutler putting a water glass to my lips. "Do you have any Theraflu?" I asked.

I sank into sweaty wet sheets. Rogue was in a closet, screaming, saying she can't feel her legs. Jenn leaned into me and whispered, "What's the worst thing you've ever done?"

I was in Buena Vista Park and there was a serial killer in the woods. I tried to run but my feet stuck to the ground, the skin stretched when I tried to lift them, like stringy glue packed with twigs and dirt. I wiggled a molar with my tongue and it popped out into my hand. All my teeth began coming loose; they sounded like dice in my mouth. I watched them fall to the ground and saw it's not really a path I'm on, but there are kids like Little Shaun submerged under the tarry glue, dead, bobbing up to the surface, eyes closed, and mouths open in a final gasp for air. I fell backward and slammed my head on a tree, thinking *they're soulless so they're attracted to death.*

I awoke with a cold hand on my forehead. It was Mr. Cutler pressing on my head. His eyes were closed, and he mumbled and shouted, clutching a brown leather book that said Holy Bible.

"I COMMAND you, unclean spirit--"

Back under. There were a million little, tiny spiky devils on my body, dancing on my skin. Their feet had barbs like fishhooks, and every hop and jig poked, hooked, and ripped my skin. Get off me, I willed. They ignored me. I decided enough was enough. I shrunk myself down to their size. I kicked and punched them one at a time.

The sound of his voice frightened me awake. "From all EVIL, deliver us, O Lord," continued Mr. Cutler. "From all SIN--"

I came fully conscious. Mr. Cutler was breathing heavily. "Turn back the EVIL upon my foes, in your faith DESTROY the DEVILS and DESTROY them like the UNCLEAN SPIRIT tormenting this child--"

The shouting made my head pound. I just need some fucking Theraflu.

I wasn't sure if I was supposed to act like a demon was leaving me in order to make Mr. Cutler stop. I had to get him to stop shouting, stop touching me ... it was like he was trying to put something inside me. I looked in his glittery eyes and pulled my head back from his hand, shrinking back like anyone would if a creepy old man was touching them without asking. He stopped and sat back in one motion; like a recoil. He glanced around the room and mumbled something

VIOLET BLUE

about restfulness, got up, and walked out without a second glance.

Taylee glared at me from the doorway, arms folded. "You don't know how lucky you are." She followed her father. I found a dry spot on the bed and wished again that I had some Theraflu. I replayed the bit of Mr. Cutler's exorcism in my mind just to be sure it really happened. I was angry at myself for not striking a man who touched me while I was asleep, vulnerable.

My fever broke that night. I insisted on eating dinner with the Cutlers to prove I was fully capable of going to school the next day. I was anxious about the thought of being left alone in the house with Mr. Cutler.

I felt woozy and weak while Mrs. Cutler drove me to school in the morning. The sun's eye pounded my head from above. I wondered if light would ever stop hurting, or if maybe that was a leftover from the flu. I practically jumped out of her Saab and beelined to the guidance counselors' offices. The crisp air and salty ocean smell made me feel instantly cleaner, clearer.

Everything in school was loud. I met with my counselor, Mr. Burtleson. I went light on details, told him I'd been placed in a new home and really wanted to fix whatever I could of the new school year. He was the "cool" counselor, the guy who was known for going to movies with students and bringing his younger daughter along. His desk was a mess; piled high with student files, books, notepads, and the floor around it was an obstacle course of more files, more paper. File cabinets sat like sentinels around us, drawers lolling open like overstuffed tongues. He ran a hand over his beard, thinking.

I was going to need credits and to be bumped back into

142

remedial math, because my low grades were a problem. For credits, he said, I could do admin and filing in his office for one period a day.

It seemed like every time I was about to decide that all adults were terrible, there was someone who reminded me that there were good ones. Yet when I left Mr. Burtleson's office, on my own in the hall, I realized how lost I was. This wasn't the first time I'd tried to start over at school; it was one of many.

It was supposed to be my high school, but I didn't go there. I saw a future where I was an adult and every time people at parties, picnics, cafes, or bars started talking about high school, I would feel like a liar saying I went to high school at all. At this point, I could barely remember high school and I was standing in it.

And none of it mattered. I had no future because my past had already destroyed it. Why was I even here?

I was back here because I knew that if I didn't graduate, no one would listen to me as an adult.

I was back here because I was chasing my faith in the system and my trust in adults.

I don't need to prove anything by going back to school, I thought. I just need all of this to mean something.

I went to a few classes and felt totally lost. I felt like I didn't know anyone, so I skipped last class and went to McCoppin to see if anyone was out smoking.

The best way to describe my reception at the playground was "mobbed." Tina Chan hugged me, then Mara, then John Gone, and Joe pressed his forehead on mine and just held it there for a minute. "I was so scared after they found Jenn," he said. "You disappeared."

Ashley Bailey strode over and gave me a bear hug. "Be

careful," I coughed, "don't kill me!" Even her trio of scary cheerleader buddies -- Paisley, Leticia, and Hailey -- hugged me. Paisley, who tried so hard to find a reason to beat me up. That was unexpected.

Ashley pushed a strand of hair behind my ear. It gave me good shivers, like when someone cares about you. She said, "You look the same."

"I'm not," I said.

Ashley hugged me a second time then, and I felt myself soften into her embrace.

I told everyone my story, afraid they'd decide something was wrong with me.

The whole tale could be read from Tina's expressions, from "Oh my GOD" horror about Jenn, to eyes-crossed snort-laughing about having Satan banished from my body. Friends, I realized, are the people who are on your side, who trust you to tell your own story. Ashley and Paisley laughing at the childishness of Mr. Cutler surprised me; it really was funny now that I thought about it.

"What if I wanted to keep Satan?" I joked, and Ashley said it kind of wasn't funny, but she said that I still should've yelled "Fuck me Jesus!" at least once. Everyone cracked up at that, not just because she yelled it too loud, but also because we all thought *The Exorcist* was a hilarious old movie.

Soberly, Joe said "You really need to come to the Magic Bench. Rogue and Jimmy have been freaking out looking for you."

"Not Zeke?" I joked.

Joe rolled his eyes.

"Fuck it," I said, "let's go now. I can still make it back to the Cutler's in time for the holy dinner."

15

THE BUS RIDE to Castro with John Gone and Joe felt like it took us through the clouds. It was only fog trickling its chilly fingers over Twin Peaks.

I thought the guys were too quiet on the ride over.

I told John his black goatee looked really Satanic, and that I knew this because I was now an expert on Satan. I sat up straighter to look superior while I said it. He managed a smile. I nodded at Joe like I had established a clever fact, tapping my right temple for emphasis.

Joe nodded back once and looked away, out the window. He had become more subdued, faded, even more of a closed book than before. I worried that Jenn's downward spiral into death hit him harder than anyone knew.

I thought some lines from *Repo Man* would fix it. We all loved that movie. If you were sitting there bored on the sidewalk asking for spare change and no one was smiling, you could always make everyone light up with a little "plate of shrimp" reference. Callbacks and movie lines would flow from whoever was around. Along with *Suburbia* and *Mad Max*, we felt that *Repo Man* was one of "our" films.

I looked at Joe and said, "I blame society. Society made me what I am."

He kept his eyes out the window as the bus burped and farted its way past another stop along the Sunset District's dull row houses. *Never mind*, I thought.

Joe pinned me with a sideways glance and said, "Bullshit. You're just a white suburban punk like me."

No smile, but it was a good sign. John was grinning.

I coughed, "I know ..." like I'd been shot. "But it still ... hurts." Joe tried not to smile, and failed, and I felt better about us.

I wasn't sure how I was going to explain being home late from school to the Cutlers. Maybe there was just going to be an adjustment period between me and them, where I had my own life and they had their ... religion. In my head, I started to go over excuses I could try out if they asked me to go to church with them. If they even went to church. Why was Mr. Cutler a preacher with no flock? What did they think of Jim Jones? Why didn't anyone ask why he was obsessed with gay men? Did all religions have such massive boundary problems? I was honestly too afraid to ask them any real questions.

My mind turned over the horror movie possibilities of my sleeping arrangements while we stepped off the bus into Castro's little hamlet. What a relief. Gay Main Street, where I didn't have to hide who I was or who I loved. *Jesus fuck*, I thought, looking at the giant glass windows of the Twin Peaks bar. Young gays I knew derided it with the cruel nickname "glass coffin." Now I understood what a righteous act of defiance those windows were. They said, *look at us. We are not afraid to be seen.*

The Magic Bench was overflowing with scraggly young punks and homeless kids. We came into view and Jimmy jumped up, ran over to us yelling "Wooooo!" He picked me up and kissed me right there in front of everyone, then hugged me so hard I couldn't breathe.

"Phew," Zeke said, next in line for a hug. "We were getting ready to call the eff-bee-eye to find ya! Missed you, Blue." I melted into his bony hug.

I hadn't thought about what would happen when Jenn's body was found, and the fact that I had disappeared at the same time. No wonder my friends had been worried.

It was a feeling like invisible fingers lightly drumming pleasant sensations up into the base of my skull. No one had ever told me they missed me. Not that I could remember, anyway.

I asked everyone, "Where's Rogue?"

Zeke shrugged. "She had some family thing," he said. He didn't look happy about it.

"Oh. That sucks."

"Yeah," he said, "we'll definitely need some booze when she gets back. Booze for my bay-beh!"

I got caught up with Big Shaun and Little Shaun, who told me the Lower Haight squat was officially over. The guys had scouted out a new building on Haight near Divisadero. "It's on the same block as that guy who's in the Village People," Little Shaun said.

I was kind of thrilled. "Wait, what? What Village People guy?"

Big Shaun said, "A guy in the Village People owns a house on Haight at Divis. It's not right next to the new squat, but it's close."

"Which one?" I had to know. "Is it the cowboy?"

"No," Little Shaun said. "It's the cop."

Zeke's gawky arms and legs approximated very bad dance moves as he said, "Well he's a macho, macho man!"

Zeke kept singing and dancing -- he knew the words. Big Shaun went back to asking passers-by for spare change. One of the two girls I'd originally thought were twins told me, "I think Village People cop is pretty cool." It was Jess, the smaller one, platinum blonde, with delicate features like a pretty little doll. Anyone could tell Jess was the younger of the two. Probably younger than me. She resumed painting Little Shaun's nails with a bottle of black polish. Lisa, the taller twin, nodded her angular face in its frame of shiny blue-black hair.

I was starting to feel back to normal. Right then, we watched a pair of tall, bearded nuns in the most unbelievable makeup walking along Castro Street. We all stopped our bullshitting and spare-changing to just stare.

Lisa was riveted. Keeping her eye on the nuns she said, "Who. Is. That?"

"Hey!" said Big Shaun. He waved at the nuns. They changed course and came over to us, and my heart pounded in my chest with nerves I didn't understand.

"Well, hello there," said one of the nuns in a smooth baritone. "How are you-all doing today?" The nuns had flyers in their hands, and passed one to Little Shaun who held it like it was breakable. I couldn't believe they were talking to us. It felt like someone famous had said hi to me in front of all my friends. Their faces looked like hand-painted, bejeweled brooches.

"Spare any change?" asked Big Shaun.

"Don't!" Jess slapped Big Shaun on the shoulder. "You don't ask nuns for money!"

The nuns introduced themselves as the Sisters of Perpetual Indulgence. They passed each of us a flyer and one said, "Is everyone having safer sex?"

Little Shaun's face turned red, and Big Shaun just said "Oh my god."

"Well," said one of the nuns, grinning, "that's certainly one way to look at it."

I glanced at the leaflet and saw that it was about AIDS and sex, but it was for guys. It was still the coolest thing, though, and showed how to put condoms on. The nuns thanked us and walked on, their full black habits floating around them down the street like houses defying gravity.

Jess called after them, "I love your makeup!"

I liked that we weren't the most outrageous things to look at in the neighborhood. While we blended in Upper Haight, with its punks, hippies, homeless, and clothes-horse subcultures, in other neighborhoods we were pariahs, treated like little criminals. Yet in Castro, we were among distinct identities that treated us like we belonged, like our visible differences were normal. Still, we paled in comparison to the drag queens who graced the sidewalk with their impossibly tall, unbelievably otherworldly expressions of powerful femininity. They filled me with the wonder of a child with all their confidence, their rarefied glamor tuned to a frequency I couldn't hear. Until my days of sitting on the sidewalk, even as a beggar, I'd never thought of gender as a performance, or more importantly to me, that femininity could be powerful without apologies.

The drag queens were also badasses. I got the impression that a good lot of them were ex-military, because people who fucked with them frequently found out it was a bad idea the hard way. On more than one occasion while asking for quarters, I'd been surprised by people in dresses with hairy chests asking me if I was doing okay, or if some dude was bothering me. There was also a constant rumor that the delicate, ultra-femme Thai queens knew martial arts. No one knew it if was true, but we loved repeating a story someone supposedly heard about a Thai queen who beat the crap out of some dude who came to Castro for gay-bashing and got bashed back, hard. I hated my life, but I loved this neighborhood.

Lisa looked up. "Hey it's Spider," she pointed. In unison, both girls softly said, "Yaaaaaaay."

Spider was at the top of Harvey Milk Plaza with a roll of packing tape and an armload of flyers, affixing papers to poles. She was in her black motorcycle jacket, jeans, white t-shirt, sunglasses and a signature cigarette hung from the corner of her mouth. I thought she looked handsome, though I wasn't sure if that was the right word.

Spider spotted us, gave a somber chin-up nod, and walked over. I could see the top of the flyers. As she came closer, I clearly made out words that read "IVAN: CHILD MOLESTER," and a photo of Ivan, the scary homeless guy we all avoided.

Zeke called out: "Sup, Spider!"

She nodded at Zeke, then said to me, "Glad you're okay."

I was so glad to see her, out here on her own, caring about us. "Thanks."

"Hey," she addressed our group. "You guys heard?"

We all exchanged looks.

"Little Joe." She plucked the cigarette from her lips. "He died."

Right then I thought of how I needed new shoes and didn't know how I was going to get them. I was scared my shoes were going to start smelling bad. I thought about my locker at school and that it would make a good place for me to stash things like panties, socks, and deodorant. I thought about how the sun was a massive fucker of a ball of gas behind the fog, and would kill us if it got a chance. I thought about the MUNI bus driver on our way over here, the scary way he grabbed my shirt and yanked me toward him when he thought I was trying to get on without a transfer. And all of it made more sense than what Spider had just said to me.

"No?" It came out of me sounding like a question at first, and trailed off.

John Gone just said, "Fuck."

Everyone was quiet then. Jimmy put his arm around me. Jess furrowed her brow, and then her little pixie face crumpled like a candy wrapper into quiet sobs. Lisa hugged her. Held her. Big Shaun stared off into the plaza's planter. Mark stared at the ground, his heart was in his eyes. Little Shaun glared at his shoes, and behind him Zeke looked around at everyone, a mixture of confusion and sadness on his face.

Zeke asked, "What happened?" His voice was so quiet, small.

Spider came closer and gently told those of us who didn't already know that Little Joe was sick. That he had AIDS, though Spider corrected herself to say HIV because that's what it was called now.

"How," I stammered, "... how did it happen so fast?" I was incredulous. Little Joe didn't look like the kindly skeleton-men in the Castro, or the boys who you'd see with bruises that weren't bruises. "He didn't look sick," I said. I hoped it wasn't the wrong thing to say after it left my mouth.

The HIV wasn't what killed him, Spider told us. She said Little Joe had said he'd "end it" if he started to go downhill. He jumped out of a window in the Tenderloin where he was crashing with his other family of gay and trans sex workers. Spider didn't falter in her explanation, remained present and calm, and right then I knew she'd done this awful task before.

Everywhere around us, where Spider had taped up her

warning flyer about Ivan, there were also HIV/AIDS prevention flyers. Everywhere, the signs of people trying to take care of each other in failed systems within other failed systems.

I saw a line running through it all to this moment. San Francisco had learned the hard way what it meant to be hated by the federal government. To be mocked when we needed help. To watch helplessly as loved ones died horribly, to live in fear while misinformation was spread and we were laughed at. If multiple presidents and their administrations hadn't abhorred gay and trans people, hadn't been indifferent to the suffering of Black people with HIV, we would have learned how to prevent it faster. We could've fought it faster.

I sat on a planter in Harvey Milk Plaza in a daze. If all that shit hadn't happened, there might've been early prevention, early treatment. Maybe even a cure. By the time Little Joe hurled himself out of a Tenderloin window, HIV might not have been a death sentence. Prevention -- safer sex education -- might've even kept him from getting it in the first place. If conservative, religious, anti-gay, racist, embarrassed-about-sex people hadn't been the ones making decisions about human sexuality, morality, and disease treatment in my country, Little Joe and I could've walked the long road of friendship together.

We could've come to know each other. Had years of recommending books to each other and talking about them, years of afternoon coffees at cafes like Mimic. Gotten old enough for one of us to drive a car to the freezing beach to share cigarettes and tears together after a breakup. To get old enough to go to bars together, and do that San Francisco thing where you talk about how you needed to hang out together more. All of it would've been worthwhile. I had been looking forward to it.

It wasn't okay, I wasn't okay. Nothing was going to be okay. Little Joe falling through the sky to die in a neighborhood of other Little Joes. His ribs snapped, his skull cracked, probably his aorta tearing on impact like if he'd jumped from the Golden Gate Bridge. I didn't get enough time with him. I didn't get to tell him how much I loved him, that he was a beautiful creature from another planet, sent here to bring us magic and glamour. I felt loose inside, fluttery.

No one made any jokes. Someone said we should go drink beer in Dolores Park and that it would be our Irish wake for Little Joe. Pain couldn't be killed, but booze might make it shut up for a minute.

We quietly negotiated pooling change and dollars. Spider said she'd buy beer for us, but after that we were on our own. Jimmy hugged Spider then, and I had to look away from the pain on their faces. Jess and Lisa asked if we could get Lucky Lager, in addition to whatever else people wanted, which was usually Schafer. People liked the ducks on the side of the Schafer cans. Jess and Lisa collected Lucky Lager beer caps, each of which had a rebus puzzle in them. With a sad smile, Jess shook her bag for emphasis, a muffled tinkling of tiny bells inside. It sounded like she had hundreds of bottlecaps in there.

Walking in a group down Castro, Aiden said "Hey, hold on." He reached down into the gutter and pulled out a wet piece of paper. Aiden unfolded it and said, "Holy shit."

Zeke asked, "What is it?"

"I thought it was a bus pass. It's a fucking fifty!"

Zeke managed a tight-lipped smile, as if to himself. "And that's why they call it the Magic Bench, everyone." Others nodded. Our version of a genuflection. He said to the group, "Let's get a case. And snacks."

16

THAT FIFTY DOLLAR bill made us feel rich. We would've been walking tall if we hadn't just had a hole punched through our hearts. I couldn't imagine us without Little Joe.

Fog billowed in over our heads, pushing wetly through the Castro on a strong wind coming off Twin Peaks. We ran into James The Snitch at the corner of Castro and 18th while we waited for Spider, to get our beer and snacks. His red hair hung in wet ringlets around his face. I was about to thank him for the phone number and all the free calls when he introduced us to the two guys he was with.

"Bob and Dan work there," he indicated a drugstore on the corner with a nod, curls bouncing as if in affirmation. Bob had dark feathered hair and a mustache that grew over his mouth. His buddy also had a mustache, a weak dishwater blonde spray of fine hairs across his top lip. We had a nickname for the hairstyle framing Dan's bony face, and it wasn't nice. He had a "ho cut" -- short for "Jose" as in San Jose, because it was the way macho dudes who came to the City from San Jose wore their hair. In the near future this haircut would be popularly renamed a "mullet." Ho cuts were always a bad sign that meant rednecks, speed freaks, homophobes, and men who treated women like farm animals. I noticed Bob and Dan both wore flip-flop sandals that cradled filthy toes.

They called each other "bra." They broadcast that they were straight guys who worked in the gay Castro. The kind of men who desperately hunted for chances to prove their straightness. Usually on other people. They wore it like violence. When Dan's slitted eyes landed on little Jess, he was riveted.

Jimmy told James about Little Joe, and that we were going to Dolores Park.

"Well, if anyone wants party favors!" Dan said this while glaring at Jess, who whispered to Lisa, ignoring his gaze. His voice was too loud and sounded like gargled sandpaper. Dan and Bob reminded me of Upper Haight's sour manchildren, and I vowed to stay far away from them.

It wasn't going to be easy because no one told them "no." I wanted to, but I also didn't want to be the one they singled out. Dan and Bob tagged along as we beelined for the park, bragging that they stole pills from work and could get anything we wanted. The two pharmacy employees hurried to look like they were walking with Lisa and Jess, who locked arms with each other to block space on the sidewalk as we made our formation down 18th Street. I took Jimmy's hand so Bob and Dan would be sure to leave me alone, though the appreciative little squeeze he gave me brought me back to my feelings.

I was mad at James for bringing guys who were clearly bad news into our scene. My irritation was crowded out by a feeling of deep sadness for Little Joe's absence, then just a flatness, like a ringing noise in your ears after an explosion or a gunshot. We passed a Victorian on 18th Street that had been converted into a restaurant. It smelled delicious and full of life. I heard a male server call out "Princess!" to someone within the restaurant. I clung to the sentiment's humor and freedom like a life vest.

Mission Dolores Park was a giant grassy hillside between the gay Castro, the Latino working-class Mission, and wealthy white Noe Valley -- which we alternately called "Snowy Valley" for all the white people, and "Stroller Valley," for all their babies. A statue of Miguel Hidalgo, the father of Mexican independence, presided over the park and its land that had previously been two large Jewish cemetery plots. The cultures intersecting in Dolores Park didn't blend. Except when people from Snowy Valley or the Castro bought drugs from dealers in gangs from the Mission, or Snowy's rich white men took a walk on the wild side for some "I'm not gay" gay cruising.

The drug dealers chiefly occupied the North side, which was the bottom of a hill across the street from Mission High School. They carved out holes under the park's grassy turf, which they would peel up like a lid and stash their product under, then lay around on the grass while conducting business. The steep grassy hillside at the park's top had an incredible view. When the sun was out, the lawn would be covered in bare male flesh, tanning and posing. That was called "Gay Beach." To the dismay of Bob and Dan, it was where we were headed to drink our beer. Gay men, the 38th parallel.

Dan started complaining; it was too far, he didn't like it over there. Lisa bit back saying, "We just lost our friend." I was glad she said something. But "lost" struck me as such a strange word. When you lose something, there's hope you'll find it again.

We had no problem finding a spot at Gay Beach on a foggy day. It was getting darker early. Our seating arrangement made a semi-circle facing San Francisco's downtown buildings, their tops fading into a grey blur that erased the skyline, the strange Transamerica Pyramid confusing perception of past and present. San Francisco was a peninsula, but it was really more of an island. Or another planet entirely. I thought that if the fog cleared, we'd see stars no one recognized. Constellations not yet named.

I watched as a meter maid's boxy little car ambled along parked cars looking for victims. Gangs of wild parrots streaked green and red feathers through the sky and screamed, chasing each other around giant towering palm trees that stood like stoic sentinels down the wide center of Dolores Street. We relaxed on the grass. I cracked open a Lucky Lager, passed my cap to Jess, and toasted the loud, crazy feathered punks careening overhead. I wondered if I was ever going to cry about Little Joe.

I looked around the group. Other Joe hadn't said anything in a while. No one else seemed to notice. He was an ice cube melting in a drink. Aiden was talking to Lisa, and Bob seemed to be consoling Jess, who was crying. Dan was still glaring at Jess, but James animatedly kept him distracted in conversation. Zeke and both Shauns were reading out beer cap puzzles to each other. Jimmy was good at it.

"It's a 'pop' like 'soda pop', get it?" Zeke smiled, proud he'd guessed the rebus puzzle.

A blanket of sadness returned in the quiet pause.

"Hey!" Zeke looked at Little Shaun with a goofy grin. "Ever notice that Dr. Pepper doesn't taste like doctors or peppers? What the fuck, man?" We all groaned and rolled our eyes. Zeke basked in the glow of his bad joke, mission accomplished.

I was going to have to make my way back to the Cutler's house soon. Instead of thinking about that, I reached into my bag and pulled out the photo I found in my mom's stuff when I snuck into Donna's garage. I wanted to ask Jimmy if he thought the guy in the photo looked like me. He shoved it back in my bag, hard, jumped up, and ran.

I heard the shouting as I turned my head. Zeke's voice: "Five-O!"

The motion of police officers coming from both directions registered in my line of sight first; next was the way the group of us exploded in every direction. Across my complete field of view, going by from right to left, went Zeke. Red mohawk spiked in perfect profile, he ran with his back ramrod straight, arms and legs pumping at angles like a puppet on a stick. He looked like he was riding a bicycle through the air. The smile didn't even start to crack my face before I felt a giant bear paw grab the back of my jacket and haul me backwards like a horror movie victim, my hands grabbing at nothing, my heels raking the grass uselessly for purchase.

I was shoved into place with my hands behind my head at the top of Dolores Park. The row included Bob, Dan, Aiden, Joe, and James. And me. In front of us were two SFPD squad cars. All I could think was to wonder how they'd rolled up on us so quietly.

The cops worked our line from both directions. They ran our IDs. Aiden and I only had our school ID cards. It was all I had.

"Alright," I heard one cop say. "These three go with a warning, the rest stay." He nodded at me. "This one has a warrant."

A warrant? I started to say, "What's going o--"

An enormous police officer hauled me up off the ground. Handcuffs slammed clanking onto my wrists behind me, constricting in pain that shot into my thumbs, seared the outer bones of my wrists. He pushed me over to a police car and shoved me toward the back door. I hit the side of the vehicle. Mostly with my face. I turned my head in time to smack the car with my left cheek.

Hysterically I thought, *that side of my face will never not be bruised.* The pain was sharp and dull at the same time. Bone deep.

There was arguing behind me. I was too scared to move. I noticed I was panting in panic.

"You're coming with me." It was a stout little cop. He was short but still a head taller than me, and his forearms were like coiled rope. He took my arm and led me to the other vehicle, my bag in his free hand. He was older. A Latino man with a million laugh lines who wasn't smiling. I read his name tag. Lopez. *Fuck,* I thought, *that gun on his belt is big.*

"Do you know why I'm taking you in?" He was straight down to business.

"No! I honestly have no idea."

"You have a warrant for your arrest. Were you aware of that?"

"No! Ohmigod no. What's it for?"

He considered me for a long second. "It's for driving without a license."

I was baffled. "What?"

His face was unreadable. He said, "We'll talk in the car."

He leveraged me into the back of his police car. It smelled of bleach and vomit. The seat was hard, and I had to angle myself sideways so I didn't sit on my wrists. They felt hot, throbbing.

From the front of the car he said, "Your warrant is from a ticket. It was on Divisadero."

"I ... I was in an accident. I was riding a scooter to school. I woke up in a hospital. I don't even know what happened to the scooter."

"They ticketed you for riding without a license. Your parents would have been contacted and gotten a copy."

"My mom didn't tell me anything about a ticket." I was in disbelief.

"Well, since you're a minor this was her responsibility."

I thought, of course it was. I sank back on the seat. The cuffs bit painfully. I had no idea what to say.

"Where do you go to school?"

I made eye contact with him though the metal mesh dividing the police car's interior. His eyes seemed kind. "I go to Lincoln. I mean, I'm trying to go to Lincoln. Mom sorta moved and didn't tell me." The urge to cry hit me in a rush, like a fist squeezing my sternum. I bit it back. It was hard. My face flushed. "I had the accident and then she moved. I didn't have anywhere to go. I went to CPS and asked for help."

He paused. "Did they help you?"

"I'm at this house ... it's weird. But I went back to school today."

"Do you know a girl at Lincoln named Rosalie? Rosalie Guerrero?"

"Yes!" She was practically the only Mexican girl in our school; I thought it was strange since my Junior High -- the one I went to the longest -- had been almost all Latino kids. Rosalie was nice to me, and I kind of had a crush on her. I said, "She runs track. She's really fast."

Officer Lopez smiled and said, "That's my girl." He started the car.

I thought he'd take me to Juvie -- the juvenile detention center on the side of Twin Peaks -- but he drove toward the Mission station. Decades of horror stories about that detention center and Haight runaways danced in my mind. Kids killed themselves there. I wondered if that's where I'd end up tonight. As we drove, I started mentally preparing myself to be tough in jail.

In the SFPD parking lot on Valencia Street, officer Lopez helped me out of the car and took off my handcuffs. He handed me my bag. "Let's talk," he said, motioning me into the station.

The officer directed me into a sparse reception area, its counter topped with thick bulletproof glass. We went through a locked door into a wide, brightly lit hallway. He steered me through another locked door along the hallway. The room was all-white, bright, with a metal table and three chairs.

"Have a seat."

I sat. He locked me in the room.

It was the first time I'd been alone since I woke up that morning. It felt like years ago. I looked at my red, swollen wrists, moving them back and forth. They were going to be bruised. There was going to be way too much to explain, or to lie about, to the Cutlers. If I ever got back there.

Officer Lopez unlocked the door and came in with two steaming Styrofoam cups. "You seem like a tea person."

"I am," I gave a little smile. It made my cheek feel bigger, more inflamed. "Thank you."

His wedding ring shone dully in the overhead fluorescents. Worn-in nicks and scratches as if it had learned something the hard way.

"Aren't you supposed to take me to Juvie?"

"What, are you a lawyer?" He was smiling again.

"I'm multi-talented. In case the whole being homeless thing doesn't work out."

He waited. "So, you're homeless."

Oops. I said, "I'm trying really hard not to be."

I gave Officer Lopez an abridged version, minus a lot of what was really going on, like the drug dealing and cartels, or that my mother was running around wearing the identity of a dead woman. Storytelling self-defense. I couldn't imagine how things could get worse for me, but I was sure life could find a way. I needed to be careful.

He shook his head, smirking. "You just walked into CPS? Just like that?"

"I guess no one does that."

"No one does that. And she put you in a group home?"

"Well, she put me in a home that takes kids in, I guess."

"She give you a contact number so you can keep in regular touch?"

"No. The Cutlers have all her information."

He thought for a moment. "Well, the state has decided you're a criminal. And the state is never wrong."

My mouth gaped. He smiled. "No. I'm releasing you of your own recognizance. Come on, I'm going to drop you off at the Cutlers, so you get back safe. But I want you to get this warrant sorted out."

I promised I would. I hoped it wasn't a lie.

He let me ride up front in the police car. The Crown Vic was warm, though it still smelled bad. I could tell it had a powerful engine as we wound around the hills under Mount Sutro's radio tower, glowing fog tangling in its tines like radioactive candy floss. After a while he asked, "You gonna have kids someday?"

"Probably not. Not on my salary."

He laughed.

I paused. I felt like I could talk to him. "Not after I've seen what people are capable of."

He said, "Yeah."

Officer Lopez dropped me off at the corner instead of in front of the Cutler's house, where they might see me getting out of a cop car. He handed me a card. "Call me if you get in trouble. So, what I mean is, don't call me."

I laughed. "Thank you, sir."

My cheek was pounding. It was waking up The Headache. I needed food and water. I walked. Thick fog desaturated the streetlights and Ingleside's flat-faced row houses. From across the city a foghorn blew a long, low blast. I was sure I could smell the ocean, clean salt air.

The lights were all on as I walked up to the Cutlers' door. I didn't know what to say, not just yet. Maybe, I thought, I should just be honest.

I opened the door and walked into the warmth and light. Mr. Cutler stood up. Mrs. Cutler remained seated on the love seat. Taylee stood in the kitchen doorway, arms folded. Glaring with those witchy eyes.

My mother sat on the couch.

Everyone was looking at me.

"There she is," my mother said. She was smiling.

17

ON ONE OF the misty slopes of Twin Peaks near the Cutler's house stood San Francisco's concrete and steel Juvenile Justice Center. The overcrowded facility, known for treating the boys and girls inside like animals, was a synonym for despair. I'd thought that's where I would end up tonight, but instead Officer Lopez had done me a kindness. I stood in the doorway, surveyed the faces of Mr. and Mrs. Cutler, their smirking daughter, and my mother, and wondered if I wouldn't be better off in that jail.

"Seems to me you got lost on the way home from school," Mr. Cutler mocked. "At least your mother hasn't been waitin' for long. Now come on in and have a seat."

"What's going on?" My voice was too high. Too freaked out.

Taylee smiled from the kitchen doorframe. Mr. Cutler said, "We're going to have a talk, and then you're going home with your mother. Reconcile and reunite."

I felt hope draining out of the room and darkness replacing it. My mother smiled. "Sit down, kiddo." She addressed Mr. Cutler. "I'm just glad she's okay. Do we know what happened to her face?"

I felt like I was the only one in the room with a bullshit meter and it was spiking. How did they even find her?

"Well, that shiner she's got came along with her." His pastoral hick charm oozed off every vowel. "We don't know exactly what happened, maybe she'll tell us about it."

Maybe, I thought, you'll change your mind about sending me home with her once you know the truth.

I looked at my mother. I was sick of everyone talking about me like I wasn't in the room. "How did they get ahold of you?" I demanded. "You didn't even leave me your number. The school said you hadn't called."

"Well, you ran away, didn't you?" Her voice was heavy with accusation. "And then you ran to Child Protective Services."

"Yes, I did."

She shook her head. She wore an off-white collared blouse tucked into a beige calf-length skirt. Taupe pantyhose, legs crossed. Business clothes, like when she would come home from her defense contracting job. The old days of being in charge. Battle clothes, circa Before The Bust. "I need my little girl at home. That's where you belong."

I felt hysterical. She was acting like everything was normal, and it wasn't. "You want to know where I got this bruise?" I looked to Mr. and Mrs. Cutler, then back at my mom. The bay window behind her was dark, the avenue streetlights pulsed like smudges in the fog. The room felt too closed-in. "It was when a cop slammed me against a cop car tonight after he saw I have a warrant for my arrest. Did you know I have one? I didn't."

If she was surprised, she didn't show it. A crumpled tissue in her hand grazed her nose in a swift motion. "What did you do?"

"I didn't do anything! *You* were supposed to! They ticketed me for my accident and you ignored it!"

"That's not true, honey."

I was stunned to silence. What she had actually just said

to me was so loud I could practically feel the window glass cracking.

She looked to Mr. Cutler and said, "I honestly don't know what she's done now." My mother was perfectly composed, the muscles of her face smooth. Everyone who mattered was on her side.

"She is a troubled girl." Mr. Cutler said, looking at me. "There's a path for her, where the lord can shine his light for her." To my mom he said, "The guidance of her mother will get her back on that path. This attention-seeking isn't good for anyone."

Mrs. Cutler nodded in agreement. I caught her eye and her gaze shot to the carpet. My mother nodded along too, as if she wasn't practically a card-carrying atheist. I boggled that he said I was an attention-seeker; my fantasies weren't about being the center of attention, my fantasies were about hot showers, hot food, and people who gave a shit about me. I wondered if "attention seeker" was something he just used on kids, or all women in general.

I looked at Taylee, who was clearly enjoying this. Randomly, I remembered her comment to me about using a separate towel. I wondered again, what kind of a parent teaches their child to think that way about their own body? Poisoning a person's sexuality had to be one of the greatest harms you could do to them. Especially when it's made to seem socially valid, or--

"Honey," my mother brought my attention back. It was her talking-to-a-child voice. Humiliating. "We need to be honest," she said, and I knew that "we" meant me. She knew I would always feel like a child in her presence. "Let's pack up your things and go home. We can talk more in the car." She looked at the Cutlers. "We really appreciate all you've done, I just don't know how to thank you for taking care of my little girl."

The Cutlers were so easy for my mom to manipulate, they might as well have handed her a liar's guide when she walked through the door. If we were going to play this game, I thought, if she's going to lie and pretend it was all about honesty, then I was going to be honest.

I said, "No."

"What?" she smiled.

"No. I did run away. I ran away from the drugs." My mother blinked. *Gotcha*, I thought. "I ran away from the drugs, the drug dealing, the violence, and you not giving a shit about anything but you. You're only here because I told someone what's going on."

My mother's smile was tight, it didn't quite reach her eyes. Her face was lined with exhaustion beneath the makeup. It wasn't as carefully applied as I'd seen it in the past. Little dots of mascara peppered her lower lids. "I don't know what she's saying," she said to the Cutlers. "I don't do drugs. I've certainly never dealt them. This is really disturbing to hear her say."

This went beyond my disbelief's limits. Our whole *life* was drugs. "Yes, you do. Don't you remember? The earliest I can remember is when you were growing pot before you started snorting coke. You grew the female plants at the foot of my bed, there were four of them and they were in buckets. They were taller than you!" I marveled how the memory was clear like I'd just been there. I could almost smell the sharp tang of resin.

My mother ignored me. "She had a head injury, as you know." I couldn't believe my mother was really telling the Cutlers I was making up the only life I ever knew.

Mr. Cutler nodded. "A child's recovery can be complicated."

My mother looked back to me, triumph in her eyes. She angled her head, softened her voice. "Honey, I never even spanked you."

I looked her in the eye.

Maybe she had won, but the Cutlers didn't matter to me anymore. She was denying everything that happened to me. And I suddenly knew why my mother had abandoned me over and over, my entire life.

My mother abandoned me because I was a witness.

She was here to lie. But I had been there. I saw what she had done. And after this insane confrontation in the Cutler's house, there would be no one left in the wreckage of our lives but the two of us.

"You always used a belt."

Her face froze.

"You started out using Dennis' belt," I reminded her. "Remember 'Uncle Dennis'?" There was a string of lights coming on in my head, and it was terrible. I wouldn't be able to ever shut these off. Part of me was saying no no no, backpedaling from the memories. But I had to go in, all the way. "He'd use it on me, too. And sometimes you'd just threaten to get the belt, even after you left him, and I'd always start crying before you even got it out." I spoke loud and fast, stacking words on top of each other. "You used the belt because you said you didn't want to hurt your hand."

No one said anything after that, so I stood up. I announced, "I have to pee."

I forced myself to walk calmly down the hall and into the bathroom. I was shaking badly. I didn't have to pee. I was remembering more about the belt, and those memories were powerful, clear, overwhelming. All the little lights coming on in a corner long dark. I ran the water and realized that if I let myself remember it any further, I was going to start crying. I couldn't let her see me cry.

I flushed the toilet. I hooked a left out of the bathroom to the bedroom. My clothes were clean and folded on the bed. I stuffed them into my bag, walked down the hall, and paused at the laundry room. I'd been pretty impressed they had a whole room for laundry. I spotted bills and change on a shelf next to the washer and stuffed the money deep, next to my clothes.

I walked down the hallway and went for the door. Mr. Cutler shot out of his seat. "Where do you think you're going, young lady?" The loud voice of a pastor.

I got to the door and turned the knob. I looked at Mr. Cutler and said, "Fuck you."

I heard Taylee snort as everyone's voices rose, saying things to me, or maybe each other, a rising cacophony of pandemonium in the room at my back, but I didn't care. I had trusted the Cutlers. I would never ask anyone for help again.

The swishing of wind and mist sounded like static as I pounded the sidewalk determined not to run, though I wanted to run, and scream, and cry. How could she lie like that? I cut across the wide, wet street and took advantage of Ingleside's emptiness at night to cross a corner diagonally, beelining for the MUNI stop that would take me to the Magic Bench. *Fuck*, I thought, *I'm back on the fucking streets.*

A big, shiny car pulled up alongside me. It reminded me of Bozie's boat, the Olds '88, but this one was new, expensive. Its passenger window rolled down as it slowed to a crawl, pacing me. It wasn't Bozie.

"Get in the fucking car." My mother was no longer performing.

I kept walking. "Whose car is that?"

"Don't you do this," she warned me.

I ignored her.

"Goddamnit, I've had enough of your shit, young lady," she shouted across the passenger seat. "The car belongs to Charles. You met him. I live in one of his houses in Oakland. He owns a bunch of houses, really nice ones. Now get. In."

"Charles, the guy who hit you?"

"Hey!" she shouted.

"You know, he came after me." I quickened my walking pace.

Trying to match my pace, she stepped on the gas pedal too hard then tapped the brakes, jerking the car to a stop. Then she hit the gas again, cranking the wheel right to leapfrog the curb with a loud crash, driving the car across the sidewalk to block me. I jumped to a stop as she reached over to swing open the heavy passenger door.

"You get in this fucking car right now."

"Or what? You'll get the belt?" I was scared now, but I was also hysterical, feeling out of my mind, and tears were flowing. I had no idea when those started.

She cranked the parking brake like cracking bones. I heard her door open. I couldn't move. She was coming for me and I was frozen in a bolt of terror.

I just stood there as she came around the car.

A strange feeling of calm came over me as I realized she was shorter than me. When did that happen?

I think I was supposed to flinch, or cower, but the shakiness of fear had drained from my body. When she got to me, I took a step forward. I cocked my head, like asking a question. I wanted to say, *try it*. But I couldn't say anything.

She backed up. "Don't ... go to the cops again."

We stood there for a breath. I walked past her, past the car, and she got back in it.

I didn't look to see which direction she drove. It felt like the whole world in front of me was empty. Out in the San Francisco Bay, a foghorn groaned its call beneath the Golden Gate Bridge. A lone cargo ship rattled back a low note. I walked to the MUNI station under streetlights casting a false dawn onto the blanket of fog above me. My face was wet; tears or mist, I didn't know.

I considered how I might get to the Golden Gate Bridge.

There was a way, without hope, feeling utterly alone, that I suddenly understood why people jumped. What happens to our dreams when we realize they will never come true?

I knew our beautiful bridge was the most popular suicide destination on Earth, so much that someone leaps to their death on an average of every two weeks. Bridge patrol confronts jumpers every other day, if not every day. People have studied the phenomenon, attempted to predict the patterns of suicides there in order to better prevent them.

It turns out there is no typical way people jump off the Golden Gate Bridge. But before they jump, they each do something different. They look at the view, or pace, or walk from one side to another, maybe set down flowers, or simply take off their watch. Then they jump.

On very, very rare occasions, they survive: The fatality rate is around 98%. I loved to swim and was an ace in the ocean; part of my love for it was how soft the water felt, how it could cradle me while being so malleable and yet strong. It amazed me that jumping from the bridge, you could hit the water and it would be as hard as concrete, hard enough to break all the bones in your body and rip your insides like paper. The fall would be slow through the air and then over so fast. I wouldn't need to worry about where to sleep anymore. No one would miss me.

This wasn't the first time I'd thought of suicide, and it wouldn't be the last, but it was certainly the strongest.

I could stay in this headspace, I thought, and it would kill me. This was a simple, direct truth.

I'd hoped someone would save me. Help me. The pain of betrayal by people who were supposed to protect me had broken something inside me. Until now, I hadn't thought I could be sadder than when I found out Little Joe died, or more horrified by life than when I woke up next to Jenn, or more scared than when Charles was coming, I think, to rape me.

Little Joe should still be here. People like the Cutlers thought he deserved to die; it made me want to avenge him somehow. And it hurt to think it, but my mother wasn't worth dying for. Love was a kind of faith. I would never be able to forgive her. But I had to figure out how to live with the cruelty of her truth, her betrayals, and not let it destroy me. I had to deny its ability to break me or shape me. I was being shattered and remade.

Nothing felt more like coming home than when the MUNI car rolled into Castro station. On the way I replayed in my head the nightmare of my "reconciliation and reunion" with mom at the Cutler's house. Going to Child Protective Services felt like the stupidest mistake I'd ever made in my life, but that was overshadowed by what my mother had said and done. How could she lie like that?

Never mind. I needed to find a place to sleep.

18

ON THE MUNI train I made a plan to see if anyone was around at the Magic Bench, or in Upper Haight, and to find out if my friends had gotten into that new squat yet. I could try to find Aiden's tarp in the park, though that was a gamble with a lot of walking involved. I was still hyped on adrenaline, but I knew I'd had a day that was about a hundred years long, and if I had a bed I'd sleep like a rock. I needed to think in strict practicalities. The fog was cold. The ground was hard. I thought about checking out the steam vents along Market Street downtown. Cardboard, that would make the ground less hard. I would need to find cardboard if I did that.

My stomach rumbled. I wished I didn't need to eat. I remembered the cash I snatched from the Cutlers' laundry room. I counted out thirteen dollars and some change. I planned to first grab a slice of pizza in the Castro. I hoped Jimmy would be there, working the bars. Maybe I could sleep on the roof at Kinko's.

I walked out of the station to find an empty Magic Bench. Dammit. My eyes burned from all the crying. I summoned Rogue's voice reminding me to *breathe*. I imagined Zeke's voice saying, *eat a food*.

Stealing money from the Cutlers to spend in the Castro at the "Mom & Mom" pizza joint -- Marcello's -- sounded like a slice of small justice. I almost giggled thinking about it and walked up the subway stairs. At the top of Harvey Milk Plaza, a brown mohawk flipped in my direction. Aiden jumped up from where he was leaning against the bank's rounded exterior wall. He smiled, saying "Hey!" We ran to each other and hugged.

"I thought you got arrested," he said. "But I waited for you just in case."

"You did?" I felt almost tipsy that someone would do this for me. "Wow."

"Hey, it's not like, weird." He had a half-smile. He started saying, "I'm ... ga-"

"I KNOW!" I howled, hugging him again. "God, finally," I teased. He gave me a look, like I was the crazy one, and I laughed, my face hurt like hell when I did, but I actually laughed.

We spent the night at his spot in Buena Vista Park. The 33 bus ride to Upper Haight was plenty of time to tell him everything that happened since he saw me slammed against a police cruiser in Dolores Park. The bruises on my wrists looked impressive. They ached deeply, down into my hands. Aiden got me caught up on scavenging news while we carbombed our way to his sleeping spot.

The Salvation Army was giving away sandwiches before noon every day now. Aiden said they were gross, which was totally not shocking. An industrial bakery called Entemann's in the Mission sold old bread and pastries for less than a dollar, but they threw more away into the dumpster in back -- and it was still good enough to eat. Unlike some other places, he explained, the bakery didn't dump bleach or put broken glass on top of food they threw out.

Aiden also told me there was a new food source in Upper Haight. The pizza place still gave out old pizza slices at closing time, but on weekday afternoons the Hare Krishnas had started coming to Upper Haight with a shopping cart and giving away food and day-old Odwalla juice. The catch was, they made you say their religious thing first. They'd give you more food if you came back to their church or whatever. I told Aiden I thought that was icky cult stuff. Like the soup kitchen making us pray before serving up their gross jail gruel. I told him it felt even worse after what happened with the Cutlers and their psychotic justifications for celebrating our friends dying.

Under a blue tarp in the park lined with gravestones, in the dark, I held my bruised wrists to my chest and snuggled into Aiden's trench coat. I slept very much like a rock.

"Knock knock!" I felt like I'd only just closed my eyes, but the blue tarp was glowing with daylight. Cherubic Alex was making her outreach rounds. I couldn't believe she did this every day. Because it mattered that much.

"Holy shit!" she said when she saw me poke my head up. "It's yoooouuuuu!" Her squirrel-cheek grin was one of the best things in the world, I decided.

I sat up like Dracula. "It's aliiiive!" My throat *sounded* like Dracula.

The sun felt cruel on my light-sensitive eyes. Very Dracula. Aiden and I ambled to Haight and started our day of asking strangers for food and money. I'd gotten to know the family that ran the Blue Front Cafe. Suhil, the youngest of three brothers who worked there, let me use the bathroom to get cleaned up and gave me ice for my eye, even though I didn't think I needed it. He was sympathetic about the cops.

By noon we had a good group assembled at Shrader and Haight, near all the punk stores we wished we could shop at. Rogue almost screamed when she saw me. Her, Zeke and Jimmy gathered around for hugs and I told my story again. I didn't tell anyone about remembering the belt though, or any of those memory snapshots. It seemed minor compared to what some of my friends had been through.

But its omission was a conscious decision, and when I remembered it later, I wondered what kind of asshole uses a belt to minimize the work of striking a child? I guess the question I was seeking to define, and someday answer, was: Who teaches us to love monsters?

Jimmy said he felt bad about running away and leaving me there. I told him it was okay. Zeke thought it was cool that I was a fugitive from the law. "Filthy screws'll never take me alive!" His announcer voice was in full effect.

I hadn't seen Rogue since I'd turned myself in to Child Protective Services.

She looked relieved. She said, "I thought you died."

"I did."

"Hey." She gave me another long hug.

"Does this mean we can fix your hair now?" It was Joe.

"Yes, jerk." I tried to hug him, but he dodged me.

"Hair time, fuck yeah." Zeke was excited. "Who wants to get buzzed?" He dug around in his bag and came up with clippers.

"Me me me me!" It was little Jess, who had arrived with Lisa. I still thought of them as twins. I learned that their identical haircuts were called a "devil lock," after the haircut worn by a band called The Misfits. Short all over, but funneling down into a long, single tail in front. It looked great on both of them, but I didn't think it was me.

Rogue peered out at me from behind Zeke, where she had her arms around him, her hands clasped where Zeke's belly would be if he wasn't stick-thin. She said, "Mohawk." Her pronouncement. Final. I loved it.

"Okay," I consented, "but you have to tell me how to make it go up."

"No problem!" Zeke winked. "Aqua Net is your new god."

"Or Knox gel," Joe said. He saw my quizzical look. "It's the clear stuff Jello is made with. But if you make it really thick, it sets super hard and you can even sleep on it. We can get it at Cala." This was the supermarket at the end of Haight Street across from McDonald's. Cala Foods was ancient.

Zeke buzzed everyone's hair who wanted it, tufts falling and swirling with the breeze into the gutter. I smiled the whole time my head was being shaved on the sides. My cheek hurt. The sides of my head felt cold and the mohawk draped into my face like boy bangs. I hoped it looked good. Changing my natural blonde color had to happen next, I hated it so much. Being blonde had made me a lifelong target of unwanted male attention. This cut and some color, I thought, would whittle that little problem down.

By the end of all the shaving, and sculpting everyone's trims and tails, Zeke's shaver's batteries sounded worn out. Those not getting shaved had panhandled and made trips to Cala for food coloring, hair spray, and water. The whole affair lasted much of the day. The trickiest bits were when one of us inevitably had to pee. Everyone had info and suggestions to share on this survival topic, which was a constantly changing situation. There were businesses you shouldn't even bother trying to ask, a couple places that might say yes if you asked nicely, and spots you stood a reasonable chance of sneaking in. Blue Front was the nicest, but it was at the far end of the street. McDonald's was nearby, but getting spotted by an employee would put the business on high alert for a few days.

There were also just alleys and stairwells, worse, always, for those of us who looked like girls or small boys -- we always went in pairs for safety regardless. No one wanted to get raped because they pissed in the bushes alone. Everyone had an opinion about where Lisa, who had to pee, should go. "Alright already," Lisa broke the discussion. "I just gotta pop a squat!" Jess grabbed her hand, and the girls walked off toward Waller Street.

Jimmy had news that made us ecstatic: Frank and Joey were doing an "orphan Thanksgiving" and we were all invited. We howled and whooped, exuberant. I'd forgotten about the holiday entirely. An actual Thanksgiving! Warm food! Little Sean jumped up and thrust out his stomach, rubbing it, saying: "I'm gonna have a turkey ba-by!"

It was a good day on the sidewalk. We shared burritos, did hair, and then makeup. A different ritual now that Little Joe was gone, and we paved our separate roads over the old altars. Big Sean came by and introduced a new girl named Scooter. Aiden and Little Sean joined them, and the group bailed to Castro.

At one point I asked, "Are we getting ready for a show or something?" I was hoping for another punk house party like the one where Rogue and I slamdanced.

Mark, the cute lead singer with the accent said, "Don't look at me! No gigs for us tonight," he smiled.

No one knew if there were any bands playing. Jimmy grinned. "That's okay," he reached in his jacket. "I know what we can do." He pulled out a baggie of something that looked like dried cat poop.

Joe said, "Whoaaaa."

"What's that?" I asked.

"Some drug dealer mom you got," Rogue laughed. "Those are shrooms, girl!"

I'd never taken psychedelics. At my mother's urgings, I'd put cocaine on my gums and once tried freebasing. I'd accidentally eaten pot brownies when I was ten, after which my mom let me smoke or eat as much pot as I liked -- which I tried off and on until I was twelve, quitting when I got worried about my memory. Booze had always been available to me. That was it.

When we finished hair and makeup, we had come out pretty good in the panhandling department. Tourists in Upper Haight, those who ventured toward the punk end by the bowling alley, seemed to enjoy our sidewalk salon. We'd been on alert for cops -- me especially -- but while the white-guy, dreadlocked drug dealers wandered Haight with pistols in their saggy jeans, there was never a cop in sight.

I was fed, not too tired, and looked absolutely nothing like I did the day before. I felt lighter, but also more in my own skin. I had made a marker for the night's trauma, planted a flag to show I'd been there and conquered it, and stepped through. Goodbye old me. Goodbye scared little girl: I was sending her away to live in her new home; the stories of the past. All these things went through my head, and I felt like the world looked better again through black-lined eyes. My head, with its shaved sides, felt streamlined. Aggressive.

Zeke warned me I needed to look out for sunburn on my scalp for the first week or so.

Jess, who had a bruised cheek that matched mine, gave me her compact so I could inspect myself. Joe had used gloppy, quick-drying Knox gelatin to given me a single row of perfect Liberty spikes. The color started out blonde near my scalp, and ended in dark blue icepicks. The blonde and blue interacted in the middle to give it a greenish-turquoise fade.

I had a new desire. I wanted to be seen.

Shadows crept and deepened in the Haight as the sun headed out to sea. It was time: everyone wanted to split up the mushrooms. I was nervous. I reminded myself that whatever happened in my head, I was the one who controlled it. It was going to be up to me how the experience went. Like lucid dreaming, I hoped.

We divvied up dried mushroom caps and stems; Rogue gave me a little less than her. We put them in our mouths and chewed. They were foul, absolutely disgusting, like stinky sock-flavored mushrooms. The more it became rehydrated in my mouth, the more it felt like a slug. An actual slimy alive slug. In my mouth.

"I want to spit it out," I whined to no one in particular.

"No! Try to keep it!" Jimmy looked like he was chewing a giant cud.

"Mmmm, so good!" Mark was making fun of me, chewing with his mouth open.

I felt a twinge of warmth inside my head, flipping on whatever switch controlled giggles and smiling. These people, my friends, were so funny. My giggles spilled over into the real world, whatever that was becoming, and everyone else started laughing too. I had forgotten what my laugh felt like or if I could laugh anymore at all. It sounded bouncy, making me laugh harder. A breeze blowing toward Golden Gate Park felt like a warm current.

"We have a mission!" Zeke announced. "Water!"

Trying impossibly hard to look like we weren't high, the group of us -- me, Joe, Mark, Lisa, Jess, Rogue, Zeke, and Jimmy -- packed up our stuff and walked to Haight Natural

Foods to buy water. It took us a very long time. By the time we got to the store, eyes like saucers, stupid grins one and all, it was dark.

The lights in the store were amazing. Everyone wandered around like cats, impossible to herd with all the things to look at, laugh at. Rogue took control and managed to get us in line with bottled water in our hands. When I got to the register, a bemused hippie college girl cashier said, "And the carrot?"

"Uh ..." I had somehow picked up a carrot and forgot to put it back.

"Yep," said Jimmy. "The carrot."

"My carrot," I corrected.

"Okaaay," the cashier continued. I let her weigh my carrot. It was hard to let go.

We reassembled outside the store. "What the fuck is that?" Rogue pointed at my carrot, smiling huge.

"My carrot!" I was so proud. I took a bite. It was sweet, and I missed vegetables so much at that moment. I chewed while everyone talked about the next plan. Chewing wasn't working out. What if I bit my cheek? Would I even know? The streetlights, all the lights on Haight had three extra halos that smeared a little like wet ink when I moved my eyes across them. I was still chewing the same bite of carrot. How long had it been? The carrot wasn't breaking down in my mouth. It felt like dry little pieces of gravel. I turned and tried to spit it out, but it came out unevenly.

"What the fuck?" Rogue was belly laughing at me. Pieces of chewed carrot had sprayed on the wall, the sidewalk, and on Lisa, who laughed, "Ewwww," trying to dust carrot crumbs off her jeans.

"I can't ... it's not ..." I started laughing, bits of carrot spilling out of my mouth, stuck in my teeth. Everyone was laughing. "Too dry!"

"Here," Jimmy gave me his water.

I looked at the carrot in my hand. I admonished it, "No more!"

"Come on," Jimmy said laughing. He took my hand. The one without a carrot. "We're going to the freeway."

Down Haight we went, toward the Central Freeway exit in Hayes Valley and where its 40-foot, double-decker spur dumped out onto Fell Street. The freeway was nicknamed "The Berlin Wall" because it was a dividing line. On one side of it was the San Francisco Opera, the Ballet, and Symphony halls, upscale restaurants and bars for the old money crowd, and City Hall. On the other side of the freeway, our side, it was hell. Like nearby neighborhoods Western Addition and Lower Haight, Hayes was an impoverished, neglected neighborhood shaped by discriminatory housing practices and a Black community that had been abandoned in the 1960s to rot.

Taxis and pizza delivery refused to service the neighborhood's residents, packed like sardines into boxy, low-income housing projects and mildewy, carved-up Victorians. The area beneath the freeway was a sketchy marketplace for sex work, and like in SOMA through the 2000's, construction workers would just pull up in their trucks and get blown like it was a fast food drive-thru.

Our stroll was moony, almost laid-back as we floated through nighttime Haight's Victorians and Edwardians. They were like glowy, gloomy fairy castles someone had decided to finish on top with silly sand, detailed with Chiclet teeth and fishbowl window eyes. When we got to Buena Vista Park and slightly out of the City's light pollution, I looked up and almost flinched when I saw the stars. They were so close, like they jumped toward me when I looked at them. Better than diamonds, shining their light just for our eyes, because I knew they were already dead.

I wondered, why couldn't the city let us go, all us generations of runaway and homeless kids? Why did it seem to protect us, and we are somehow allowed to remain? The only answer, I thought, was that the city was under a spell cast by its own history. Bewitched by its own myths.

People occasionally checked in on my carrot, and I appreciated that. We were both well, thank you.

The Central Freeway's exit ramp emptied out at Fell and Laguna Streets. Its on-ramp twin fed in at Laguna and Oak. Laguna, and all around it seemed darkly desolate. Ice plant, a type of thick succulent, was planted along freeways everywhere in California, and here it covered the pie-wedge hillsides between the Central Freeway's ramps and neighboring streets.

There was a plan, but I didn't know what it was. I was excited and a little scared as we walked single file up the off-ramp's minuscule shoulder. I put my carrot in a pocket for safekeeping.

Under Zeke's direction we crouched down along the side and waited for traffic to pass. A clump of cars came out of the dark around the arc, winding down their speed only slightly for the exit. After the vehicles raced by, their headlights streaking gloriously across my field of vision, there was another lull in traffic.

"Okay ... Now!" Zeke led the charge. He ran to the freeway's guardrail, a thin ribbon of concrete. We all followed him. Zeke hopped up and stood on a post. Jimmy jumped up on the next one, and we all stood on posts, in a line. In front,

Zeke called out when he saw them coming. "Cars!" he shouted.

Everyone posed, freezing like statues. Zeke did his best "Walk Like an Egyptian." Rogue had her arms out and head cocked down, like Jesus. Jimmy did a ballerina pose. Wanting to keep both feet on my post, I went with an old-fashioned bodybuilder pose. I couldn't see what anyone else did.

The headlights all came on us at once, racing by. Cars blared their horns, making my heart shriek in my chest. "Okay, clear!" Zeke jumped down as the last in the traffic cluster disappeared, and we all ran back to our hiding spot.

I had road grit in my eyes, felt the fine grains on my face when I touched it, and I smelled like exhaust and sweat. It was terrifying and thrilling, the sounds of multiple vehicles bearing down on me flanked by a chorus of horns. The light trails of headlights and taillights were incredible. The city's freeway was a riotous artery of light and sound, pulsing over rooftops, awake while City Hall slept nearby.

We struck a pose for commuters three more times, until we had to rest at the top of the hillside. We sat in the soft ice plant, which made our butts wet. No one cared. Joe said he wanted beer, and everyone agreed; it sounded amazing.

Rogue said, "No! Do this first!"

She flopped over onto her side, crossed her arms across her chest like a corpse, and rolled herself off the top of the hill, bouncing down cushioned by crunching ice plants, rolling and laughing. Every time Rogue bounced, her laughs barked a little louder, and she went ha!-ha!-ha! down the hill. Everyone tried it, and soon we were all racing back up the hill to go again.

Zeke and Rogue tried a combo, where they hugged and tried to stay hugging each other as they rolled together and bounced downhill, smashing apart at the end. I tried it with Rogue and we broke apart halfway down. Jess crashed into me once; I accidentally rolled over Mark; Joe tried it end-over-end like a cannonball. For the finale, Zeke had four of us try to hug and stay together as we rolled and bounced over the crushed ice plants, breaking apart violently, quickly, and landing on each other laughing, only to roll the rest of the way down on our own.

Everyone was soaking wet, slimy. We linked arms and held hands on our long journey across neighborhoods to Our Lady of Safeway. We were all homeless. Walking the ruins of San Francisco's dreams. I'd felt so lonely and beaten I wanted to die, I had slept under a tarp in a public park, and now I was with this family. Who had almost been destroyed in similar ways, by darknesses that cross-faded into each other; parents, authority figures, crazies, white knight citizens, each enforcing their twisted moral justifications on us. Everyone blaming us for what we were going through.

Yet we remained. For each other. With our control over our bodies and genders, with our music, loving who we loved. A family of dignity and pride, of caring and respect, warding off the bogeymen, together.

19

IT WAS GETTING COLDER and San Francisco's tourists had made their exodus. Sleeping outside worsened as the air chilled and the ground hardened. Rooftops and the park were okay, but mornings were achy, painful.

I was completely homeless now. It was life lived at one extreme or another -- I was either dead tired, or amped on adrenaline and hyper-vigilance -- yet the hours stretched. And I'll tell you: Boredom and hopelessness is a toxic cocktail. To dull the pain and kill the boredom, people around me did dope, speed, or anything and everything. I understood why. But I was determined not to become my mother.

Rogue and I were working on a D&D campaign one morning at the cafe when Frank and Joey sent us on a mission to rustle up their late dog walker, Jimmy, who was apparently sleeping one off in Frank and Joey's van, which we called the "murder van" -- because it looked like one.

I walked with Rogue along a row of rummy-junkies laying on the sidewalk at various angles, men warming themselves in the South of Market sun. SOMA's windless heat cooked their odors into the air, turning our walk down the alley into a noxious gauntlet of piss, shit, and rotten shoes. We were the early morning search and rescue team. Rogue spotted the murder van and we honed in.

"Wait," Rogue said quietly, holding up her hand. I smiled, thinking she had a plan to prank Jimmy. An oversleeping penalty. We stood two parked cars away from the van. "Stay here," she said. I stayed.

Rogue walked over and looked at the side mirror, then quickly peered inside. Her mohawk looked like a rooster comb in profile, peeking in the van's window. She turned around and walked back to me. She wasn't smiling. "Let's go."

"Wait," I said, "what's going on?"

"You don't want to know," she said. "Let's just go."

"What do you mean?" I started walking to the van. Whatever it was, I had to know.

"Don't!" Rogue hissed, barely above a whisper. "You don't want to look in there."

I followed Rogue's previous steps, carefully looking in the side mirror first. It was hard to see into the van's dark interior. After half a second my eyes caught movement. Slow, rolling movement. I blinked the image into focus. Lisa moving, arching her back on top of Jimmy, and Jimmy's hands rising to meet her pale skin.

I backed away from the van. "Oh," I said quietly. Rogue came over and took my hand, leading me back toward the cafe.

Rogue could've said 'I told you so' when we were walking but she didn't. Instead, she just said, "I'm sorry."

I asked if we could walk for a little bit. I waited for her outside the cafe while she went in to tell Frank and Joey that Jimmy was on his own. She came out with two mochas in paper cups. "Soy, like you like," she said, handing me the treat. We walked.

"Do you want to talk about it?" She asked. "I'm fine either way."

I asked myself out loud, "Do I want to talk about it?" She waited, walking with me.

"I don't want to talk about anything ever again," I said, "and I want to talk about everything. It ... hurts. I'm so tired of hurting, Rogue. I'm so tired of losing things that were never even mine in the first place."

"I know what you mean," she said. "It's not like he cheated, I guess, but he did betray you."

"Yeah. He did."

"And every time I think of betrayal," she said, "I think of my asshole mom."

"Ha, me too."

"Our moms are a lot alike," she said.

"I'm sorry."

"I know, right?" Rogue sipped her coffee. "Down was up. She got so used to lying to everyone about the shit she smoked, who she was fucking or whatever, that she just lied about everything all the time. Took me a long time to get it through my thick head it wasn't me getting shit wrong, it was her reality distortion. 'Cept shit got bad, really bad over there."

I knew Rogue meant the projects, which she avoided like the plague. She took a deep breath. "I just don't trust anyone. Can't. Except Zeke, of course. And you."

"Thanks." I thought about what she said. "I think it's the shame that makes them lie. Our moms. They're like, ashamed of everything."

"That's how women were raised back in the day."

"Totally," I said. "But it's still how the world works. If it was an engine, shame would be, like, its oil. Like, with my mom, I think she's so wrapped up in how ashamed she is about drugs and sex, and stuff she's done, and how trapped she is in all these lies, she's always in these relationships where guys beat on her and yell at her. I think she thinks she deserves it. And that scares me, Rogue, that I came from this person who only knows love as abuse. I hate betrayal, and that's deep for me, like, betrayal makes someone dead to me. But I also expect it. What I'm afraid of is being doomed to repeat this shit. I don't know if, before my accident, if I knew what was happening to me was wrong. I do now, but it's so fucked up."

Rogue was shaking her head. She said, "A fish has no word for water, I guess."

I thought about that as we strolled through chilly morning shadows between San Francisco's downtown skyscrapers. I looked around. We'd walked all the way over to the Transamerica Pyramid. I wasn't afraid of trusting people, not really. I wanted to upend the economy of shame that made people do violence to themselves and those they cared about. Shame was what made you let people hurt you.

We stopped and looked up. "I love that we live in a city with a gorgeous fucking pyramid in it," I said.

Rogue smiled. "Me too."

Walking back in the cafe with Rogue, I felt sad but grounded, and like I was seeing the cafe through different eyes. I saw a place I belonged. People who cared about me in all the loneliness. And as a point of pride, the 'zine rack had my poetry chapbook for sale, and my writing was in a few of other people's 'zines, too.

One night after Rogue and Zeke went up on the roof of Kinko's to sleep, I went inside the shop instead. It was around two or three am at the 24-hour copy and print chain.

The employees were all UCSF students. Those guys really liked their amphetamines. When I walked in, Mike, Dave, and Ryan were working madly on a contraption using two metal stanchions, the kind normally used for keeping customers in a line. Their wide eyes reflected the overhead fluorescent lights, sweat popped on their temples, their grins manic. Overly friendly bees buzzing in blue polyester uniforms. They'd knotted thick rubber bands into a chain between the stanchions. A crude slingshot. They launched X-Acto knives at a "Line Forms Here" sign. It wasn't working as well as they'd hoped, and they were arguing about height and tension.

The copy shop was a box of boxes. Squat cubes of warm plastic housed machines that clicked, sifted paper, and purred nonstop. A faint buzz hung in the background from the fluorescent light tracks overhead, giving shadows nowhere to hide in their white-light blare. It was an exposed space limned with corporate colors and bland posters advertising services for fleets of equally flat-hued office workers who were nowhere to be seen after midnight. Only its black-clad, torn t-shirt occupants indicated that Market Street's slice through Lower Haight and Castro was right outside.

Punks and art nerds had taken over the copy machines, making chapbooks and 'zines. For free. An all-you-can-eat of DIY publishing.

That Kinko's was where San Francisco's 'zine scene lived and breathed. 'Zines were a global phenomenon of independent publishing that, by the late 1980s and early 90s, were vital to art, music, politics, sex, and gender. Through punk culture and 'zines, we learned about corporate greed, global warming, factory farms, propaganda, gender identity -- and so much more. Things you'd never see in The *San Francisco Chronicle* or on TV. 'Zines offered something we desperately needed as American kids: different viewpoints.

We hungered to be part of the world. Punk and 'zine culture didn't reinforce our beliefs, it challenged them.

After a reassuring glance at the 'zine rack, I settled into a game of gin with Spider and Alex. There were bruises on Spider's neck and lip, but that was none of my business. Frank stood in the doorway, his face relaxed in a gentle smile. He was our mother hen, Joey was his grumpy ballast. I'd never spent friend time with them until they closed the cafe for a day last week and we had our "orphan Thanksgiving."

That was the night I found out why Frank walked like he was in pain: he was. One night, he told me, he'd stepped off a MUNI bus in the Mission District and it plowed into the crosswalk over three of its passengers. An elderly Mexican woman didn't survive. Frank marveled that you could live to seventy-five and still die in such a frustrating, pointless way. The other man suffered a broken arm. Frank's left hip was broken and his internal organs were damaged.

Years later, here they were. Still tied up in litigation against the City of San Francisco and its stupid drunk MUNI driver, all their money hopelessly sunk into hospital bills and legal fees. Frank was in constant pain. Jimmy and Zeke scored him pot. Frank's doctor said he may not live to see a settlement. In the middle of all that, starting an underground cafe was Joey's idea.

Today, Zeke and Joey cranked out food and drinks behind the counter and a tip jar that read "Don't fear change, put it in the jar." A song by The Vandals played, and Zeke sang "I Want To Be A Cowboy" while they worked. He stopped singing to ask a customer, "Do you ever wonder if you've had milk from the same cow twice?"

Before I understood what was happening, Spider's legs shot straight out under the table, knocking over an empty chair. Her hand flew out and cards fanned in the air for an instant, falling as her shoulders thrust back and her body stiffened, jerking her out of the chair and onto the floor.

I had never seen a seizure before. But Alex had. She shouted instructions to move furniture, give room ... And then to call an ambulance. Because when it was over, Spider couldn't get up.

We were all pretty shaken up after Spider was carried out. Quiet and sad.

One week after her seizure, Spider would be back at the cafe with a manilla envelope of color photographs. In the photos we would clearly see the boot prints SFPD had left in purple, red, and green on her back.

I asked Rogue if it might be a good time to get a D&D game going. "I'm too beat." She and pointed to an empty chair next to her. The gesture meant, *You, sit.* I sat. On her other side was Tamara, a punk girl from New York. She had a deck of tarot cards and was giving Rogue a reading. Her boyfriend was in a punk band, Fang. It was stenciled in giant letters across the back of her leather jacket. I remembered Tamara from meeting her outside Planned Parenthood the previous weekend.

The clinic building was a tidy, fortified box in the middle of a block near City Hall on Eddy Street. Its location made it convenient for both clients to access by bus, as well as "pro-life" protesters who screamed and threw blood on women trying to walk in the clinic as we arrived.

I'd been to Planned Parenthood once before; I wanted to make sure I knew everything I needed to know to bang without getting sick, so I got my first annual exam and those tests, a breast exam, and all the birth control -- and information about sex -- I could handle, for a sliding-scale fee of $5. The bullet-proof glass inside the clinic, just after its blast-proof doors, was intimidating. Though it wasn't anything different than a liquor store or some Chinese restaurants in Oakland.

The women who worked there were not intimidating at all. When they learned I was homeless, they said to pay what I could. The woman who examined me was funny and kind, and told me to come back if I got sick on the streets. Later, I would, and she gave me antibiotics. I made sure to get an exam every year after that.

The day I met Tamara though, the scene in front of the clinic shocked me. The protestors greeting us had giant signs with bloody, horror-movie photos of things I couldn't quite make out, and some held jars with liquid and unidentifiable, formless, fleshy shapes inside. What freaked me out most was that they brought their children. Little kids. Some of the kids looked scared. Others held gory signs and screamed on cue with their parents at the young women and their mothers trying to walk into the clinic.

Worse, they were all white. And in a minute, they would all be screaming at Rogue when it was her turn to go in. This was an extra layer of terror. It made me furious.

We paused across the street from the clinic to take in the insanity before Rogue and Zeke braved the shrieking lunatics. We couldn't all go in. Everyone was tense.

I scanned the crowd looking for Mrs. Cutler and Taylee. It seemed like this would be one of the only places they could exhibit their emotionality, and that was probably by their religion's design. I became distracted by a group of about ten punks and goths threading through the protesters. When I saw what they were doing I had to stop myself from thrusting my fist in the air and yelling "San Francisco!"

Half of the goths held armloads of wire hangers. They handed them to surprised anti-abortion protestors who didn't seem to realize what they were accepting. Two of the goths, a couple I'd later meet named Kim and Elanoir, held signs. Elanoir's sign said, "EAT YOUR CHILDREN" and had little drawings of forks and knives on it. They were all so calm. Zeke said, "Fuck yeah," and I saw that Rogue was smiling, too. Tamara had been one of the counter-protestors.

Tamara was tough and beautiful, the kind of girl I wanted to be. Like Rogue, she had a reputation of being a ruthless street fighter, the girl you didn't mess with. I wished Tamara had been around the day after Thanksgiving, when three skinhead girls decided that Rogue and I didn't belong panhandling in "their" end of Haight Street.

At first, we laughed them off. "What are they doing here?" I asked Rogue.

"Maybe they're starting a band," said Rogue. "The Dickheads."

They cornered Rogue and I near the bowling alley. They said unrepeatable things about Rogue's skin color and hair, kicking our feet to make us jump. Skinhead Sarah was one of them. They called me a "race traitor," and other things related to Rogue that had me vibrating with anger. I wanted to jump up and flatten them on the spot, but I knew Rogue was exhausted and consumed with sadness. Her and Zeke both were. It was going to be her call on anything we did.

Rogue said, "Let's get out of here," so we walked toward McDonald's and Golden Gate Park. The skinhead girls followed. Rogue was pissed, though I hoped that maybe if we walked far enough, they'd just leave us alone. Instead, they followed us, mocking and hurling invectives.

Rogue and I walked to the park's beginning and Hippie

Hill, an open space of lawn where hippies congregated with their drugs and dogs. We took a trail that forked where the artery of traffic from Kezar Drive cut across the park. One fork went up, another went down. We wordlessly chose going up, toward cars and light, which was obviously a better idea than underneath the overpass, surrounded by tress, absent of witnesses.

The three skinhead girls kept coming.

We reached the road. It was like a mini-freeway. Cars raced by in a steady stream; there would be no crossing it. Rogue and I turned right, walking on the shoulder along the top of the overpass. Halfway across the bridge, Rogue stumbled into me. She'd been shoved.

Turning around put Rogue face-to-face with one of the skins, a well-fed brunette with a "bash cut" and black Docs. Her green bomber jacket made her look bigger. She looked dried out, tired up close, but energized by hate.

Traffic howled by on our right; to the left was a low concrete barrier and a fifteen-foot drop onto the path we didn't take. Skinhead Sarah stood on my left. My heart pounded; Sarah could push me into oncoming cars. The third skinhead was a tall blonde in a newsboy cap and tight white jeans with thin red suspenders; she had a tight-lipped smile and stood between her mates.

What happened next happened fast. The big brunette reached out for Rogue's hair, and Rogue slapped her hand away, while stepping back. The girl tried again with her other hand, and Rogue slapped that one away, too. The two of them locked into a struggle, gripping each other's arms in a tug-of-war.

I saw the tall skinhead cock her arm back and put all her

weight into a sucker-punch that Rogue had no way of stopping.

I'm not sure how it went this way, but whatever happened in my head was faster than what I was seeing. I thought, *three of them and two of us. One is busy with Rogue. Take the big one out and it's just two-on-two.*

As the tall one followed through punching Rogue, I pulled back and put everything I had into punching her. I remembered my training; shoulder first, imagine your target is the back of the head. She was already coming forward to meet me thanks to her wide, sloppy swing. My fist crunched something, her head went back, and she went down. I could hear cars honking.

But Sarah had done exactly what I did, punching me while I punched someone else. *Her swing is still crap*, I thought, steadying myself on a step backward. I took in a little wave of hysteria washing through my brain informing me that I'd been hit on the left cheek again, and would forever have a bruise there.

I think Sarah expected me to go down, or maybe fall into oncoming cars. Anything other than what I did. I punched her back. Something snapped in me then because I kept going. I grabbed her green nylon jacket at the shoulders, threw her into the concrete barrier, and popped her on the mouth with my left fist.

Really though: When you hit a skinhead once, you just want to hit them again. I grabbed her shoulders and pressed her into the railing, and up, somehow, off the ground. I know I did this because it's where I found myself when, seconds later, a blinked tear ran down her cheek, and she said "P-please ..."

Later, while icing my face with a cold beer I would plead

my case to Rogue that I didn't actually intend to throw Sarah off the bridge. I just wanted to scare her into leaving us alone.

I set Sarah down. Everyone was frozen, watching me. "C'mon, let's go." Rogue took my arm, and we left them there.

That fight on the bridge cemented my reputation on the streets, for better or for worse I didn't care. My scars were armor now.

It helped as San Francisco's days got darker and my friends started to disappear.

20

SAN FRANCISCO'S fog on my face was the sweet, cool kiss of home.

I went back to school to hustle kids for sleepovers. Ashley Bailey got in my face the minute she saw me. Hands on hips in a cheerleader skirt, she beelined for me. She was in full uniform. Her eyeshadow approximated school colors in gold and burgundy.

"Why didn't you call me?" Her brown eyes sparkled with mirth, but refused to break with mine, so I wasn't getting off the hook. I didn't have a good excuse. She wanted me to come over. "No" wasn't an option.

That meant I needed to get my cover story straight for her parents. Like other kids on the streets, I had refined my story into three versions. None were too far from the truth, but needed to be different, depending on risk.

The version I told people I thought might be harmful was one I called "All Good." This was for people who broadcast problems ahead; they had all the answers, were casual bullies (or homophobes or racists), had extroverted insecurities, or basically told me up front -- one way or another -- why they weren't accountable for their behavior. People tell you who they are pretty quickly, but some were louder than others. I was getting better at picking those people out faster.

In "All Good" my parents were going through a rough patch and I was giving them some space. Saying the word "parents" was always a novelty for me. In reality, I had no emergency contacts. But "All Good" told people there was someone waiting for me, that I would be missed if something happened.

Another version called "Mom's My Friend" was for people whose couch I might want to stay on again, or a friend's family. People to keep at a distance, but not enough to make them want to help me too much by, say, calling anyone. In this version, my father was dead (I didn't know if he was or not anyway), and my mom was a Silicon Valley engineer currently out of town on work trips. A lot.

In my mind, it was like rolling back the clock. As if my life had been allowed to unfold as it could have; I simply imagined what life might be like if my mother hadn't become an addict.

The final version was for the very few people who had earned my trust. It was called "This Sucks." It was a story closer to my truth, but one that omitted details and plot points that might get me killed by the cartels or turned over to the police. So, hardly anyone ever heard it.

Ashley made me stay through the end of the school day and took me home with her. I didn't usually let anyone make me do anything, but I was amused at being bossed around by a cheerleader, flattered too, and also marveling that I felt strangely vulnerable when someone -- Ashley -- insisted on doing something nice for me. My urge was to run.

We were a mismatched pair on the bus ride to her house in the Outer Sunset, though this was San Francisco, and the only one who seemed to care about it was me. Ashley abruptly switched gears to greet her mom. Then it was all I could do to keep my jaw from hitting the floor while she smoothed out every question regarding her surprise house guest.

I should've expected that Ashley already had a cover

story for her mom and dad as to why I was coming to stay over -- and she did. I admired her for coming up with one close to "Mom's My Friend."

The Bailey house was a giant, three-level family home. A mansion compared to everything I'd lived in with my mom. Still, the whole place was a mess of spilled Cheerios and children's toys. Her mother was a tiny little Catholic woman who had birthed five boys in a range of ages, and also Ashley, whose age was right in the middle. Being a typical Irish Catholic father, Ashley's dad was tall, weathered, gruff and generally absent. So, when she brought me over, I was just more of the menagerie, which, it pained me to see, had Ashley fated to be a largely ignored surrogate parent for all the younger ones. This was a place where girls were mommies, and boys were little men.

Ashley cleaned the house, got the kids ready for school, she got yelled at by her dad, and her brothers tried to push her around. I immediately understood how she learned to fight and why she sought it out. It made sense that her friends -- Paisley, Leticia, and Hailey, who all wanted to beat me up at one point -- were the toughest girls in school. If I learned anything, it was *don't fuck with the cheerleaders*.

We went upstairs after all her idiot brothers were put to bed. She had her own bathroom. Ashley made space for me to sit with her on the counter. She turned on the fan, pulled cigarettes and a lighter from her purse, and we lit up over the sink.

"What do you want?" I asked her.

She smiled, shaking her head. "I want to be your friend, dummy. It's not rocket science."

I laughed. "Okay, but you don't really fit in with my friends."

Ashley looked at me sideways. "You're an ass."

I giggled. "Dick."

Ashley asked about my mom. Point-blank. And then everything poured out, like my body was venting a fever. It felt good to tell someone. Ashley didn't judge me, and I thought that we all try so hard to make family what we wish it could be, and it wasn't fair that we only got what we could steal from life in moments like this.

I told her, "You know, I used to beg the universe that someone would help me, that someone would save me. Like, an adult would help me. But that night my mom practically ran me over, afterward I decided I was going to be the one to save myself. No one can save me but *me*."

Ashley looked hurt and I couldn't figure out why. I said, "I want to believe she loves me more than anything in the word. I wish for that harder than anyone could know. I feel like a puzzle with so many missing pieces I don't even know what the picture's supposed to be."

She looked into my eyes. "I can't believe you live out there now. I wouldn't even know ... how."

"It's harder than it looks," I joked.

"Well, I have something you probably don't want," she sighed. "Mr. Burtleson gave me this." She pulled a piece of paper from her purse and handed it to me.

"Oh," I said. It was my mother's most recent name, and a phone number. "Huh, I guess she's in Oakland now," I said, looking at the area code: 510. I emitted a rueful laugh. "I bet she's still worried I'll rat her out."

"That's the thing though," Ashley said. "My mom is a bitch, and too old-fashioned, but I know she loves me. So, I just don't get it." She seemed to be struggling, but continued.

"When I have kids ... I can't even imagine doing that. Like with you, and with Joe, and John ..."

"What do you mean? I'm not like Joe at all." Thinking about Joe hurt and made me angry at the same time; after a weekend of partying with Santa Cruz skinheads, Joe had decided to become one. It was a betrayal no one had words for. Now he was radioactive.

She could tell that upset me. "No, no, that's not, oh god no." Ashley explained that Joe lived with his dad who ignored him, and hit him. I found out that John Gone slept alone in a trailer behind an apartment building in the Mission; he'd been placed with family who lived in the building but for some reason he lived in the trailer out back. These were things I didn't know about my friends, because you never asked people personal questions on the streets. It was too risky for everyone. In that moment, I realized that this was also how I was raised by my mother in our world apart from everyone else.

Ashley interrupted my troubling train of thought. "Ever notice John never wears short sleeves or shorts?" Ashley said, "He's covered in scars."

"What? Wow. I didn't know."

"No one does, but I asked why he was always covered up. Not in front of anyone," she waved the air, exhaling smoke. "And he told me. I think he just wanted someone to talk to."

I raised my eyebrows, nodding, and said, "or you have boobs."

Ashley laughed. "I'm like the boob channel." She grabbed her own breasts. "Eyes up here, lady!"

I pretended to be hypnotized by her boobs. Then I stopped. "But John. Do we know why?"

"Yeah," she took a deep breath. "His family -- not the place he stays now, his other family. They're really religious."

"Oh." I was getting a sinking feeling.

"Uh-huh. Well, he said that they were really, really religious. They raised him really, really religious. So, he said that every time he had a sexual thought, like a real thought, like I think he was trying to tell me it was when he wanted to jack off ..." she shrugged, "John would cut himself to make the thoughts stop."

"Oh no," I said. "Oh no," I said again, wanting to say something better. "He's our guy."

"I know," Ashley said. "But at least he got away from them."

"God, what the hell is it with sex," I said. She laughed and asked what I meant. I told her about Taylee and the two towels. Ashley raised her eyebrows, opened her mouth, and shut it again. She looked down at her crotch and back up at me, cocked her head.

I smiled. "I know, right?"

"I'm Catholic," she said, "and I know we're not strict or anything," she indicated the house around us, "but I can't imagine anyone making a girl hate herself like that. She's gonna take it out on people, too, I bet. Look I know you're not religious or anything," I shrugged but she kept going, "but I can tell ya, that's not what God's love is all about."

"You should've heard them go off on gay people," I was venting now. "They're like obsessed with gay sex. As if gay and sex were the same thing."

"It is to them," Ashley said. "And lots of people. If they knew how boring our gay friends are," she laughed.

"It's a fucked up way to keep someone afraid, or not in control of their lives," I said, nodding, then shaking my head. "I just feel like everywhere I go, practically everything bad I see happening to people leads back to people being made so afraid of sex, of their own fucking bodies ... it's insane. Like how we could practically stop the spread of AIDS if everyone just used a condom. Why is that so hard?"

Ashley snorted. "Hard."

I laughed, "so hard."

"Hey," she interrupted. "Want to pierce each other's ears?"

"Oh, are you a tough punk rocker now?" I was teasing her, but I knew she was tough. She had the capacity to be open, and to let me in. If that wasn't a kind of strength, I didn't know what was. "What about your mom?" I asked her.

She rolled her eyes and left the bathroom. She came back with ice and, puzzlingly, a little potato. "Um ..." I smiled.

"Don't even start, I know what I'm doing. Here, put this ice on your ear."

I did as I was told. "Can you believe Joe does this without ice, just for fun? One time I asked him how he did it all the time, and he insisted I watch while he pushed a safety pin though his cheek."

"His cheek! Holy crap," Ashley said. She was pouring rubbing alcohol over a safety pin, and I wasn't feeling reassured. "But you know what? I get it. He hurts more inside. It's pain he can control, plus the rush."

I stopped looking at what she was doing, and looked her in the eye. Ashley was actually telling me that inflicting pain was about powerlessness. I really needed to know what books my cheerleader friend was reading. I said, "When did you get so wise? Ow!"

Turns out, the potato was to steady the thin skin of my ear

when Ashley shoved the safety pin through. It went through with a gross little "pop" sound.

"That didn't hurt," she scolded me.

I looked in the mirror for blood, found none, furrowed my brow. "It's crooked," I said.

"Now you'll never forget me!" She grinned.

I slept in her bed. It wasn't sexual, but we kept talking about sex.

We'd both had it and weren't impressed, yet we still wanted to do it, and this was hilarious. I told Ashley that my first time was with a guy so I could just get it out of the way, to know for sure that it wouldn't mean anything. She said she understood exactly what I meant, which relieved me. The man I'd done it with was a friend of Cassie's, the woman whose Vespa I'd crashed, and when I told Cassie I'd had sex with him, she didn't believe me. He was the son of a prominent local Asian politician and engaged to Cassie's sister. The second time was with a man my mother had wanted me to have sex with after a drug deal. It hurt. Ashley's first time was with a theater nerd, and I loved that.

She asked if I'd had sex with Jimmy, and I said yes. Sex was more like just a thing we did together, almost a sport or performance for liking each other, which was fine for ego-stroking and getting off, but not what I was still convinced it could be, a thing where you get real with someone. I told Ashley that, and added, "I mean, he's all photogenic and takes the sexiness seriously." She giggled at that. I said, "He's hot. He actually wanted to talk about sex which no one had ever done with me before. So that was fun."

"Was?"

"Yeah. Frank and Joey sent Rogue and I out to find Jimmy

last week. We found him. With my friend Lisa grinding on top of him, in the van he sleeps in."

"Oh booboo, I'm so sorry." Ashley stroked one fuzzy side of my head. "I'm so so sorry. God, that really sucks."

"I didn't think I'd feel hurt." I forgot how betrayed I felt, and sad. I wasn't mad at Lisa. I was disappointed in Jimmy. I added, "I think he wanted to be my boyfriend?"

"It's okay to not know what you want."

"Thanks, O Wise One." I was joking, but it was good to hear that. I'd never had a boyfriend. But now that I was thinking about it, I'd never had anyone consistent in my life for this long, ever, like the way I had Zeke, Rogue, Joe, Aiden, John, Ashley, even Mark and Jess and Lisa, and yes, even Jimmy. Not counting my mother, of course.

"Is he ..." she made a fist and dropped her forearm like it was a dead weight. The universal hand sign symbol at our school for "horse cock." Ashley, with the important questions. I screamed into a pillow. When I was sane again I said, "Yes, dorklet. Yes. It was just like in the movies with the talking horse."

"Wiiiihhilbur," she snorted through laughs.

As we talked through half the night, even after Ashley's mom warned us to go to sleep, I realized that by being on the streets I was losing touch with TV, music, movies, news, and technology. It was like being in an involuntary time capsule. Ashley's references to new music and TV shows were totally lost on me.

I wondered if the distance between myself and the way normal people communicated, lived, and went through the world was becoming a gulf I risked losing the ability to cross. It meant I'd have to fake knowing what people were talking about even more than before when they talked about things they considered "normal." It also meant I had to work harder to have compassion for people who took all that for granted. It was so easy to want to hate people for having homes, food, opportunities, and family to fall back on. That resentment was a specially cultivated side effect of living on the streets. Some kids had it bad, and encouraged it.

The next morning Ashley's mom was guarded, almost suspicious of me. I didn't blame her. If she was as old-fashioned as Ashely said, by the looks of me she'd be worried I would steal something. It made me try harder to make Ashley look good by cleaning up in the kitchen, traditional gender roles and all. Ashley had to show me how to load the dishwasher because I'd never used one before.

Her mom warmed toward me a bit when I helped Ashley get the boys ready for school. Ashley made a point of waiting until no one was looking and pinched my butt, and I got in a good elbow to her boob. Then I pretended to go to school with Ashley, hugging her goodbye when I stayed on the bus, continuing to the Castro.

21

EVERYONE WAS EXCITED when I got to the magic bench. When I was at Ashley's, Jimmy met some rich brat from Specific Whites (Pacific Heights) whose parents were out of town. The brat wanted to party with us tonight at his mom's house somewhere up in the mansion-lined neighborhood of Ashbury Terrace. I wondered what we should call the punk version of a Trustafarian.

It was great news, and not just because I needed a place to stay that night. Or that I might see the inside of an actual mansion. It was rare we got to stay in one place all together. Sure, we'd show up with booze for partying and to make nice, but we were thrilled about the prospect of showers and a kitchen with food. Lisa and Jess looked at each other and said in a unison sing-song, "We can make Kraft dinner!"

Staying in one place together made us feel like a family. Sometimes other homeless kids would find out about a vacant house, or someone whose parents were away for a weekend and wanted to have a party, and we'd all go crash there. Zeke and Rogue, our punk rock mom and dad, were always adamant that we not fuck up people's houses, and we stuck to that rule.

If the house was empty, we called it "housebombing." There would be no need for housebombing tonight. We were invited guests. According to Zeke, who'd gotten the details from Jimmy, the house was huge, and the rich kid didn't give a shit about it.

We spent the day preparing by panhandling and fixing

our makeup and hair, trying to be careful about who to invite. Or who not to invite. For example, Scooter was nice, but she was a junkie and they always screwed something up. By the end of the day we gathered Mark, Lisa, Jess, Jimmy, Zeke, Rogue, and me.

Jimmy met up with us at dusk and together we combined our knowledge of San Francisco's secret stairways between neighborhoods to shorten our hike to the terraced mansions above Haight. Jimmy held hands with Lisa, which annoyed Jess more than me. I took one of Jess's arms and Mark took the other.

Jess and Lisa, "the twins," were officially over. It had nothing to do with Lisa and Jimmy hooking up. Lisa had broken one of the most important loyalty covenants of street family: when Jess needed help, Lisa abandoned her.

It happened when I was early morning panhandling in Upper Haight with Lisa. Our soundtrack was the hydraulic whine of the buses. The clap of a girl's boots on her way to work at Buffalo Exchange. The annoyed buzz of flies disturbed over a pool of vomit in the gutter. The hiss of water pushing back the smell of last night's piss from the storefront of the drag queen store, giant legs on its sign kicking the sky. The warming up of the city's orchestra, a prelude to a day like any other in San Francisco.

Jess walked up and her gait seemed strange. I guessed she was high or drunk. But then, the smell. It was foul and coming off her in waves, growing stronger the closer she got. She got up to us and I saw her makeup was uneven. It looked like half was missing.

"Ugh, what is that?" Lisa held her nose and waved her hand ineffectively.

"I need to get cleaned up," Jess said with a voice like broken glass.

"What the fuck," Lisa said, standing up. She walked around Jess and exclaimed, "Oh! What the fuck!"

Jess looked at Lisa, pleading. "I just need to--" she said, trailing off.

"What happened?" I asked. I got up as Lisa backed away from Jess, her face pinched and squeezed in revulsion.

Lisa grabbed her bag, saying: "I can't deal with this."

Jess turned and I saw two pieces of information. A fresh scrape on her jaw, and what was undeniably human feces on her back. She looked at Lisa, lip quivering. "I need you."

In shock and confusion, I watched Lisa leave. I grabbed my bag and went to Jess. "Can you make it a couple more blocks?" I asked her. She nodded, biting her lower lip.

I took her hand and led her down Haight Street to McDonald's -- I'd gotten good at sneaking into their bathroom. I realized she wasn't high; she was just having trouble walking. I pushed that to a corner of my mind and got her into a stall, plugged up a sink with towels, and began filling it with water and liquid soap from the wall dispenser. She struggled with her coat behind the metal door and her bag dropped to the floor, Lucky Lager bottle caps chiming their spill across the tiles.

"I'll get those," I said. "Here. These are for you." I passed her a clump of paper towels under the door. "Hand me what needs to be washed," I told her. "I'll pass you wet towels and soapy towels next."

The smell was beyond awful. I was breathing through my mouth but it was thick, in everything. I had to really concentrate on not gagging. But maybe what was worse was thinking about what might've happened to Jess, and realizing that Lisa had abandoned her.

"Do you ..." I started. "Do you need panties? I don't know if my panties will fit you," I said, "but I have some clean ones in my bag."

Jess sobbed and I almost lost it. I knew what it was like to be hurt and to be abandoned, where your heart caves in and crumbles to pieces. These were two fears that had crippled my judgement in the past, had hobbled my ability to navigate properly. I wasn't transgender like Jess, but I knew there were other layers of violation and pure wrongness here, beyond most people's comprehension, and I could only feel helpless about it for so long until it would turn into despair or anger. But I knew we shared the trauma of being abandoned by the people who were supposed to care about us at the moment we needed them the most.

I said, "Hey Jess?"

"Yeah?"

"I'm not going anywhere."

I meant it.

* * *

THE HOUSE WAS WAY UP over Corona Heights and along Buena Vista Park, on one of the steep hills. Next to where I slept in the park with Aiden. The kind of hill where you think sidewalk should be stairs, and when you stop to catch your breath, you turn around and the view takes your breath away, again.

The neighborhood's tony little collection of mansions never failed to fill me with envy and longing every time I walked through them to sleep in the park or carbomb. I dreamed about what it would be like to live in one of those houses. Walking among them alone on Christmas Day, with nothing to do but stare in the windows, became a yearly tradition for me that stretched far into adulthood. Sometimes sad, sometimes not.

Jimmy said, "This is it."

I stopped in my tracks. "Wow," I said.

Urns and columns flanked wide front steps of white marble, contrasting ruddy Spanish-style architecture leading the eyes upward. It looked like there might be a roof deck way up top. Behind black iron gates at the sidewalk's boundary, the mansion had a small, curved driveway tailored with wisteria that had closed up shop for the foggy winter. According to Jimmy, we were to enter through a side door.

One of us had to hop the wall and open an iron garden gate. Mark volunteered for the initial breaking and entering and lithely hopped the boundary. The air was cold and wet, but I caught the scent of something night-blooming in the garden as we passed into it, lacing the air with a wonderful sweetness. I couldn't believe people lived like this. Once we were all through the gate and shut it behind us, we found our way along a path illuminated by lights shining out of what I thought must be a downstairs game room.

I didn't even hear the dog until its growl flew across the lawn in a flash of black. I turned to practically catch the heavy German Shepard in my arms, falling down and pushing in blind terror at a pure mass of fur and teeth. Growling in my ear, wet grass through my pants. I felt pain on the side of my face. And then warmth.

Giddily I thought, *at least it's my right eye.* Then I heard a dog squeal, a high-pitched, ear-splitting tone going away, away from me, but still somehow keening in the dark. I was on my knees in wet mush, with my eyes closed, unbreathing, waiting in my own darkness to come back. The scree of sound continued. I slowly opened my eyes, and I saw light and my friends, then my right eye obscured with a red spot as a spreading pool of blood took my sight away, like a theater filmstrip burning and spreading into black.

Just before everything went from red to black, I saw where the sound was coming from. Jess sobbed and held Lisa, who stared at me, face crumpled around the screaming "O" of her mouth.

I knelt in wet grass outside the Ashbury Terrace mansion telling my body how to remember to breathe. I felt warm fluid running down my face and couldn't see. I knew it was blood.

In some rational part of my mind, I was breaking down what happened into pieces of information. You need information to navigate. On the streets, everyone compares notes on survival, endlessly. I had recently been reading about navigation by triangulation. How do you know where to go when you don't know where you are? To my understanding, or more for my purposes, triangulation was a way of determining something's location using the locations of other things; finding a path by establishing perspective. Generally, I was constantly trying to figure out where I was going -- with my life. Worried about who I was going to be in the future. Unknown destinations that could be calibrated by where I stood now, and where I didn't want to end up; who I am angled against what I don't want to become. Two points of information with which to hopefully navigate a path to something better.

At that moment in the grass, I was in a very familiar place called trauma. Trauma isn't personal. It just happens, like an earthquake. Trauma is a piece of information. Fear is another, and we know what fear is because we have information to compare it to in the form of desire, or what we want.

And what I experienced in that long (but actually short), terrible moment was a trauma unlike anything I'd experienced before. But it was still an earthquake. I was born on a fault line, I reminded myself, and I have so many frames of reference for trauma, each in their own little snow globe in my mind. What happened at the Cutler's house was also trauma, one that nearly pushed me to suicide. After I decided not to jump off the bridge that night, I next decided I needed to figure out how to navigate and create stability inside myself while living a completely unstable life. I could ask, and ask, and ask why trauma happens to me. Or I could use it as information to help me decide how to get through all of this, better. I chose the latter.

With my friends, I had broken into a wealthy person's private property. A dog attacked me. Point one.

Hearing Lisa screaming at the way my face looked really scared me. Figuring out what we're afraid of is usually the easy part. So, there was my other navigational point. I was injured.

Point three was unknown, but it would be what I wanted to do about it. How I chose to react now that I established perspective.

IT DIDN'T SURPRISE me that Lisa fell apart while Jess, the little one, the young one, didn't. Like me, she had never been a child.

Helping Jess in the bathroom flashed in my mind while I

knelt in the grass, struggling to get past fear wrapping me like a straitjacket. I was injured but I didn't know how. Would Jess help me, or would she abandon me?

Mark helped me up off the grass, the Ashbury Heights mansion towering over us. I could tell it was him by the gentle way he put my arm over his shoulder and his New Zealand accent softly saying, "I got yeh." I was so glad it was him and not Jimmy.

22

JESS AND MARK helped me get upstairs into the mansion.

We were in Travis's mansion. More correctly, it was his parent's mansion. One of them. Travis's dad was a well-known plastic surgeon who lived in their other mansion, in Specific Whites. This one was his mom's mansion. Mommy was out of town. Her junkie punk son wanted to party.

Travis was a grade-A specimen of rich San Francisco bad boy disaster. I wondered where Jimmy found him.

"You shouldn't do that to your eyebrows," Travis slurred at Jess as he leaned in the doorway of an upstairs bathroom the size of a Tenderloin apartment. I could tell he thought he was being playful, but couldn't tell the difference between being mean and being funny. His dark bangs hung over hooded brown eyes, lifted with a dimpled smile I thought would've been handsome on anyone else. "My mom plucked hers and she reeeeally regrets it now. Had to have it fixed."

Jess raised her eyebrows at him, almost as if she just noticed he was still talking, then turned back to blotting my right eye. Brandy -- the German Shepard -- had just started to bite my face when Travis dragged her off of me. Looking at Travis now, I couldn't believe he could've moved that fast. Brandy was okay but I wondered about the squeals I'd heard, and Travis calling her a "stupid fucking dog."

My moment of panic on the lawn was short once I did my internal triangulation. Dog attack. Something wrong with my face. My destination was to assess damage as practically and as soon as possible, and decide what to do about it.

There had been a lot of blood. Mark reassured me that faces bleed a lot after he picked me up off the lawn, and Rogue, who came running with a really nice, monogrammed towel, said the same. With help from Jess, the trio led me though a sliding glass door into the mansion to its kitchen, where we rinsed my face. My sight returned once we cleared the blood out of my eyes. The kitchen had a sink in the middle of the room. I remembered I hadn't been anywhere with a sink island since my mother's glory days of coke parties in wealthy Valley homes. It felt like someone else's memories.

Everyone else had toddled away with Travis to wherever the booze was, though he came back in to bring us a couple of bottles. "You should go in one of my mom's bathrooms upstairs. There's places to sit and apparently the light is really good. Use whatever the fuck you want, I don't give a shit," he snickered. He also offered everyone food and heroin.

"Yay," Mark hissed under his breath, grabbing bottles and glasses, following Jess and I out of the kitchen. Our footfalls were silenced by red Persian carpets in wide hallways lined with antique wooden chairs and tables, with mustard-colored walls featuring framed paintings and gaudy sconces dripping silk flowers. It looked like no one lived there, like a real estate show house.

I stopped us on the way upstairs at the sight of a giant painting in the mansion's entry, where one stairway came up, turned on a landing, and a second stairway coiled higher. On the wall stretching to the ceiling was a framed, hand-painted depiction of the Sutro Baths in the 1890s, when the sumptuous Greek, glass-encased pavilion on the beach was the world's largest indoor public bathhouse. I'd only seen it as it was now, a haunting, rocky ruin flanked by treacherous cliffs. It had been destroyed by fire in 1966. The painting showcased the building's architecture, dotted with frolicking bathers in caps and swim attire on slides, trapezes, springboards, and a high-dive. The painting had to be taller than me.

"Man, everything sucks now," Mark said.

"I bet it sucked back then, too," Jess tugged on my arm. "C'mon Dollface."

We found the bigger bathroom and made camp. It was a spotless showroom of white marble and gold fixtures, the bottom half of the walls in shining mint colored tile. Travis was right about the better lighting, and the bathroom's mirrors were on another level. "Fuck," Jess said surveying the room. "I am so doing laundry in here."

Rogue left us to find Zeke while Mark, Jess and I found an apocalypse-ready first aid kit under the sink and settled in. Mark poured whiskey into glasses "for the ladies" and kept a bottle for himself. When Jess shooed him away, Mark plopped into a huge bathtub, arms outstretched and booted feet over the side, and told us terrible jokes while we did damage control on my face.

"Hey, how many punks does it take to screw in a light bulb?"

"Mark," Jess had already started giggling. "Why do you hate us?"

"Five to screw it in," he answered himself, "and two to argue about who did it first."

I pulled a mirror toward me that was attached to an extendable arm mounted to ... another mirror. I was going to have some new scars. My right eyebrow had a dotted line of gouges from arch to hairline, which had its own set of wounds. There was a long cut in the exact crease of my eyelid around one centimeter in length. A small piece of skin on the outside of my lower lid near the tear duct was missing.

Jess shoved a glass of booze into my hand. "Take a shot, then we clean it all. 'S gonna hurt."

"Hey, how does a skinhead tie his Docs?"

Jess rolled her eyes and dabbed my eyebrow with an alcohol swab. I sucked air between my teeth and said, "I'm not sure what hurts more right now."

Mark grinned. "In little Nazis!"

This was when Travis appeared in the doorway. "That's good scotch," he said to Mark.

Mark raised the bottle to Travis in a mock toast and downed a gulp. "Cheers mate," he said. "Thanks for all this."

"No problem, man."

Travis was a malignant pinball bouncing around a life where everyone would take care of him and I wanted him to leave. I tried to keep my reflexes under control as Jess dabbed my closing cuts. It felt like Jess was applying fire to my face. All of life seemed to be an exercise in not showing anyone that I was in pain.

"Heeey," Travis said to me. "I'm really sorry about Brandy."

I really didn't want to fuck up our chances of staying here tonight. "It's not your fault," I said, which I didn't know if it was true but was something I could live with myself for saying and would give a guy like Travis what he needed, which was to feel good in the moment. "Thanks for grabbing her."

"Who gives a dog a hooker name," he said to Mark, and I

cringed inwardly for Jess. Travis looked at Jess and said, "It's mom's favorite booze."

"Okay," she said to me. "Let's let that dry out for a sec." Jess picked up the first aid kit's instruction card and fanned my face. That's when Jess got Travis's unsolicited eyebrow grooming advice, and then he wandered off. "Come downstairs and join the party," he called out from the hall, "And make ye merry while ye may!"

When Travis was away from earshot, Jess said in a cynical monotone, "Super glad for the lack of foursome request."

I looked at Mark in the mirror. He was staring at the doorway with a look I couldn't figure. His eyes met mine. "Hey," he said.

"No-" I was worried Travis could hear us but Jess and I were smiling now.

"How do you get a bitter rich boy out of a tree?"

Mark wasn't smiling. "You cut the rope."

* * *

MY EYE WAS SWELLING up pretty badly, and some of the cuts seeped. I didn't really want to be seen by anyone downstairs where the party was, and it suited Jess just fine to stay upstairs with me. We moved our camp to the bedroom adjoining the bathroom. Mark left us to get ice for my eye.

The large guest room had furniture and appointments that looked as unused as all the other furniture we'd seen. A giant king-sized bed stuck out of a wall inset like an overstuffed tongue, next to a breathtaking set of floor to ceiling windows with a view of the Golden Gate Bridge across the neighborhoods. The cream-colored carpet was so thick it felt like walking on a layer of marshmallow. Ornate baby-food-beige wallpaper with cream scrollwork matched the patterned fabric of the bed, throw pillows, and sitting area's chairs in color only. It was strangely tacky.

"Yuck," Jess said, plopping on the massive bed. "Can you imagine having this rad room and decorating it like this?"

I opened the walk-in closet. "Holy shit," I said. One section was robes. I pulled one out to show her, a fluffy beige terry cloth monstrosity. "Let's do some laundry."

"Okay, but make sure that no one comes in."

"Is Mark safe?" I knew protecting her boundaries about being transgender was a matter of life and death.

"Yeah, he's cool. But definitely not Travis."

She trusted me, but I still turned my back while we changed to wash our underwear, socks, and smaller items in the bathroom's two sinks. We rolled our garments in towels on the floor, smashing them to squeeze the water out before hanging them over every available surface for drying. My face felt hot, heavy, and throbbed whenever I bent toward the floor. We both jumped when someone kicked on the door with a boot.

"Who is it?" I asked with a tone like I was mad.

"It's Mark, open the door!"

I went to the door as Jess said, "Took you long enough."

Mark held a tray piled high with sandwiches, glasses and another whiskey bottle, more stuff than I could see. "They didn't have Kraft dinner," he smiled. "But there's plenty of blow downstairs if anyone doesn't want to eat. Whoa," Mark angled his way into the room with the tray, looked at all the underwear hanging everywhere.

"I'll have you know those are my work panties," Jess warned him. She came out from around behind the walk-in closet door as I followed Mark into the bedroom.

222

"They're too small for me anyway," he said, setting the tray on the bed with effort. "Here, now let's put a sammie in your filthy face holes," Mark was already unburdening the tray. "Ice for the face," he passed me a plastic cold pack.

Mark sat on the floor with a bag of chips and a bottle, and relayed his experience checking out the scene downstairs. More punks had shown up, he told us. It was a full-on party with Travis providing all the party favors. The place would be thrashed by morning, he said, so our time here definitely had a looming expiration date. He absently clicked on the room's TV. "Chilling up here's more my scene anyway," he said. "Travis wants to be in a band," Mark's inflection told us just how not-excited he was to be Travis's new punk-band buddy.

Jess and I smiled and made "oh wow" noises, like bored kindergarten teachers. Jess asked, "Did you wish him luck?"

"Nah, he's got a bank account full of luck, he doesn't get any of mine."

I was glad Jess and Mark were staying with me. I was bummed that no one else had come to check on me, but my face was an ugly mess. The ice held back some swelling around my eye. The sight in that eye was swimmy, felt like there was oil in it. I tried not to think about how much it freaked me out while we all three got under the bed's covers, passed the whiskey bottle, and watched some late night horror film on TV. It wasn't Creature Features, the midnight horror double-feature of my childhood, but it was kind of perfect, even with the yelling and music whispering up from downstairs. Every time I looked at the view outside our windows I felt pulled downward by longing, jealousy for the kind of life Travis took for granted.

"Do you believe in karma?" I asked my friends.

Jess looked at me. "Like good shit happens to you when you just make sure to be a good person?"

"Yeah."

"Nope."

"Really?"

"Too many assholes who do evil shit are running around doing just fine. So, nope."

I slept between Jess and Mark. Through the night, my eye bled on the pillow and when I awoke, my eye was sealed shut with blood. Completely. I had to will myself not to freak out so I wouldn't cry, because I didn't know what would happen if I did. With my one eye I could see in the mirrors that I looked like a monster. Try as we might, soaking it with water and a washcloth, Jess and I couldn't get it open.

Jess helped me pack up. I had to get to a doctor. It was the worst, most helpless and frightened feeling in the world. I had no money. Hospitals would refuse to treat you without insurance, plus what if they called the cops? I didn't think I could get to Planned Parenthood, if they could even help me, and there was no way I was going to try and get to the Tenderloin to hope Larkin Street Youth's meagre clinic could help me.

Mark walked me to Haight Ashbury Free Clinic but couldn't stay because he had to check in with his mom. The clinic would be gross; it was where tweakers and crusty kids with scabies and old box-dweller guys with skin rot went. I wanted to fall apart and disappear into nothing as Mark held my hand through the neighborhood of mansions down the hill, only able to see out of one eye. For the guy I knew as a live wire of fury onstage, he was way more funny and caring than I could've guessed.

I sat in the clinic and waited. That's something us poor

people do so very well, I thought, surrounded by depressed, sick, and other homeless people in varying states of pain inside and out. We wait, bored and slouching, packed in a waiting room where hours go by as we sit there sick, wounded, strung out, bleeding, and hope to be seen by a real doctor, or hope for antibiotics, an inhaler, insulin, or some aspirin. We sit and wait and hope for an accurate pronouncement -- it's a gamble -- because otherwise we'll end up back in those hard plastic seats to wait some more, worse than before.

After five hours, a nurse practitioner cleaned my eye with boric acid. It scared me that it was acid, but I had to trust him. He said he suggested stitches but that it was up to me. I had no idea if I'd had any of the shots they asked about. I didn't know my family medical history, and I reflected inwardly that I had no way to find out. Who would I ask?

I left with no stitches and a bandage over my eye I'd never be able to change the way I was instructed to. They said to come back if it showed signs of infection. If I slept in the park that night, I was sure that was an eventuality. I was already a day behind in finding food, a place to sleep. I was certain that showing up at any of my friend's crash pads looking like I did would freak people out so bad I'd probably lose that connection. No one wants a cute, no-hassle street punk when she's not cute and needs real help.

I couldn't find anyone I knew along Haight Street. I couldn't imagine that anyone was still at Travis's house, but how would I get in? Travis seemed like the kind of guy who would definitely pretend not to be home when the girl his dog attacked showed back up in worse shape.

Navigating the street with one working eye was hard, harder than I thought. I tried to panhandle on Haight at

Ashbury. People were really freaked out by my face. Within a couple hours my eye and face felt hot. The clinic was closed. The cafe was closed today, too.

A seasickness of hunger became a chill in my bones that made my teeth chatter. I was so hungry I was freezing from the inside. I didn't know what to do. I felt like I was going to die on that corner. I was desperate.

I remembered the slip of paper Ashley gave me. I didn't want to do this. But I needed to be indoors, and possibly more medical care. I was afraid my eye would get worse, and I knew someone would hurt me, rape me like this, out here, take everything I had left. I used those two awful data points to triangulate my way forward.

I went to a pay phone and pulled out my journal, dialed the number James the snitch gave me. Then I called my mom.

23

I PUNCHED the long string of numbers into a worn and dirty pay phone, another free call courtesy of James The Snitch. My mother's new number began with 510, so I knew she was somewhere in the East Bay. This was impossibly far away for San Franciscans, another state entirely. Whenever my friends tried to talk me into going to a punk show in the East Bay, I always said I'd go when they paved the Bay. So I could just skate over.

Of course I occasionally crossed the Bay for my friends anyway. I had a fond memory of watching Mark's band play outside on the steps of Sproul Hall on the UC Berkeley campus. Punks tried to make a circle slam-pit on the steps, and they just got tired, tripped going up and down the stairs, and fell down a lot. Rogue and I surveyed the scene from our seats on the ground nearby, completely amused.

My eye was swollen more now, hot, and felt oddly sweaty. I let the call ring twice and I hung up. Then I entered the mess of numbers in again and let it ring. This was one of mom's secret signals, agreed to so long ago I didn't know anything else.

I grew up with many rules about contact with the outside world, far away from the carefree movie everyone else seemed to live in around us. Never talk about mom or her friends, or where she is at any time, to anyone, and especially never on the phone. If people ask about mom, lie. When mom lies, back her up. It was the lying that made my memory work around the concussion even harder. I was hard-up for reliable witnesses to my own past.

The rules of operational security were threads I could follow to remember a chain of reasons for their existence. They were ingrained in my head from experiences with dealers up and down a hierarchy of importance, drug runners, good and bad "clients," and finally, DEA agents. Never talk, never tell anyone anything real. Always make sure no one is following or watching. Watch for people just sitting in their cars, look out for people lingering without anything to do. Never answer the front door or the phone unless you're expecting someone. Ever. Pay close attention to who sees you coming and going from home base; if someone seems like they don't have somewhere to be, keep walking. If you're being followed, call mom to warn her.

And if you have to call mom, ring twice. Then call back.

She picked up, and there was silence. My mother was there, but she wasn't ever, not really. Drug dealers don't live in the normal world. She'd taught me that people hate gaps in conversation, they can't stand silence when there should be talking. It was one of the ways she hustled people in conversation. If callers encounter silence, they'll always tell you who they are first in one way or another. My phone call was a paper airplane across a hostile border into grubby paranoia.

"Hi mom," I said, to put her at ease.

She snorted, a laugh. "Hey kid. Howya doing?" I heard the hiss of a cigarette drag.

I said, "I think I'm hurt."

"Are you in trouble?"

"No, I'm not in trouble. But I might be-"

"What," she interrupted.

"My eye," I sputtered. "I got attacked by a dog and I think I need to see a doctor. It's hot and swollen shut."

She exhaled, saying: "I can't just drop everything, you can't just expect me to stop working when you decide you want to come home."

"That's not it," I said, "I-"

"Did you even try to take care of it?"

I blurted, "I went to the free clinic but now they're closed and I think it's getting worse. I just-"

"I can't come get you."

That was at least a concession. She wouldn't interrupt whatever she was doing, but there was an offer in her words, and I thought that maybe if I went to her, she might help me. I imagined my eye becoming infected. Being half-blind on the street already made me way too vulnerable.

Besides, I thought bitterly, if she offered to come pick me up, she'd be four hours late anyway -- if she showed up at all. I knew how this went.

I hated to give her this word, but I had to: "Please."

There was a long pause, punctuated by another drag on her Marlboro Gold. "Take BART to Fruitvale. I'll have Deshawn pick you up."

"Who's that?"

"He drives for Charles. He'll come get you in an hour."

The day's panhandling had been bad, like scraping crumbs under a bus stop bench. I got to the Van Ness station with just enough money in my pocket to make the Oakland trip one-way. Fluorescent lights flashed on my hot, heavy face while I rode a humming BART car through the tunnel under San Francisco Bay, hugged by the stale air of the train car's fabric-and-carpet miasma. People avoided looking at me. I tried to hide in an old paperback copy of

Hero With A Thousand Faces, but reading was hard with one eye.

I hoped I was doing the right thing by asking my mother for help. I hated how desperation made me so vulnerable.

Fruitvale BART wasn't a place I wanted to end up, let alone get off a train at night and go stand outside waiting for some guy I don't know. What I'd heard about Fruitvale wasn't good. Everyone on the streets, in my circles at least, talked about how you had to keep clear of the Guardian Angels at all costs. They were a group of self-appointed anti-crime vigilantes who hung out at East Oakland BART stations. But everyone knew them as a bunch of thugs in militaristic uniforms that didn't need any excuse to beat the shit out of people they didn't like. Which they did, often.

I saw a group of their tell-tale jackets and berets when I got off the platform. I turned away, skipping my stone of eye contact across their surface, hoping they didn't see me. I walked with purpose toward the parking lot where I stood alone looking conspicuous as hell, with every shady person in the world checking me out. Great. Thanks, mom.

It was nighttime when I arrived. A lot of people were hanging out along the rim of the parking lot like it was their job. I was well aware that I looked like a beat up little white girl trying to turn tricks at Fruitvale BART.

Oakland's Fruitvale neighborhood was orchards until it experienced a population boom of traumatized and destitute refugees from San Francisco's 1906 earthquake. It later housed scores of Black families who flocked to the Bay Area for the World War II employment boom. Like with communities in San Francisco who ended up in housing projects, they came for the equal opportunity jobs but got stuck in a discriminatory housing situation where the "opportunities" were anything but equal.

It was familiar as a San Franciscan to see East Oakland wore its history on its sleeve.

"Damn," said a big mountain of a man walking toward me across the parking lot. He wore jeans with an untucked, brown work shirt. It made him look like one of those carved out hundred-year old tree trunks tourists drive cars through, but somehow ambulatory. As if a stump in Guerneville had decided to go see the sights in Fruitvale, maybe make any left-over fruit trees feel insecure just for kicks. "I'm Dee," he said. "Deshawn. But just Dee."

I said, "I guess I stand out."

He chuckled, a low rumble that in any other setting would be a 3.9 on the Richter scale. His smile made me realize this guy was actually younger than his size suggested. "She said you was hurt."

"Dog bit me."

"Shit, on the face! Dogs," Dee shook his head.

"I'm not much of a fan anymore."

"Well let's get you where you're going."

Dee drove a big, old, empty white van, and he drove it slow. East Oakland's wide, cracked streets disappeared under it as we traveled block after block of neglected houses, weedy lots, and boarded-up buildings, slowly climbing our way up to the Oakland hills. Eventually we crossed a freeway and I saw signs for the Oakland Zoo. I tried to remember if I'd ever been to a zoo. I hadn't, I realized, as the van clanked and bumped its way along the freeway's frontage road, past a church, rumbling into a different bit of Oakland suburbia where houses were getting bigger, but not nicer.

I looked at the street sign. "You gotta be fucking kidding me," I said as we turned down a side street.

"What?" Dee rumbled that laugh again. It was a great laugh. "Yeah, Rifle Lane. You hear 'em up here just like everywhere else."

I thanked Dee as he dropped me off in front of a fairly largeish house with peeling paint and a yard that looked like a post-apocalyptic film set in miniature. What was once a long hedge standing in for a fence seemed to be angrily corralling a rectangle of weeds clearly willing to fight for their rights. The house lights were on. My mother opened the door before I finished walking up the steps.

"Jesus," she said, blowing a cloud of smoke under the porch light. I guessed she meant my face.

She held the door open and stood aside. I guess I didn't really want a hug anyway, I thought. She looked older, tired. I could tell she'd been partying by the creases of makeup around her eyes. As I passed her, she remarked acidly, "All that beautiful blonde hair." In another world that would've hurt my feelings.

The house was much bigger inside. An open-plan living room dominated the lower floor with a kitchen to the left and a dining area in back whose double doors opened onto a back deck. It was too dark to see the yard. She had the whole house to herself, she explained as she led me to the kitchen. My mother said that it was one house of many that Charles owned, and Dee, his driver, also helped manage them. She told me all this with a cigarette hanging out of her mouth while she put ice in a plastic bag. "Put this on your face."

I did as I was told. The cold plastic bag gave a tingly sort of relief to the heat and tightness of my face. "Here," she shook out two Tylenol and handed them to me. "There's a mattress upstairs for tonight. I'm going to rent that room out so you can't stay unless you're gonna pay rent."

"Okay. I'm just worried about my-"

"We'll see if you need a doctor in the morning. Sheets and towels are in the hall closet, I'm going to bed."

The mattress was on a hardwood floor in her large spare room. She'd closed her bedroom door, so I felt alone in the house. It was sparsely furnished. I could hear the freeway one block away, a constant background hum. I grabbed cold chicken from the refrigerator, the kind sold from a supermarket rotisserie. The Tylenol toned down the throbbing of my eye, yet when I took a shower, I was careful to keep it out of the hot water -- just the thought of anything touching it scared me. Restless, I flicked on the downstairs TV. I didn't recognize any shows. I was now really, completely outside the rest of the world's version of normal life. I didn't belong here, or anywhere anymore.

I gave up and went to the flat mattress on the hardwood floor upstairs, which actually felt like heaven. I made mattress angels. Privacy is better than pornography when you're homeless. I didn't realize I'd fallen asleep until my mother woke me up and sun streamed in the bedroom windows. Even with one good eye, it really was a beautiful room.

My eye was swollen shut again. I could feel the pressure in my cheek, my sinuses.

My mother was having her usual breakfast at a dining table by the French doors: black coffee and Marlboro Gold 100s. She told me to ice my eye and take more Tylenol, and started making phone calls, a stack of notes in front of her. I held the repacked plastic bag of ice against my face and looked out at her enormous backyard while she told me that "we'd see later" if I needed to go to a doctor. The backyard was rocky, abandoned, with a handful of sick, diseased fruit trees sticking up from the barren earth like rotten sticks.

In between calls my mother said, "Charles wants you to clean his house. He'll pay you twenty dollars."

"Clean his house?"

"Yes," she glared at me. "His personal house. It's really nice. Don't be a little shit."

My cheeks flushed with heat. Anger or humiliation, it was dealer's choice. I hated it when she called me that.

I really didn't want to see Charles, at all, and the thought of leaning downward to scrub anything made my face pound in anticipation. Worse, the whole thing started to feel like a set-up. Like she was just going to delay me and stall me, use my desperation up until I was back into her indentured servitude. I stood there saying none of this and my silence was taken for agreement. Drug addicts pop other people's consent like pills.

She told me, "Charles is out all day and Dee will come pick you up." I felt relief that I wouldn't risk seeing Charles, but still.

"Then after," I said, "I'm really worried about my eye-"

She was already back on the phone, nodding an absent agreement and waving me away like I'd interrupted her concentration.

24

WITH ONE PHONE call asking for help, I was back in one of my mother's complicated traps. With her, everything had a price. I had to talk my way out of being taken to her drug dealer boyfriend's house and forced to scrub the toilet of the man who raped her. The man I last saw coming into my bedroom in the middle of the night who stopped when he saw I had my mom's gun, and it was pointed at him. I wondered, did he tell her about that?

Morning sun streamed into the kitchen through French doors whose paint peeled with neglect. Rather than warm and cheerful, its light only brought out the flaws in everything around me. My mother's stained coffee cup, the overflowing ashtray, her nicotine stained fingers and teeth, the pocked and scarred kitchen table between us.

I reminded myself I wasn't afraid of her anymore. I wanted to ask her why she wouldn't just take me to a doctor, why this had to be a trade where I paid in advance. Why she couldn't tell me what was really going on with her. If this was the life she wanted. I had a whole other life she hadn't even asked about. In a short amount of time on the streets, I'd seen that there were many ways you could choose to live your life, like Frank and Joey, and even Spider and Alex.

But here I was. Standing in another strange house while she ignored me until she got her way, or I angered her. "I just need your help," I said quietly.

She halted her attention to notes and phone calls and shot me a dark look. "Things don't just happen because you decide to show up, young lady. Not that you even look like a lady anymore. And you don't take that tone with me and then ask me for help."

My heart started pounding. Before I could stop myself, I said, "You moved and didn't tell me." I was going too far back in this already and I knew it.

"And you wrecked everything when you crashed that fucking scooter. Then you had to go fuck me with that Child Protective Services bullshit. I almost didn't get out of that. Despite what you think, not everything revolves around you. Not all of us can just flounce in and out when they feel like it." Her words were sharp hooks; I felt them pulling me down into the swirling darkness of a cyclical argument I could sense changing the room like weather.

My head pounded, my eye throbbed. I suddenly felt desperate to stop this. "Charles scares me," I pleaded. "I'm sorry!"

"I'll make you sorry if you keep using that tone with me, goddammit."

"I'm sorry," I had to take a breath to keep from crying, the pressure in my face was hot and hard.

"And I'm not sorry. Do you think you can take time out from your busy schedule to do some work for a change?"

I could only repeat, "Charles scares me."

"You want to be the one to keep all of this running?" She chopped a hand at the forlorn house around us. "Do you know how much of your life has been paid for by me? What makes you think you don't owe me for being born? I'm the reason you even exist. I spend every waking hour of my life taking care of you and you should be grateful. Don't give me that take me to a doctor shit until you've earned it, you look like you can walk and clean a house just fine to me."

I stood mute while she continued. "You used to be so smart," she lit a fresh cigarette. "Now look at you. Get your shit together. Dee is on his way to pick you up. Don't embarrass me." She picked up the phone and started dialing.

I felt empty inside. I floated back upstairs to the bathroom. When she was like this, trying to beg or reason would just make her more angry, and I didn't want to delay any chance, however slim, I might have of getting her to take me to a doctor. My mohawk was down and faded to a dirty turquoise and my face was red. I pushed strands of hair behind my ear and just stood there, breathing. I blamed myself for questioning her, for not just taking the easy way out. Asking for help was always such a bad idea. I would never be able to understand why for some people it was like waving a red flag in front of a bull.

I missed Rogue so much. Her mom was like this, too. I missed Jess, who knew how to deal with people that tried to manipulate her and had boundaries to know when things went too far. I missed Mark, who listened to me and cared about what I thought and felt. I missed Zeke who could make fun of every mean person, and Aiden, who trusted me and always had my back. I missed my friends and their colorful fuzzy hair. Mostly, I missed being hopeful.

I can do this, I told myself. I would be back with my friends soon.

The bathroom mirror was dirty, but I looked bad. My right eye wasn't swollen all the way shut anymore, but it was puffy and hot with cuts I worried weren't healing. It looked like a drunk had dipped a brush in dark red and painted scabs in clumsy strokes along my eyebrow and in the crease of my eyelid, then finished it by stabbing messy brush marks along my upper and lower eyelid. I looked like hell. I wondered if my mother was stalling on taking me to a doctor because she was worried they'd call Child Protective Services. Wouldn't that be funny.

Coming here was a mistake, I thought. I still wasn't sure why I was agreeing to go along with her.

I couldn't believe I lived like this before. Being on the streets had changed me in so many ways. I felt like I was finally seeing people for what they were. There were questions I was turning over in my head now with every interaction I had, to determine if people and situations were harmful or safe. Situational inventory. This place was isolated. My mother was isolating. Yet it was the way I was raised. It had kept me from being able to compare her to other adults. Now, every time she opened her mouth, I could see what she was doing. She was running so hard from accountability for her own actions. And as a result, she had become the cruelty that decimated her own life.

I went back downstairs. She was still at the kitchen table. Black coffee and cigarettes. I sat down.

"Dee will be here to pick you up in twenty minutes," she said. "He'll take you to the house and show you what needs to be cleaned."

"What's his deal?" I asked.

"Who, Dee?"

"No, Charles." I was courting danger, I knew it.

Her entire face changed right then. Softened. *Oh great*, I thought. She thinks she's in love with this guy.

"He takes care of me, sweetie. Wait until you see his house. He owns houses all in this neighborhood."

"Do you work for him?"

"A little bit," she said. "I'm at the Volkswagen dealership in San Leandro three days a week. The guys there can't believe my hustle! I couldn't stay on Van Ness, they fucked me out of my commissions too many times. After all I did for Jan, that asshole."

I took that to mean she was working her way back up the ladder as a coke dealer, and that she left the San Francisco dealership in a flameout. Of course she was still selling cars. It stroked her ego to make people do things they didn't want to do, plus she could drive a different car with dealer plates anytime she wanted to. It was great cover for a drug dealer.

"Are you happy?" I asked. I figured my bravery was no less irrational than the fury she leveled at me a few minutes ago.

She got up and went to the kitchen saying, "Of course I'm happy. What kind of question is that?"

There were so many things I wanted to say to her right then. I wanted to tell her it would be okay if she said "no." I wanted to tell her I was pissed at her for turning her back on me, but that dimmed with the sudden realization that she actually had no friends. My friends were dying on the streets over in San Francisco, and being ignored, silenced, lied about, and physically attacked for being homeless, for being gay, for having HIV -- and here she was doing all those things to herself.

I didn't respond. I knew she'd see that as her victory, and while in the past it would've burned me up with anger and shame, now it was starting to feel sad.

Then Dee arrived to pick me up. He was bigger than I remembered. He drove me down into East Oakland's flats, passing house after dilapidated house. Plastic bags and furniture and strollers lined cracked, weedy sidewalks. Forgotten Victorians came apart around the people living in them, as did housing blocks and one-story walk-ups circled by cyclone fence. Dee didn't talk much and I was fine with that. I was trying to figure out why we let people we love make us do things we don't want to.

I could tell which house belonged to Charles. Along a block of houses pocked with all the hallmarks of multi-decade poverty, his was neat, well-kept, and had two big shiny Cadillacs in its long driveway. There was an eerie quiet in the way that you could feel how, in a neighborhood that wasn't short on graffiti, apparently no one messed with this property up to the lines.

Dee let me in, and I could see why my mother was impressed. It was well furnished in the way you'd expect an older bachelor with a sense of style would make his house. Not what I expected at all. A red sectional couch wrapped around two low marble coffee tables in matching hues of slate, all facing a large TV in the living room. There were plants, a few hanging lamps, framed prints, driftwood, and statues.

It was all so tidy I wasn't sure what I was supposed to clean.

"Over here," Dee said, leading me to the kitchen. "Cleaning supplies are under the sink and there's more in the hall closet. Come over here." He ambled down the hallway; his shoulders were so wide they practically touched the walls. I trailed him like a tiny duckling. He gestured into a room along the hall. "This is the business room. You clean it but don't move anything, don't touch nothing. Don't move that mirror."

We stood in the doorway of a second bedroom outfitted as an office. A large two-pan balance scale sat in the middle of a big dark wood desk. To the side of the desk stood a tall, freestanding, full-length mirror. A leather office chair at the desk was turned to face it, while a second, lesser-quality chair sat alone on the side of the room. It also faced the mirror.

"He only talks to people with the mirror," Dee explained.

"What? Why?"

"It's how he does it, that's all."

I didn't understand. But I decided that room gave me the creeps. It was spotless.

Dee left me alone and I got to cleaning. My dread deepened with each passing hour. It would be past normal office hours for a doctor's visit by the time I was done unless I went to urgent care.

The drive back to Rifle Lane went by in silence. Dee, who seemed like an okay guy, paid me twenty and tipped me ten when he dropped me off. Dee was errand boy, driver, and live-in muscle for the neighborhood drug dealer.

I stepped out of the van into the nearby freeway's constant hum. The sound reminded me I'd woken up in the middle of the night from a nightmare about a serial killer.

I shook it off as part of growing up in California, where serial killers are as much a fact of life as year-round citrus, seven-year droughts, or Spanish in your daily vocabulary. All kids knew about the Zodiac Killer, Charles Manson, the Trailside Killer. They were locals. When I began living on the streets the Golden State Killer was active. So were many others. Generations of women in California grew up fearing these men.

I shook off the memory and walked up to my mom's house. I stopped when I heard party sounds over the freeway noise. She was partying.

All my hope of having a doctor look at my eye sunk into a hard pit in my stomach. Being here was a series of moments strung together by despair.

I decided I'd go straight to the room with my mattress and hide there. In the morning I'd get to BART. I had some cash now, I could figure it out. Maybe go to the cafe and Frank and Joey might be able to help me ... No, I thought, I'd just go straight to Larkin Street Youth Services. They'd know what to do.

I walked into a scene out of some dated 1980s coke party playbook. The TV was on, the stereo was on, everyone was on. A room full of adults drank, talked over each other, and snorted lines off a framed "Michelob" mirror on the coffee table.

"There's my little girl!" my mother shouted.

"Shit girl, look at your face!" I felt myself step back into the closed door behind me as Charles cut through loudly chatting people and came over to peer at me up close. He wasn't much taller than me. Weird, I remembered him as so much bigger. He smiled at me. He was terrifying. Did he even remember I'd held him at gunpoint? If he did, he didn't show it.

"Ooo, that's pretty bad honey," he said peering at my eye. "I'm Charles, I'm with your momma now." He looked over his shoulder and shouted at my mom, "You gonna get her taken care of?" Then back to me, "She's gonna have to get you fixed up. We'll take care of it," he winked. "C'mon, you want a drink?"

"I think I just want to go to my room for a bit."

My mother floated over. Her makeup was fresh, her hair up. A loose, flowy, low-cut tawny blouse hung on her thin frame over a skintight pair of burgundy slacks. Her clavicles looked like wing bones. "Dee moved your bed downstairs honey," she told me, exhaling smoke.

"Uh, okay-"

"You put her down there? You can't put her there, you got mice here," Charles snapped at her. "I told you I killed one today!"

"She's fine with it," my mother told him. "You know I need to rent that room." She looked at me but said to Charles, "She can't just come back here and expect to live off me. She can take care of herself."

He looked at her, hard. When he turned back to me his features had softened, but there was a glitter in his eyes that made me want to dissolve into the carpet, the drapes, the ether.

"C'mon," he said to me, "it's through here." Charles turned and I followed. Wishing I would turn around and go out the door. *Run*, I thought, just run and never stop.

Charles walked me through the party to a door leading downstairs at the back of the house. "Well, we got one less mouse now," Charles laughed, like we were friends now. He told me, "I caught that little fucker up here, runnin' around the kitchen. I got it under a bucket, you know? Then I didn't know, I'd tried bug spray. You think, it kills bugs, right? But it didn't work! So I dumped it in the sink and got the water as hot as I could-"

"I think I'll stay up here for a minute, have a beer?" What he'd said made me want to scream, and maybe vomit, and then cry. Alarms blared in my head. I wasn't going downstairs with this guy.

"Alright!" He liked this change of plans. "Let's get you handled."

I got the beer then slipped away from Charles and into the living room. Sitting at the far end of the couch, I begged the world, the trees, the gods, that no one would talk to me.

The "party" was mostly men. I felt doomed. Within

seconds a short, sweaty little guy zeroed in on me. He sat down next to me and started making small talk. I tuned it out while imagining what I must look like to him, a teenage girl with a mutilated face having a beer, and I wondered what kind of creep would hit on me. People think kids aren't aware of this stuff. They're wrong.

His voice interrupted my thoughts, and he was saying "... but you know, I don't get regular days off."

I blinked and said, "What?"

"My job," he said puffing up, smirking. "Can you guess what I do?"

I looked at his clean-shaven face, hands, watch, belt, the outline of an undershirt, and his shoes. "You're a cop," I deadpanned.

His back straightened. People within earshot stiffened, conversation dipped. He said, "No, well, not exactly."

I let the silence stretch.

He said, "I'm a CO. Do you know what that is?" He was either too gakked on coke to wait for my answer, or felt it was his duty to explain things to girls. He plowed forward saying, "I'm a correctional officer. I work at San Quentin. You know, we have Charles Manson there. Do you know who that is? But that's not the most dangerous thing about my job."

He scooted closer to me on the couch and said: "You know, they don't care in there, they're all lifers. They have nothing to lose. The thing you gotta look out for," he said leaning in, "is rape. All they want to do is get us. They figure if they get us once, they got us, you know? And they don't care, they laugh when they're being put in solitary, because they got one in us. It's a game."

I was trapped. All of this, from the front door to the couch, happened within about twenty minutes. Fortunately, I thought, I have a lot of practice in not reacting to things no matter how much they shock or scare me. There had to be something good in the world I could someday use it for. I wondered if you needed a high school diploma to become a paramedic.

I set my beer down and made a face. Touched my stomach. "You know, I don't ... I don't feel so good." I wasn't completely lying. His breath was rank.

"Uh oh," he said. "So, is making out, out of the question?" he smiled, leaning close. He was sweating through his light blue dress shirt.

"I've had it coming out both ends," I lied. "I gotta go." I stood up.

"Can I get your number?"

"Yeah sure," I said. "It's the same as my mom's."

"I'll call you later," he assured me.

I threaded my way through the partiers like a mouse finally seeing its escape route. I could hear my mother and Charles arguing in the kitchen as I closed the door. I picked my way down creaky wooden stairs in the dark, feeling the air change to cool and damp. I felt along the unplastered wall until I found a light switch.

The stairs ended in a sunken garage. A cement floor was piled with boxes in which a path through towering cardboard ended in a doorway, minus its door. I found another light switch inside the doorway, bringing on a single bulb hanging from the center of the unfinished room's low ceiling. It was a musty, carpeted square lined with wood paneling. Two small windows near the ceiling showed I was below ground level.

My mattress was in the far corner. I saw my bag and felt a wave of relief. I fought the urge to run over and hug it. More boxes sagged along the room's walls. The carpet, the color of a dirty pudding cup, was specked with hundreds of little black pellets that grew dense toward the baseboards. I doubled back to the garage where I'd seen a broom. When I swept the pellets, the mouse droppings just jumped and danced, bouncing off the carpet and walls. I gave up and flopped onto the mattress.

I listened to the party. Glass clinked on a table, laughter trailed down the stairs. A soundtrack backed by the constant hum and whoosh of freeway white noise.

I thought about my mother. She reminded me now, in so many ways, of older women I saw on the streets. No: she was more like women who were five minutes away from being on the streets. Not runaways like me, but the mean, sad addicts she snidely called "bag ladies." The ones I saw fighting with their dirtbag boyfriends in the Haight or Tenderloin. Like every drug addict the world over, she was trapped in a snapshot of her life. *What happened to you*, I thought. Did it happen all at once, in some unknown trauma? Or was it gradual? Did you even know it was happening?

Of course, I had asked her when I could, and asked, and asked. But I'd gotten years of answers that didn't make sense, stories that conflicted, stories with what felt like threads of truth, all of it disturbing. I knew she'd been hiding things from me all along, like the identity of my real father. Like what it meant when she once told me she'd been "disowned" by her own mother, my grandmother.

But then I sat up. I looked around. I was surrounded by brown cardboard objects that might hold answers.

25

PARTY SOUNDS upstairs drifted down into the drafty, door-less basement room that was now my sleeping spot at my mother's house. I sat on the bare mattress and surveyed an assortment of cardboard boxes, their corners denting a dirty gold carpet specked with mouse droppings. Everything down here was cool and damp. I got up and went into the garage, its air defined by the smell of old tools and mold. I spotted an old rickety tool table. It had a scattering of rusty gardening tools, abandoned by whoever lived here before. Someone once loved this decrepit place.

I grabbed a flathead screwdriver and went back to the little room. Gripping the tool like a knife, I slashed open box tops, stuck the screwdriver into my back pocket, and dug in.

All their contents needed to do was tell me more about my mother. Threads tying together the story of how I ended up here. I tunneled through box after box of macrame lamps, hippie knick-knacks, pieces of decorative driftwood. I pawed through wadded-up newspaper to expose pots and pans, china, teacups, candleholders, my mom's books. It was all familiar but light years away from where my memories were strong and most recent: Our life of constant moving around and leaving everyone behind when, for whatever reason, we had to go.

It took me an hour to get a sense of all the boxes in both rooms, but the contents were definitely our stuff. More precisely, it was her stuff. My mom's junk from our previous life, things boxed away by whoever the DEA hired to move us.

There was no kid stuff here. I'd had records, posters, stacks of science magazines, oodles of horror and sci-fi paperbacks, stuffed animals, and a Barbie collection that included a coveted Black Barbie and a GI Joe doll. I remember having slot cars and racetracks, a microscope and slides, more video games than anyone alive. And brain puzzles, like heavy steel horseshoes with a ring stuck between them, and Japanese puzzle boxes. All the stuff you give a child with a busy mind when they're not allowed to have outside friends. It was all coming back to me -- memories as strings of lights, coming on, and on, and on -- yet none of my stuff was here.

I moved heavy stacks to be sure I got my hands into every single carton. I was still finding unexplored boxes. I was sweating. I wondered if it would ever be safe for me to take a shower in this house. Not with Charles around, I rued. And definitely not during this stupid party.

I ripped open a really heavy box hoping to find my books.

Several paper envelopes held stiff yellowed photos with white borders, they spilled into my hands full of people I didn't know. Photos of an old white Corvette and a very stylish woman with a smart bouffant-bob ... it was my mother. She looked amazing. In photo after photo she wore wild paisley vests, fringed jackets patterned like tapestries, denim bell bottoms, rusted suede miniskirts and knee-high leather boots. The Corvette was her car. Some photos were labeled in black pen with dates and places: It was all a colorful fog of life in San Francisco, Stanford, and Silicon Valley. My mother was undoubtedly the center of every party, at least according to the photos of happy people orbiting this young, beautiful, hazel-eyed engineer.

She was with an incredibly fashionable older blonde woman in a few photos -- was that her mom? One Kodak photo showed her smiling, absolutely beaming at the baby girl she held. It had to be me, though it's true I had no way of knowing for sure, but I felt it. My grandmother was a stylish Doris Day lookalike, who at one point in time was overjoyed to have a granddaughter.

I examined a photo of my mother kneeling next to little-me in front of a giant, lush Christmas tree amid a pile of presents and wrappings. She was draped in a wild mustard-and-jade colored robe patterned in Indian flourishes, her bouffant-bob still messy from bed, helping me unwrap presents. The ghost of my mother smiled from the photo at her gleeful, flaxen-haired daughter, and something in me broke.

I felt stuck, just staring at the photo. I thought, *this is all so wrong.* I never got to meet her. Who were all the people in these photos who got to hang out with this cool, smart, ebullient woman? I hated them all right then in that moment, those assholes. And somehow, I felt sorry for my mother. That dreamy, independent lady engineer has no idea of the madness that lies ahead of her, and that little girl knows nothing of the dark rooms and horror coming for her. My heart twisted and folded in on itself at the utter, sheer unfairness of it all. I felt sadness and anguish all rolled up in my chest, warring for dominance, flushing my face with heat. A lump blocked my throat, so I swallowed it back down hard.

Angry, I pawed deeper into the box and blinked back tears. I found more photos, thick prints of myself as an infant, grinning like a tiny hairless weirdo. My mother's writing on the back of one photo exclaimed, "Such a happy girl! She loves holding her feet!"

My age increased through the photographs, and I marveled at images of myself that I'd never seen. I came across a photo at around age five or six, my hair in ridiculous pigtails. I was dressed in some bizarre outfit with a huge bow on the front, and I looked extremely pissed off. Whatever was going on, I was no longer oblivious to it, and I liked the girl I saw in that photo very much. I set it aside and began a small pile of images I'd take and keep for myself.

The entire box was a time capsule. Vintage San Francisco. There were photos encompassing her marriage to "Uncle Dennis," taken in his house, where my earliest memories of violence resided. Then there was a gap, nothing for several years. Photos showed us resurfacing at a house in Mountain View. There were pictures of me, of scales, of drugs. In one photo my mother held three giant stacks of wrapped bills -- I remember this, the time she let me hold thirty thousand dollars in cash.

I looked closely at her smiling face in this photo. Something was off. Her face was different from the other photos. It was like the muscles on one side of her face weren't cooperating, just enough to look like one side was smiling more than the other. The other side was kind of melting. I compared it to earlier photos, and yes: There it was. What did that mean?

I was at the end of the boxes. The party upstairs had wound down, those noises were gone. All I could hear now was Oakland's oceanic white noise, the freeway. Part of me hoped I'd find some of my old stuff in the last box. Something to show I hadn't been excised from her life. I slashed the box tape, pulled open its cardboard leaves, and dug through layers of crumpled newspaper to find an odd-shaped item wrapped like it was made of glass. I unwound the paper. In my hands I held an animal skull. It was the leopard skull from the photo of my father. It was missing teeth, yellowed, stained. It was real.

I had to know who my father was. What happened to him. I stood, cradling the skull in my hands, anger simmering up in me pushing aside all the little-girl feelings of hurt I'd been steeping in. I had some questions for my mother, and she was going to answer them this time. Really answer them.

Determined, I set the skull on my mattress and went upstairs into a house that was now dark. I stood by the stairs leading up to her bedroom and froze. I heard sounds. Icy needles splashed the back of my neck and trickled down my arms. I had momentary sensory confusion; these familiar sounds meant terror. The sensation was so jarring I wondered for a second if I was on mushrooms again. Lights in my mind flew on along a memory-string like they were screaming down a hallway.

Cold fear stuck the breath in my lungs as I listened.

My mother was being hit, this was clear. Though when I was a little kid, there was a time when I couldn't tell the difference between those sounds and the sounds of adults having sex. Standing there, I remembered being a tiny girl outside a closed door while my mother had sex with her boyfriend, shrieking for him to stop it, stop it, picking up books and cups and an ashtray and throwing everything at the door and walls, crying and screaming.

I remember my mother coming out in a robe and being furious with me, and a beating to make sure I never did it again.

Which, I realized standing there, was why I couldn't move in that dark house on Rifle Lane. I felt like I was seeing it from above.

251

It's amazing what happens when we unlock trauma and explore it from the future. It's terrifying. But there's power in this, power we can use.

It's why I was so obsessed with my little concept of triangulation. *Maybe I don't know where I'm going,* I told myself, standing there, trying to figure out what to do, seeing dark trees around the house from above, but I have two points to navigate from.

I know where I am. I know who I don't want to be.

I've never been the kind of person to have trauma come at them and wonder, oh god why me, or any other waste of time. That was a luxury other people could afford. I had come to understand that in moments of insanity there are really only two things: Survival, and who we become during these moments. It's who we are when we look back, how we acted -- but more importantly how we feel about how we acted -- that makes us who we are.

I went upstairs toward the sounds. To the closed door of my mother's bedroom.

Through that cheap, hollow door I could hear thumps, wet smacking noises, and the breaths, grunts, and groans of someone being hit. A whining whisper faded in of my mother pleading for him to stop. I heard Charles saying what a mess she made, that she didn't know how to be a mother ... In a queasy instant I realized he was pretending to do this for me.

I heard a thump I guessed was her head hitting the wall. And this must've been what it was like last time I was trapped in a house with these two, when he came for me next, I knew it was, so it would happen tonight, too. I knew with every certainty that this shit would happen again and again, and forever if I stayed here. My mom would get away from him eventually, but for some inexplicable reason she'd find another one just like him. There wasn't anything I could do about that.

But I had choices. My destination still contained mystery. Hers did not. His did not. And where there were men like him, there would always be a girl like me.

And I was so tired of seeing people I cared about being hurt.

The doorknob was locked. I pounded my fist on the thin door shouting, "Hey! Knock it off!"

The sounds stopped. Charles yelled, "You go back, you hear?" Then, he said to my mother: "You fuckin' hear that shit?"

I heard her head thump the wall again. He roared at the door, "Don't fuckin' tell me in my house."

There's a lot to be said for enrolling your kids in martial arts classes when they're young. It builds confidence, sure, and in my case probably way more than I needed. But one thing my mom did right was placing me in combat classes as a child. Which is why my body changed the second I decided I was going in there, no matter what.

My knees unlocked and my joints went fluid; my center dropped with my chin as I put my weight just forward of my hips and stepped one foot back. Like that, it was easy to target the area next to the knob and aim for the back of the door. Each strike of my heel was thunder; it took two kicks to break the door's thin veneer and flay its doorknob out of position. A grunting third kick threw the door all the way in.

The bedroom's air was hot and thick, humid with the smell of body odor. Charles stood over my mother, who was half out of the bed herself, where she'd been getting her head slammed into the wall. Her red satin pajamas shone in the dim lamp light. Charles wore nothing but white boxers. He glowered at me through his glazed, almond-shaped eyes. He was high. And I was in trouble.

He yelled at me "The fuck did you just do!?" and took a step toward me. *This was dumb, this was so dumb,* I thought, now what the fuck am I going to do? I was frozen in place.

I didn't even notice I'd come all the way into the room. He took another step at me, more sure of himself now in the absence of my response.

My mother stayed where she was, quietly crying. I looked at her there, and for some reason I thought, *you don't even realize that we are the only people in this room.*

Charles boomed at me, "What you gonna do now, huh?" He faced me fully now, seething.

My pause, a few jetting heartbeats, was enough for Charles. He stepped toward me with purpose.

But everything I had once been was in me now, all the things I could be were there too, and everything that had happened to me had brought me to this moment. And trying to scare me was a waste of his time.

I did the first thing I thought of. I filled my lungs and I screamed, stepping at him like there were a million knives coming up out of my throat to meet him. I met his eyes and screamed fat from bone. I screamed up into his startled face, not the screams of some horror movie frail, or a terrified girl getting snatched in an alley, but screams of war, of purifying anger. He took another step forward and started to speak, and I refilled my lungs in a gulp, stepped at him further, and I screamed my blood opera into him, pushing him back, back into the corner of the room.

We all three stayed like that for a moment. Silent against the white noise of the freeway outside. I looked at my mother again. I didn't know what to say. Charles didn't move. He just stared at me.

I went back downstairs with a coppery taste in my mouth.

Later, I would wish I had done more.

Later, I would wish I had done nothing at all.

I found a packing blanket amid the boxes, threw it on the bare mattress. I remembered the screwdriver in my back pocket as it bit my ass while rolling into my makeshift bed. I slept with it, and I slept fully clothed, not that I slept well.

26

I WOKE up on the dirty mattress with a throat that felt like sandpaper. Daylight came into the room from ground floor windows near the ceiling, filtered through whatever dead grass and leaves had collected against them outside. I remembered startling awake at one point when I felt something touching my leg, only to find a little grey mouse had wandered under my blanket. It probably had fleas.

I sat up and surveyed the room, listened to the house. It didn't seem like anyone was here. The room smelled like old cardboard and things people wanted to forget. I wanted the opposite. I had gone upstairs last night burning with questions and ready to demand answers. I had grown up not knowing who my family was. My mother wore the identity of a dead woman. I didn't know how many times she had changed my name, or who it even belonged to. My past was a black box. All I had wanted to know was where I came from, and if I was truly alone.

Groggy, I began hauling on my boots. A terrified mouse launched out of my right boot toward my face; I jerked out of its way. I didn't know mice could jump so high.

My mother was waiting for me at the kitchen table when I got upstairs. She had her customary cigarette and black coffee. She was dressed in tight blue jeans and a red zip-front hoodie. I could see a sad backyard through the French doors behind her, hued cool grey in Oakland morning light.

She said, "That was quite a little stunt you pulled last night." I resisted the urge to raise my eyebrows in surprise.

The screaming had abraded my throat, sure, but my facial wounds were re-inflamed and stiff with fresh swelling. She shot me a furious, sideways look. "Who's gonna pay for that door?"

I thought, *No good deed goes unpunished.*

She took a drag, studying me. She said, "Get whatever you need, I'm taking you to the doctor."

Relief washed over me: I was finally going to a doctor. I dashed to the kitchen for bread and a cheese slice.

"Hurry up," she said, as I crammed my mouth and jogged downstairs to grab my journal, sunglasses, and cigarettes. She was getting in the car by the time I came out.

It was a dealership car, the latest silver Volkswagen Jetta. My mother drove fast and recklessly, pushing the car's limits. I wondered if she was trying to keep our time alone together to a minimum. I refused to be scared or distracted. I asked her what the photos were in the basement.

She waited a beat before answering. "Those were not for you to look at."

I tried a different tact. "Was that your Corvette?"

"Goddammit, what did you do?"

I didn't say anything. She straightened an imaginary flyaway. "I loved that car. That was my car."

"What happened to it?"

"I totaled it on 880. Before you were born. No one could believe I just walked away. But no one could believe a girl drove that car like I did. They looked surprised every time I got out of it at Stanford. Split rear window."

She pulled into the medical center parking lot. "You know, one of those photos is your father."

"What?"

"Remember that guitar? That was his."

The memory of the acoustic guitar came back in a rush while my mother parked the car, but my brain hijacked it to wonder what happened to it. Did she sell it?

She turned off the car and turned to look at me. I searched her face for bruising or swelling and found none. Then she told me my father's name, and it was the one on the dog tag I stole from her boxes at Donna's house. "He came to see you after you were born. At your grandmother's house. He just stood over you, you were a little baby in your crib, and he cried and cried. Then he left."

My mind exploded with questions. "Why did he leave? Was my grandmother, was she the blonde one in the photos?"

"Come on," she was already out of the car. I struggled to keep up with her through the parking lot. She told me my grandmother's name. "But that's not her real name. My dad died in the war. She remarried into a family that didn't want me. Did you know that?" Her tone was acid, bitter. I didn't know what to say. But then, I wasn't sure what to believe. She told me, "My mother married a Coppola. Your great aunt was Edith Head. You're Nick Cage's cousin, not that it matters."

I followed her across the parking lot, completely speechless. I thought that had to be the craziest thing she'd ever said to me. We got inside the lobby, and I was dizzy. I worried she was telling her stories again, the ones woven from facts, but took you in a direction away from the truth to distract you from whatever parts she didn't like.

I asked her again, "Why did my father leave?"

"I don't know," she said. "He was real messed up. He just said he had to go and he left you."

I didn't believe her, and I started formulating questions to try and get at what really happened. I wasn't ready to stop this conversation but now we stood at the medical center's admissions desk.

Like lights flooding a dark room, my mother shifted into her car sales charm. "Kid had a run-in with a mean dog," she smiled to the nurse. "Poor kid," she ruffled my mohawk. I hated it when she did that. I quickly smoothed my hair back into place.

The nurse looked at me, waiting. My mother jingled her car keys.

"It was a couple days ago," I said.

The nurse said, "Okay, well..." She pulled out a clipboard and small stack of papers, and handed them to my mother. "Let's get her looked at." She told us the wait time, and we sat. My mother filled out paperwork, and I wondered what she wrote. I realized I should ask her about my medical history; I didn't know anything about it.

Because we have rules about talking in public about anything, I asked if she'd go outside for a cigarette with me. Uncharacteristically, she said no. "We can talk later," she assured me.

Years later as an adult, I'd track down the woman who was my grandmother. She and her husband, whose last name was indeed Coppola, had retired to eastern California to run a drive-in diner. The woman told me that yes, my great aunt was Edith Head. She also said my mother had lied to me about my father, that my mother told my father to leave and never come back, and no one knew why. My grandmother then told me she and her husband had lived for years with the peace of having disowned my mother. Then she told me to never, ever contact them again.

Many years after that, I'd get a copy of my father's Navy records and discover that my mother married my father when she was already married to someone else. My father discovered this during his service as a nuclear engineer, finding out his marriage was a lie when the US government told him the marriage was annulled.

I probably had an inkling of all this as we sat in the lobby. My mother nodded when the nurse called me, and then I followed a little woman in scrubs down a long hall into a numbered room. She weighed me, took my blood pressure and temperature. My entire body sighed in relief when I saw I didn't have a temperature. We struggled past the inevitable moment of awkwardness when I'm asked about my family health history, and allergies or shots, and I tell them the truth: I have no idea. She left. I sat on the crinkly paper-covered bed and dangled my feet.

A few minutes later an even smaller person came in, a man about my height with dusky skin, wild salt and pepper hair, and dark lashes that framed twinkling ebony eyes. He appraised me.

"That poor dog," he said.

It was that moment when you haven't smiled in so long you wonder if you've ever smiled, and you're just smiling. I was so glad to talk to someone with a sense of humor. I tilted my head back. "It was ruff," I deadpanned.

He smiled, warm eyes meeting mine. "Oh, now I see what we're working with here." Looking at a clipboard he added, "Is there anything you want to talk about?"

I said, "No, it's not like that." I added, "It sucks, but no."

He set the clipboard down and gently put a finger under my chin to tilt my head, saying: "Okay, well if you change your mind, it stays between us."

He looked me over, and he called me One Eyed Jack, and I really, really liked him. So, I felt comfortable telling him that I didn't have any money and might not make it back for a follow-up. He didn't miss a beat, saying: "I'll send you out with a few things, but you come back and see me no matter what, okay?"

"Do I need to?"

"I don't think so." He explained that I was really, really lucky the dog's teeth had broken my skin but nothing further. "Your eye is inflamed," he said, "and I want you to keep the swelling down."

He left and came back with an ice compress, some pills for me to take now, and a pack of antibiotics. "These are just in case," he said. "Now, is there anything else you want to talk about?"

I shook my head no, wishing I could tell him everything. I knew that doing so would somehow end up with me placed with Child Protective Services, or arrested, or both.

"Thank you for being so nice to me," I blurted out. I felt like I wanted him to know I could see he was trying to make a difference.

To my surprise, he hugged me. It was, I guess, a fatherly hug. That was new. I bear hugged him in return. "Here," he reached into a coat pocket and handed me a business card. "Alright, you're free to go."

"I don't get an eye patch?" I joked as he hustled me out of the room.

I walked out to find my mother's seat empty.

The admissions nurse said, "You can wait here while someone comes to get you if you like."

"Wait. Where's my mom?"

"Your mom?" she looked confused. "The woman who brought you left when you went in to see the doctor. Was that your mother?"

I didn't answer and went out to the parking lot. Her car was gone. I started shaking, willed myself to get it under control.

I took a deep breath and walked back into the medical center lobby. Faking calm, I asked the nurse, "Did she say she was coming back?" I willed myself to ignore the fact that my voice was too high.

"I don't think she said anything," she told me. Concern furrowed her forehead. "Is there someone you can call?"

Good question, I thought. I held the cold pack to my face and racked my brain. If I had been in San Francisco, I could just walk out the door and figure my next move as I went. But over here in the East Bay I didn't know where I was, I didn't know Oakland at all. My mother just ditched me at a medical center. I felt unmoored. I took a deep breath. I had to think fast and stay cool.

I asked her, "Can I use your phone?"

"Of course," the nurse was now visibly distressed. Another nurse joined her. They both looked worried and confused.

I paged through my journal while doing a panicked run through the rolodex in my brain, thinking, *who do I know over here (no one), okay, who has a car, who has a car ...*

Bozie.

I called Bozie.

I masked a physical rush of relief when he answered. "Bozie! Hey! I know this is random, but ..." I turned away from the nurses and told him I needed a pickup and that I would totally owe him one, like big time.

"You wouldn't believe your timing," he told me. He said he was on his way.

I didn't want the nurses to call the cops on me or

anything, so I told them my ride was coming and I'd wait outside.

Fuck this, I thought as I looked at all the shiny cars in the parking lot. Fuck her, fuck going home, fuck fuck fuck. The cars were all nice. I needed to get back to people who gave a shit about me. Where I was safer. But dammit, the rest of my stuff was still at her house. I'd have to go back and not be too mad, so I could get in, get my stuff, and just get out.

I waited for Bozie and counted the Mercedes. The BMWs. Expensive sedans, I didn't know what those were, so they didn't count. I squatted against a concrete wall and held the cold pack to my eye. This was a white, rich-in-the-hills part of Oakland. I hoped no one would call security on me for loitering.

A white Porsche pulled up to the curb. Ugh. I looked away. *Ignore me*, I thought, *ignore the little scumbag*, I willed the people in the car. I wished I was invisible.

The car honked. I gave it a look. A bleach-blonde head bobbed up and down in the driver's seat, waving at me. What the hell?

Bozie rolled down the passenger window. "Your chariot!" He grinned. "Your chariot arrives!"

I jumped up and ran to the car. "Holy shit Bozie!" I lowered my voice, fumbling with the door handle. "Did you steal this?"

He laughed, "No! This belongs to a ... hairdresser." That last part was downright sheepish.

I slid into the car's soft leather interior. "Wow," I marveled. I'd never been in a Porsche before. "Wait, what hairdresser?"

"Um," he pulled out of the parking lot. "It's this older woman I'm kind of ..."

"No way!"

"Oh, way. Marina." He meant the Marina District in San Francisco, indicating she was from the old-money, conservative side of town that was so different from the rest of San Francisco we pretty much considered it a separate city. LA by the Bay. He said, "She's pretty cool. Lets me drive her car."

"Dude, this is awesome. Thank you. Thank you, you brazen hussy."

"Well, it'll make up for something else." Bozie went on to explain that everyone was going to be really mad at him, but he'd gotten a job. Not just a job, but that he was a security guard. For the bank at Harvey Milk Plaza.

"Wait, what?"

"Yeah, they want to keep panhandlers away from the bank. I'm sorry, I really need the job."

"Huh," I rolled this over in my mind. Already scheming. Maybe I could find out what days they didn't have security, and the magic bench could still be magic for us, just not every day. I eyed Bozie as he drove. He was such a good guy. And he was so ... he looked great, like all the time. He bit his lip, worried about what I'd say next, and he was the nicest thing I'd seen in days with all his interesting boy angles. Damn Johnny Perfect. Gotta watch that, I thought. Friends last longer.

"Bozie -- wait. I need to go back and get my stuff."

We managed to navigate back along the freeway to Rifle Lane. The street's name was not lost on Bozie one bit.

The driveway was empty.

"You want me to come with you?"

"Sure," I said. I was so glad Bozie was with me.

No one answered the door. Bozie said, "What do we do now?"

I thought for a minute. I asked him, "Do you have a card, like an ID or a bank card I can borrow?"

He pulled out his wallet before his better sense kicked in. "What are you doing?"

"Come on," I grabbed his ID and cut out toward the back of the house. We got to the French doors on the back deck. I slid the card into the latch, muttering under my breath. "It's a little trick mom taught me."

"Fuck," Bozie exclaimed as I wiggled the card and popped the door open. "Can you teach me how to do that?"

"Yes, absolutely," I grinned. The house was empty. Still, I didn't want Dee to show up and get the wrong idea. I told Bozie, "Maybe you should go wait in the car right now."

I ran downstairs to grab my bag. The room was so gloomy it took my eyes a second to adjust. I found my pilfered stack of photos and stuffed them in my bag as I took the stairs up two at a time.

I stopped at the back door. Then I went back.

My first stop was my mother's bedroom. The Beretta was in its box, under the bed like always. I ejected its heavy bullets into my hand. They were hollow-points, made to explode in a person rather than travel through. My mom was an idiot, but I didn't want her dead or going to jail for murder. I put the bullets in my pocket, left the clip out to show it wasn't loaded, and went back down to the garage, my final stop. I found the last box, dug out the leopard skull, and stuffed it into my bag.

Bozie made the Porche's tires squeal when we peeled off Rifle Lane. The house seemed to get bigger in the side mirror as we got further away. I was so glad to be going back home.

27

BOZIE and his housemates let me stay on their couch for a couple of days. Their Upper Haight apartment had the kind of baked-in disrepair that old railcar-style San Francisco Victorian flats seemed to hold a trademark in; ratty carpets, peeling kitchen and bathroom linoleum, dirty walls covered in punk band, comic book, and Klimt posters, windows and lamps draped in craft store black lace and Indian patterned fabric.

A large fish tank along one wall containing a very friendly boa constrictor named Medusa kept the living room warm, where I slept on the couch. Bozie's housemates included a Satanist stripper, a vegan Industrial Workers of the World organizer who worked at an organic food store, and a raver hairdresser, who all shared the flat. If I played it right and didn't overstay my welcome, I hoped I might convince Bozie and his housemates to let me come stay one day a week.

Everyone at Bozie's thought the leopard skull in my bag was really cool, but I needed somewhere safe to put it. I called Ashley and asked if she'd meet me in the Haight.

I hadn't been back to Cafe Mimic yet. I decided to stay close to Bozie's place in the Haight while I could crash there, panhandling, hustling food, and seeing friends in the neighborhood.

Some of the 'zine scene Kinko's dwellers had couches I could crash on, for a night at least, in their Fulton Victorians and Haight apartments. There was even a house full of hackers who welcomed me in the "goth ghetto" -- a violent neighborhood that gentrifying real estate agents would later rename "NOPA." Couches were gold in a city where I had to wait in line for the chance just to make reservations (at a later time!) for one-night shelter beds. Which I really needed since I had no ID, no address to get one with, and a warrant out for my arrest.

Being in the Haight helped me feel centered; its familiar places and people whittled down the hurt my mother left in me. Comic Relief held friendly faces, a few bucks for some poetry books I'd sold, and the happiness of new comics they let me read in the store. It was tempting to trade my chapbook earnings for a copy of *Stray Toasters*. In these worlds, evil occupied the packaging of normalcy and could only be destroyed by its victims, who could smell poisonous intent oozing from the corrupted. If there was anything I could relate to, it was the way the main characters sent cheery postcards from hell.

My journal absorbed me. I wrote about feeling hollow, and how my ordeal in Oakland felt, like I'd sweat out toxins at the same time. The ways I felt now was sort of like the way it feels to finally go outside after a really bad, painful fever. San Francisco's wind, cooled by the water on three sides of us, cleared the sky and sharpened me.

I was so glad to be home, even if I didn't really have one. I had a laundry list of people I needed to see in order to feel normal again. After a few days, the ebb and flux of Haight's homeless faces had turned up Big Shaun, Little Shaun, Scooter, the Jess-Lisa twins, Mark, and Aiden. The hugs were long and warm, and Mark kissed me on the forehead. But I still hadn't seen Spider, Alex, or any of the Cafe Mimic crew. I was especially jonesing to see Rogue. I'd talked to Ashley on the phone, and we made plans to meet up in the Haight after she got out of her last class of the day.

I met her at the bus stop on Ashbury. After a big hug and her inspection of my slowly healing eye, I said, "Here." I took the newspaper-wrapped skull out of my bag and handed it to her. "Can you hang on to this for me?"

"What is it?"

"A skull," I said.

"Ew!" Ashley shouted and for a skipped heartbeat I watched her hot-potato the package.

"Don't drop it!"

"I won't! But ...whose is it?" She grinned. "Is it one of your enemies?"

"No dingleberry," I smiled back. "Buy me a sandwich at Blue Front? I'll tell you all about it."

"You know I love going places with you." She loved teasing me about the way we looked together. The joke was that I was embarrassed to be seen by my cool punk rock friends with a blonde cheerleader, a "normal" person.

I whined, "But you never hold my haa-aand." She took my arm, and we walked close like that to the deli. I think she loved the way we seemed like opposites. Ashley wasn't in uniform that day, but still looked the cheerleader part in white tennies, bouncy long blond hair, and some guy's football jacket. Poor lucky jerk, I thought.

My chest tightened when we got to the Blue Front Cafe. Three skinhead girls lingered out front. One of them was Sarah.

Ashley straightened her shoulders as we stepped to the door.

Sarah said to me as we passed, "See you at the cafe. Bitch." My blood froze.

Chivalrously, Ashley held the door open for me while she glared daggers at Sarah. But this was bad news. Skinheads ruined everything because they could, and if they'd found the cafe ...

Ashley asked me, "Did she mean that cafe you go to, with all the art?"

"Yeah," I said. "Shit, I need to warn them."

The Blue Front's smells greeted me like an old friend, a mixture of coffee, chai, falafel, hummus, and toasting bagels. Its layout reminded me of a San Francisco apartment. Most tables were in the center and side of the room; at the back its deli-style counter displayed Middle Eastern salads and dishes like a museum of delicious objects. Its old wood paneling felt cozy. Its creaky wooden chairs with torn vinyl seats were a warm cup of comfort in rundown Upper Haight.

We ate falafels and I told Ashley about my horror show in Oakland, as well as being ditched at the medical center by my mother. My story of sleeping with mice grossed her out. I fleetingly wondered why it didn't bother me as much.

After a moment of thoughtful silence Ashley said, "You can't go back there." We looked at each other across the table. "Ever."

I didn't know what to say. She added, "I guess some part of me wanted you to work it out with her. I'm sorry. I didn't get it."

"It's okay." I knew she had something I could never understand, with her home that never changed, and even having both parents around -- a rarity for anyone I knew. It made sense to me that she thought everyone should just have a mom. I didn't even know how to be a daughter.

"Do you think," I asked her, hesitating, "do you think

your mom would let me stay with you guys one day a week?" An idea was forming.

"Hmmm," she nodded, narrowing her eyes. "Clever, clever girl."

She said she'd try to make it happen. We finished our falafels. I had to get to the cafe, find Rogue, and warn everyone about the skinheads. Joey would know how to handle it. The skin girls were gone when we walked out and hugged goodbye. I kept my relief to myself. I wanted to avoid trading blows with anyone until my eye was better. I knew Ashley could handle herself in a fight, but I knew that if those girls tried to lay a hand on Ashley, I'd bring down the sky to protect her.

I hopped on the 71 bus to SOMA. The bus took forever to halt and belch its way down to Market Street.

The bus was nearly empty. One of the L-shaped seat clusters held two girls and a guy dressed in a way I'd never seen before. Their giant backpacks were covered in some kind of tightly-packed scrawl written in white ink pen, and their bags took up extra seats around them. I noticed all three seemed to be dressed the same, in black, with scarves covering the women's heads. They caught me looking, but I thought, *whatever*.

My peripheral vision was interrupted when one of the girls sat next to me. I cringed, not wanting to talk to anyone. I scowled at her. The other girl sat behind me.

The girl sitting next to me said, "Hey."

I gave her a nod. "Hey." I went back to looking out the window, pulling my bag closer in my lap.

"How are you today?" she asked.

I ignored her.

"I mean, how's life going for you?" She said. "I think we're all fellow travelers here."

I sighed inside.

"Have you eaten today?" she asked.

"I don't really feel like talking, thanks."

"Well, I just want to make sure you're okay," she smiled. "Not everyone needs a home when they have a light to guide the way."

The girl behind me said, "Can you pray with us right now?" I turned around to scowl at her and noticed her jacket was covered in the same ink-pen handwriting as their bags. She smiled at me. "We have food," she added. "Jesus gives us so much when we give him ourselves."

Cults fascinated me, but that didn't mean I wanted to talk to people in them. I really didn't like being cornered by the same refrain I felt like I got when the soup kitchen asked if I was hungry but just wanted a little piece of my soul in trade. To some god I was pretty sure I didn't believe in, because it sure seemed like the same god who was glad my friends were dying of AIDS. I shook my head at her while I thought about this. I was thinking I didn't like this god, who prayed on the weak and hungry. Which isn't to say that I hadn't thought about higher powers and fate. People who think those of us that aren't religious don't have a complicated relationship with faith are wrong. We do. But then there were these fools.

I glanced at the guy, he was watching us intently, then I looked back to the woman behind me. I stood up, shouldering my bag. I told her, "I just can't see myself worshiping a man." Then I began moving to the front of the bus.

Out of the corner of my eye, both girls went back to their

previous seats, talking to their male companion in low voices. The bus had finally got to Seventh Street. *Methadone alley*, I thought.

Then the singing started.

The women had conferred with their ... boss? Manager? Jesus pimp? And now they sat behind me singing some religious song.

If they were trying to expel something they considered unholy, it was working. I decided to take the next stop and jetted out the door. I felt relief that they didn't try to follow me, but it was a concern. I jogged all the way to the cafe, and started to smile to myself about what Rogue and Zeke's reactions would be to my story about the singing Jesus freaks.

I thought I somehow had the wrong address when I got to the cafe and its door was shut. It was the afternoon, so why weren't they open? It had been almost a week since I'd been in, but it felt like a year had passed. I banged on the building's double-doors. The street was quiet. I didn't like it.

I called out, "Frank! Joey?" I was about to start wandering in a circle in the alley when the cafe's door cracked open.

Frank's large, bespectacled form filled the doorway, his pale eyes blinked in the light. He pulled me into a hug faster than I could ask what was going on. Something was wrong, my intuition was screaming, my breath felt short. "What's going on," I said, my voice muffled in Frank's massive, aproned belly.

"Honey," Frank moved to hold my face in his hands. Joey came up behind him.

It was now that I noticed Frank's eyes were bloodshot, puffy.

"Zeke," his voice broke, and Joey finished for him. "Zeke hung himself."

I'd been thrown into an icy lake. Is this what it feels like to pass out, I wondered. Frank walked me inside while Joey closed and locked the door behind us. "You were gone, and we were so scared," Joey said, embracing both of us. Frank was crying.

"What?" I couldn't understand anything.

"It's okay if you need to go away sometimes. It's okay. But please." It was Frank. "Just tell us so we know you're alive. Just tell us."

My attention went to an island, this place I'd never seen before, where these two men cared about me so much they were upset. I was swimming to get there, but I was also drowning.

"Zeke ... ?" *Shock, this is shock, I'm in shock.* Somehow we were now sitting on one of the cafe's couches, and I'd never seen the place closed, empty of people. Hollow. Terry came out from the back, hustling on his cane with a box of Kleenex.

"Four days ago, the boys got caught-" Frank started.

"Boys?" I asked.

"Jimmy and Zeke tried to rob a liquor store," Joey filled in. "Jimmy got away, and we have no idea where he is."

"Zeke hung himself in his cell," Frank said gently.

"Where ... oh my god, where is Rogue?" I practically screamed.

Joey said, "We don't know. No one can find her."

28

PAISLEY LOOKED MORE INTIMIDATING in street clothes than her cheerleader uniform, and I was glad for it. We were at a punk show in the Potrero neighborhood, outside a warehouse under two freeway onramps. Inside it was hot and muggy; at the side of the building where we stood the air was frigid with thick, wet fog.

We were a search team for Rogue. Mark's band was playing inside; he'd had the idea for us to canvas the show asking if anyone had seen her. Paisley had come along because she was now a Cafe regular -- thanks to Ashley. After the skinhead girls tried to intimidate us in Upper Haight, Ashley decided her scary cheerleading buddies had a new location for after-school homework. I was definitely not going to argue with Ashley. I'd have an easier time draining the Bay than changing her mind once it was set.

I wasn't really in the state to construct a cohesive argument. At any given moment my insides felt like the top of a roller coaster, or a gravitational singularity pulling everything into an impossibly heavy weight. I rocketed between extremes of grief, fear, panic, and anger over what had happened to Zeke, Rogue, and Jimmy while I was in Oakland.

I did have the sense to ask Ashley what the hell she was doing, in a nice way. The four cheerleaders had walked into the Cafe, spread out their homework, and settled in like it was their own. Ashley's answer was about the skinhead girls: "If they're not afraid of you, then they should be afraid of your friends." Once I saw how smitten Frank and Joey were with Lincoln High's toughest femmes, it was already decided anyway.

Now Paisley and I shivered in foggy cold outside a shitty punk club called "The Farm." The club was in a compound of similar chock-a-block, roughly assembled warehouses circling a deeply sunk parking lot at its center that flooded like a toilet when it rained. Mark's band played inside. As much as I wanted to go back inside to watch him yell, sweat, and work up the moshing crowd, Paisley and I were on a mission.

The Farm's compound sat in confluence of neighborhood badness. Its barbed wire fence bordered a public park that was a gang territory battle line. Two blocks away was San Francisco General Hospital. At the top of the compound was a public garden that had been farmed by city hippies who neglected to put in lights. A building at the far side of the warehouses, under the freeway's on- and off-ramps, was a notorious chop shop that blended into concrete pillars and homeless encampments. It was where the copper thieves lived with their shopping carts. On the hill behind us sat a set of housing projects with a reputation so violent that I didn't know anyone who'd go up there during the day.

This is where Paisley and I had come to continue our search for Rogue. My world had been shattered, again. The pain of Zeke's hanging and the absence he left colored everything I looked at. When people die, they really take a piece of you with them. It would be several years and many more deaths until I'd come to understand that this missing piece is okay; it's theirs to keep wherever they are. That they live forever because I remember them, and I bring them with me everywhere I go. But it would take a very long time for me to not feel frustrated by grief, so mercurial, which only stops when you suddenly notice it just doesn't hurt anymore.

I wasn't there yet. Everyone was sad. Jimmy was still missing too, but it was Rogue I was freaked out about. Her other half was gone, and then she'd vanished in a moment of what must've been pure pain. And I wasn't there for her.

I stood next to Paisley and thought about the last time I saw Rogue. She was playing house in a kitchen with Zeke. We were in the Upper Haight mansion, and I was preoccupied with holding a towel to my bleeding face, laughing and doing shots with Mark and Jess.

I had to find Rogue. Three days is a long time. We'd looked everywhere. I felt like everything I did was wasted energy if it wasn't somehow part of the search.

When I panhandled, I asked if people had seen Rogue. Aiden and I went to stores and cafes in the Haight and asked anyone working to look out for her. Bozie was our eyes in the Castro at his new post guarding the bank. Alex chatted up her needle exchange "clients" and talked to people when she did outreach to give away free condoms and distribute HIV test information. Spider went to shelters, clinics, and homeless outreach spots in the Tenderloin, including the church Glide. Jess kept an eye out in the Mission when she turned tricks.

I called Officer Lopez. He made me aware of one problem. No one knew Rogue's legal name or her family. It was the same for all of us, though: It was taboo to ask each other in the first place, dangerous to know or share. Our names were a vital, and sometimes last, line of defense against people who would hurt us, drag us back to hell.

Plus, names and family information were too painful. You just didn't ask. You gave a person back their autonomy and their ownership of themselves by using the name and gender they told you. When someone tells you who they are, you believe them. For most, it was the only kind of respect as a human being they got. So, there was a lot I didn't know. Officer Lopez promised he'd keep an eye out anyway.

Mark went everywhere else with me. We visited all the homeless tribes in the city we could find. The violent punks on Market and Powell, where Dido's Liquors sold to anyone (we called it "Dildo's") and fist fighting was a sport. I traded blows with a few girls to earn respect so they talked to me. I stopped caring about fear after that, and didn't hesitate to approach skins to ask if they'd seen Rogue. After a couple leering skin boys said I should fuck them to find out, Mark started holding my hand when we approached groups of men.

We went through the Tenderloin a few times, talked to amputee homeless veterans while they panhandled, checked with a few kids we knew doing sex work on Polk Street, and asked around the Ambassador Hotel -- a flop for homeless addicts run by trans women who were the block's mother hens. I told Mark I didn't care if we found her high, hooking, or whatever. Just as long as we found her.

We ventured into the Haight's abandoned Polytechnic High School on Frederick Street, nicknamed "the mansion on Parnassus." This was one place I'd never sleep in, no matter how desperate. Polytech squat was one of the roughest hellholes for homeless in the city. The building had once been a beautiful Art Deco masterpiece of sweeping, sharp-edged columns and stylized geometric decorative details. Even in its decay the building managed to evoke Fritz Lang's *Metropolis*. Rumor had it that the school was shuttered for asbestos.

Inside it looked like a mental asylum in a horror film, lit in places only with candles. The school's warren of hallways was confusing, though Mark knew its tricks, and I let him lead us past closed doors, walls streaked with filth and cratered with holes. The whole place smelled like a dead man's shoe -- one that had stepped in feces. We wound through a dark maze of human rats' nests, room after room of ruin that reeked of urine, rotten boots, spilled beer, garbage, and worse. Since there was no plumbing, the squat had designated "shit rooms."

All we found were lazy junkies, crazy hippies with leathery voices and skin, a handful of resigned gutter punks I mostly recognized, and a couple skinheads trying to start a party, aggressively crushing beer cans when they saw us. It was the most hopeless place I'd ever been. But still, no Rogue.

The punk club I was at with Paisley was coming up dry, too. I was glad for Paisley's help, even though she tried to beat me up when we first met. I couldn't figure out why she wanted to be my friend, but I was so sad about Rogue that I just went with it.

We left the cafe together, on one of the extra-long MUNI buses, which Paisley called "the shame train." It was the first time we'd gotten a chance to talk, just us. She asked me point-blank about being homeless. The way she asked, kindly and privately, didn't make me feel like a freak show. Next thing I knew we were comparing favorite authors, and I could tell she was a writer. Maybe just not ready to talk about it yet, but a writer all the same. She was really into *Vampire Lestat*, and told me that Anne Rice wrote that book in a Victorian on Divisadero between Upper and Lower Haight. Basically, the neighborhood where I sort of "lived."

I knew right where that was. I thought that was so cool. For no reason, I told Paisley: "I saw a shootout there one night. Two cars just driving slow down Divis, one going the wrong way, both just shooting at each other like in slow motion."

Paisley looked at me sideways and said, "Shit just follows you around, don't it?"

When she put it that way, I was feeling more and more like I was cursed. "Yeah, that's me," I told her. "Like some fucked up lightning rod."

We smoked, watching groups of well-heeled punks avoid our eye contact while leaning against The Farm's weathered exterior. The music scene punks looked down on us street punks and I could feel it. Punk was comprised of many tribes and these shows were where they all intersected in a who's-who social clique centered around a 'zine called *Maximum Rock 'n Roll*. A lot of those punks had cars they trashed to look cool, nice homes they pretended not to have, and money to spend on looking perfect. It reminded me of the high schools I never went to.

I didn't have anything against them. I had just become more aware of what to expect. Trying to talk to punks at these shows about Rogue just made the differences between punk's social classes more distinct to me. I didn't understand why outsiders had to go and start their own pecking orders, and create more outsiders to step up on. Plus, the dynamics of all these white kids not having the time for Paisley was starting to piss me off.

Paisley looked perfect for a punk show. She wore jeans and a black jacket. Tonight, she'd put on a black D.A.R.E. To Keep Kids Off Drugs t-shirt and glossy purple lipstick. Her short natural hair accented her high hairline. I felt like a little boy-girl in comparison. She looked so pretty it sort of made me feel left out.

The way they treated us hung in the air like a bad smell, which is how Paisley and I ended up outside with my cigarettes and her cloves. We'd talked to as many of these assholes as we could and came up with nothing.

The *pop-pop-pop* of gunfire snapped us to attention. It came from behind the fence next to the club. Paisley and I dropped to the ground, not caring about rocks ground into my palms, wetness through the knees of my jeans. We stared at each other for a heartbeat. She said, "You okay?"

I nodded yes, and we looked around the compound's lot. A group of coiffed punks stood a few feet away, oblivious.

Paisley called to them, "Down! Get down!" We looked at each other again in disbelief. The smokers either didn't hear the gunshots over the music, didn't hear Paisley yelling, or didn't care.

The three girls glanced at us. We'd interrupted their chatter with two guys in baggy chinos with skateboards drinking something out of a paper bag. One cherry-redheaded girl in a crew cut wore a fake fur leopard coat that went to her knees, ending at the tops of shiny black boots covered with silver buckles. A shorter girl with black and purple Betty Page hair stood with her hands on her hips, no coat, in a tight little black dress over a ripped fishnet bodysuit. A very tall blonde woman with perfect Egyptian eyeliner regarded me over their heads.

They lost interest in half a second.

Paisley watched them, but said to me: "Fuck this." Her face was disbelief mixed with anger.

"Yep," I agreed.

Paisley took my arm as we stood up, "C'mon."

"We're done here anyway," I told her.

"Besides," she remarked, "they got what, like four Black people in the club?"

I narrowed my eyes, deadpanning, "You saw *four*?"

She clicked her tongue at me, smiling, and pulled a fresh clove from her pack. "Gimme a light."

Looking for my lost Black friend with another Black friend in a very white scene that thought it was subversive felt like madness. My friend was missing, and she was Black, and so the cops wouldn't give a shit. And really, neither would any of the girls at The Farm with perfectly dyed hair posing as outsiders, otherwise their scene would be diverse and actually challenge any status quo because they'd actually have some Black friends. They'd know what it was like to love a friend and feel her go on alert for self-protection at shows like this -- beyond that of simply presenting as female. The more I looked around, the more annoyed I got with everyone.

The club's door opened and a torrent of sweaty, energized suburban punks poured out. A very sweaty Mark came bouncing over to Paisley and me. He asked us, "Any luck?"

Paisley said, "Nah, we're through."

I said, "We just heard a bunch of gunshots over in the park."

"Yikes and fuck," Mark said. "What now?"

Paisley stubbed out her clove cigarette with her heel and said, "I gotta get home. I'm an actual schoolgirl, you know."

Mark offered us an elbow each. "I shall escort the ladies safely to the nearest bus stop." Smiling, Paisley and I hooked our elbows with Mark's and started walking toward Potrero Street.

Everyone at the bus stop was bathed in a sallow yellow glow under the sodium streetlights. We waited. Mark put his hands on my shoulders from behind, and I got a tingly feeling behind my ears. He leaned close and said, "Where are you crashing?"

"I ... I don't know yet," I realized as I said it that I hadn't really let myself think about that. Every time I thought about where I was going to sleep, I wanted to cry. I couldn't go to the Kinko's roof anymore.

"Hey," Mark turned me around. "Stay with me."

I looked at Mark standing there, smiling at me. Short brown hair, sparkling almond eyes, toffee skin, Ben Davis work pants and a black Derby jacket over his Social Distortion t-shirt. He'd always been there, right next to me. I smiled too, and he knew I was saying yes in the way that two people being pulled toward each other just do. The bus pulled up and we said goodbye to Paisley, who gave me a hug, a smile, and an excellent eyebrow raise that told me I'd have some explaining to do later. Fingers intertwined, Mark and I walked toward Bernal Hill, a pocket of suburbs in the city where his mom lived.

Mark lived in an in-law apartment behind his mother's two-story house above Precita Park, which we all called "Patty Hearst park" -- it was where the heiress was apprehended by police after a short chase. His mom's house was dark. Mark cautioned me to be quiet as he undid a gate latch into the backyard. We walked along the side of the house in shadows until we reached a door.

"It's just a room and bath," he said. "But I'll get kicked out if she knows I brought anyone over."

There was little more than a bed in the small space. A collection of books, albums, tapes, and CDs were scattered around the floor; a side table had a glass of water. His bed was pushed up against a window that overlooked a small backyard.

"My dad lives in New Zealand," Mark explained. "They don't get along. She kind of ... doesn't want me here."

I took my bag off and set it on the floor. "Can I take a shower?"

"Yes!" his face opened in a giant smile. "I'll go after you."

When I came out of the tiny bathroom in a towel, Mark was fussing with something by the bed. "I snuck in and got us this," he beamed. By the bed was a bottle of wine, two glasses, and a box of cookies. "You can start," he blushed.

He showered while I changed into panties and one of Mark's t-shirts from the floor. It smelled like boy, was worn into his angles, and I liked that. I plopped on the bed and grabbed a book. It was *A People's History Of The United States* by Howard Zinn, which is a giant book and not casual reading at all, and tried to look relaxed and occupied when he came out in a towel. I was so nervous I was reading the same line over and over.

"Got yer light reading on, eh?" He was grinning.

I was embarrassed. I didn't know what to say. Mark sat on the bed next to me, poured two glasses of wine, and handed me one. His hands were shaking.

"Here's to you wearing my clothes," he clinked my glass. "Just don't steal 'em, I don't have a lot."

"I won't, I promise," I said. It felt like the stupidest thing I ever said in the history of people saying things. I *wanted* to steal his clothes. I loved the way he dressed. But I wanted to steal them, so he'd be part of me, so I'd never be without this feeling.

"Nah, I don't care." After a moment he said, "Can I ... can I kiss you?"

I set the glass down and moved my hand to his face, traced the bones at his cheeks, down his jaw. I squared to him, sitting there on the edge of the bed, and touched his lips with both hands, my fingertips following the curve of his mouth and back up to his temples, outlining the sockets of his eyes. His entire body relaxed then; he closed his eyes and exhaled. I brought my hands back behind his ears and into his damp hair, relishing the feel of him, his textures.

Mark opened his eyes and said, "Now you."

His fingertips came to rest on my jawline and his thumbs traced the bottom curve of my lips. I closed my eyes. I sensed that I was floating in a timeless place as he found invisible patterns on my face along my eyebrows, my hairline, gently traced my third eye. I opened my eyes and he smiled. I smiled back. We moved our smiles closer until our lips barely touched, not kissing, just breathing each other in and out. His hands held the back of my head, but I knew they were really there to stop me from falling into the endless night forever.

We kissed, and it was gentle, sweet. It was peace. It was trust. We became hotter very quickly; his hands graced my back, my waist, my hips. I found the muscles along his back and the line of his spine, blanketed stones in soft skin. I wrapped my legs around him and we arched together, pressing against each other, finding healing and the sustenance of joy between lovers, somewhere in the hollows of each other's throats and in each other's eyes, and all other thoughts were lost in smiles, kisses, sweat, and moonlight breaking the fog through a small garden window.

29

THE SUN STREAKED a bloody pallor on the San Francisco Bay's calm mirror as it rose behind the Oakland hills. I watched light creep forward, sparking in little glints off commuter cars in their mechanical trudge over the Bay Bridge. I stood on the edge of Pier 33 outside a half abandoned industrial warehouse space used only in part by fishing boats. But not the side I was on. I could hear men shouting on the other side of the old structure, through the corrugated metal walls, over a din of machinery and the beep of a reversing forklift. You had to be careful where you stepped here. The floorboards were soft. Fish guts and oily rot permeated the air.

I looked at the bullets in my hand. Hollow-points, "stopping power." Good 'ol mom.

I rewound the tape in an old-fashioned Walkman Mark gave me before he left, thinking, I need to start from the beginning, again.

Mark and I were never more than two steps from each other unless he had band practice or a check-in with his mom. When he'd pull me close for no reason at all, the nape of his soft neck smelled like safety and sea salt, and other good things that were at once familiar and foreign to me on some instinctive level. I snuck home with him every night. His capacity for bad jokes was terrible and fantastic. I was falling into him, it was scary, and I consumed every minute like stolen candy.

There had been a few days where I thought things might

be okay. We couldn't find Rogue. Zeke was gone forever. Jimmy was still missing. Our tribe had settled into a resigned gloom. The terrible things that happened to each of us were still happening. Same playlist, a different song.

I felt cursed. My friends felt cursed. The city was cursed. People were dying all around us like some great Catherine Wheel of AIDS rapidly draining San Francisco's population. The streets had less people on them than just a few years ago, and I could see it. Especially at night. My friends and I roamed neighborhoods emptied of hundreds, going on thousands of people taken indoors, and then away, by the plague. The effects of the federal government's public health abandonment of San Francisco were everywhere. The weight of it threaded through the neighborhoods, hid among the ancient redwoods, seeped into the landfill under homes.

And here we were, growing up in it. Invisible, forgotten, hated, alone, begging for food, but wide awake. While blobby tourists munched baguettes and bought Ghirardelli chocolate, Trustafarians played hacky sack on Hippie Hill, and the complacent hid in mindless TV shows that told them how to think, how to ignore the suffering within and without. We grew up under terror of nuclear annihilation and slept in empty schools with shit-rooms while our mayor stuffed his pockets with money.

At Mark's urging, I started up a D&D game to get everyone back together. I got my players together on the cafe's corner couches. Frank and Joey were delighted we got the game going again. We were absent Joe and Rogue, but we hammered out new characters with John Gone, Aiden, Bozie, little Jess, and to my surprise, occasionally Paisley, who I worked in as a teleporting Swamp Witch.

With Zeke gone, there was a new punk boy working the

counter, a runaway named David. Pale, thin, with a lock of black mohawk always down in his eyes; he had a limp that didn't slow him down and an adorable smile. He might've been around my age, maybe fifteen. He was from Hawthorne, Nevada. Hitched his way here after running away from a "reeducation" camp his redneck parents placed him in because they thought he was gay. He wasn't. It blew my mind to learn that those camps were real. He never explained the limp, and we never asked.

I got a coffee refill. David's tip jar said, "You know what they say about the size of your tip." He was perfect here.

David said, "You see Alex?" He nodded over to where Alex and Spider played gin.

Alex heard her name. Smiling, always, she stood and walked over.

I tilted my head and said, "Are you strutting."

Her round cheeks turned rosy. "What!" She feigned mock insult. "Me, just minding my business-"

I suppressed a giggle. "If you don't stop trying to look at Paisley, I'm gonna call the Creeper Cops."

"Am I that obvious?" She was so sheepish, so guilty. Alex nodded her head "yes" while saying, "Is Paisley gay, by any tiny, remote chance?"

I raised my eyebrows and looked away, pretending to suppress judgment.

"What about you and Mark," Alex derailed. Mark and I had become the group's couple in only a few days. I wore his Social Distortion t-shirt nonstop. My mouth dropped open, and she kept going. "No no, me likey, me likey. But you know, you two should come in and get tested. All the cool kids are doing it." She winked.

"Oh." I had thought about getting an AIDS test, but it was

so scary. Everyone I knew had sex with condoms because no one wanted to die, but still. I knew it was good to get tested. For my generation, an AIDS test was like the San Francisco version of patriotism. It was your duty. It showed you were a responsible community member.

"Here," she pulled a card out of her back pocket and handed it to me. "It's a drop-in, evening hours, it's in the Castro, and if you want, I can be there with you. They draw a little blood, and then it takes a week for results. Then Bob's your uncle!"

David wrinkled his face. "What does that even mean?"

"Okay," I said, "I'll do it."

On my way to get tested that evening, I went to see Bozie at his post guarding the bank. I was nervous, hyper, and I needed to see a friend. He stood tall in a rent-a-cop uniform and his signature bleach-blonde buzz cut on Castro at Market. He was red meat left at the edge of a wolf's den. I walked up out of the underground station marveling at the way men on the street nearly walked into light poles looking at him.

He smiled when he saw me. I said, "You should wear black eyeliner when you're in uniform."

He rolled his eyes. "Oh, fuck's sake."

I couldn't suppress my grin. "No, it would look hotter."

"I really don't need your help with this!"

We hugged. I told him I was about to get tested. He asked where, and what was involved, and as our conversation got going, we watched a tall Black man in a suit walk into the center of Harvey Milk Plaza, right in front of us. In one hand was a battered blue milk crate, and in the other was a megaphone.

I said, "What the fuck."

Bozie shook his head saying, "*This* fucking guy ..."

The man set his crate down and climbed up on it. He adjusted his megaphone, and began bellowing, "Romans 1:27! And likewise, also the men, leaving the natural use of the woman, burned in their lust toward one another! Men with men working that which is unseemly, and receiving in themselves that recompense of their error which was meet! AIDS is the judgement of God!"

I shouted to Bozie over the noise. "This is awful!"

Bozie said, "I know. He comes over on the 24 bus from the Baptist church on Divisadero and Haight. They sometimes come in a group and leave their shitty flyers everywhere."

I felt terrorized and mad all at once. "Aren't you going to do anything?"

Bozie folded his arms and said, "Hang on a sec."

The preacher's voice boomed. From around the bank's corner, a tall, very dark man in a strapless white dress with a wide fluffy skirt slowly walked into the plaza carrying a heavy boombox. He calmly set the boombox down opposite the man of god, and made an exaggerated show of pressing the play button.

I recognized the song's opening trill immediately. The man in white struck a pose, waiting. And loud, as loud as the preacher man, lyrics sprung the be-dressed fellow into action; he began a series of tightly choreographed and obviously well-practiced dance moves.

Madonna sang, "You must be my lucky stah." The dancer knew his moves. "Cuz you shine so bright wheh-eva you ah," the boombox blared. "Stah light. Star bright! Make everything ah-right!"

In surprise, I told Bozie, "That's just like in the video!"

He said, smiling, "The Castro is a self-filtering organism."

I left to get my AIDS test while a small Harvey Milk Plaza dance party formed. Testing was done after hours at a medical center a few blocks down Market, and Alex met me there. I could immediately tell everyone was a volunteer. There was a focus and consideration, a compassion, in every word spoken that let you know they were there because they cared. I'd never seen anything like that before. Fighters in quiet armor.

I couldn't look at the needle going into my arm. A moment later, the man drawing my blood gently said, "You can look now. All done." It wasn't as bad as I thought it would be. It was the waiting, the fear and suspense that was going to be the hardest part. Alex chatted me through the process, interjecting little hints about joining her for outreach. She kept pitching me as we said goodbye. "Hey, and if you wanna get wild, you could come with me on my rounds. It's aaaaa-wsooome, doooo iiiit." Alex was practically bouncing up and down. I gave her my best YOU CRAZY look, before breaking into a laugh. Alex giggled, a deep laugh that finished as a rumbling smoker's cough.

"Besides," she said, "We're supposed to be going in pairs. I could use the backup sometimes."

That struck me. Our family, our baby-dyke cherub was risking her life to help our communities fight to take another breath. I'd just seen it as background noise this whole time. I had to go meet Mark back at the Magic Bench, but I told her I was in, and quickly got details about meeting up for training. This would be good. I'd feel like I was doing something about it.

It was dark when I got to Bozie, who was ending his shift but said he'd wait for Mark with me. I was buzzing from adrenaline, and began telling him the test was really no big deal when we were interrupted.

"Hey!" Some guy, a drunk, wobbled his way toward us from the bars. "Hey!"

As he got closer, the shapes became recognizable. A black leather jacket, a curly black mohawk. My heart flew up into my throat.

I yelled, "Jimmy!" *He was alive, he was alive, and he was still here!* I put my arms out for a hug, and had a flash-memory of the time he found me here, scared and alone with a bruise on my face, and he got me pizza and beer. Jimmy wove a zig-zag across the sidewalk like he was avoiding invisible obstacles.

His weight fell on me when we hugged, and I almost fell. "Whoa," I said. "Oh my god, I'm so glad to see you! Everyone's gonna be so glad-"

"Huh," he pulled back, looking at Bozie like he was trying to figure out who Bozie was, and how, exactly he had just appeared next to me.

"You," Jimmy pointed at me, then at Bozie.

"Jimmy, where have you been," I went on, too excited. Jimmy leaned in at me for a kiss and miscalculated, swerving in a wide curve. I stepped back. His eyes were glazed. Jimmy blinked slowly, saying: "You shh ... come with me, baby. C'mon," he reached for me.

"No Jimmy," my heart sped up, beating hard. "I can't."

"Shht," he shook his head like he was trying to get water out of his ears. I looked at Bozie, who looked utterly confused, and back at Jimmy.

I'd read in old crime novels, books I'd borrowed from the cafe written by James Ellroy and Raymond Chandler, about guys who telegraphed their punches. I never knew what that meant until Jimmy's fist barreled a wide arc out of the night, sailing toward my face. It wasn't hard to just take a step backward, through my disbelief, which I did. Jimmy missed me by a mile, stumbling on his follow-through.

He recovered his stance. We all stood there for a second, too stunned to move.

Jimmy made an angry face at me, then turned toward the bars and wobbled back in the direction he came from.

I looked at Bozie. "Some security guard you are!"

"I'm sorry," he apologized, "I ... it was so weird."

He was right. I was vibrating on adrenaline and panic. "No, I'm sorry," I said. Hurting Bozie was stupid, it was the last thing I should've done. I pulled him into a hug repeating "I'm sorry."

Mark found us a few minutes later. He saw our faces and pulled me into a tight hug. "Are you guys okay?"

We told him what happened and shared our disbelief at the whole thing. "Fuck that guy," Mark said darkly, looking toward the bars. "God, it's the fucking night for it, eh."

That's when I felt something was wrong with Mark. "Hey, what's up?"

He looked at me, really looked into my eyes. "Mum ..."

Mark startled me, pulling away and turning to the plaza.

"FUCK!" he yelled, causing passers-by to turn toward us. "Fuck,"

Mark looked at me with tears in his eyes. "Mum is sending me back. She-" his voice cracked, "she's sending me back to live with my dad, and she just told me today, but she bought the fucking ticket a while ago. I leave day after tomorrow."

We held each other in the plaza, broken up briefly by Bozie who said, "God I'm so fucking sorry man," and the two young men held each other for a minute.

I knew from the lazy morning I spent in Mark's in-law, in between sex and eating pilfered cookies, that his Māori dad lived in New Zealand, where Mark was from. I'd traced a long scar along his forearm to the back of his hand and asked where it was from. Working in his dad's car garage, he told me. It was somewhere on a very long road outside a town, far from everything, a place Mark described as "boring as fuck" and "full of sheep."

Mark and I spent every last minute together. It felt like my heart was being ripped from my chest, a heart I thought was too broken to break anymore. We said our last goodbyes in early morning darkness, waiting for the airport shuttle in front of his mom's house in Bernal Heights. Later I'd reflect that I never did meet his mother, because she didn't bother to come out and say goodbye to Mark.

At the end, he gave me the old Walkman. "It was mum's but fuck it," he said. There was a mixtape in it. Alone, I walked down the hill and put it on.

I pressed play.

That was when I walked to the piers. I felt empty, hollowed-out, like the bullets in my hand.

30

THE SUN WAS RISING opposite of the pier where I sat, the sky a stark orange against a midnight blue continuum of water and sky. Water lapped beneath me as if it was a day like any other. It wasn't. Everything was lost. I had never felt so alone, it crushed me from the inside.

My plan was to walk to the Pacific Ocean on the other side of San Francisco. Maybe I would finally just keep walking.

The salt air along the waterfront warmed with the sun, spreading light as it rose over Oakland, fading the broken clockface moon into a blue sky. The water was calm as glass. Fat sea lions flopped around through barnacle-covered pilings as I picked my way over rotted boards back to land. The screech of gulls blended with the scree of brakes from city parking and traffic trucks pausing at trash cans along the wharf. No one else was around. I dug my hands deep into my jacket pockets to keep them warm, lowered my head, lengthened my stride, and wondered why I couldn't cry.

My favorite building poked into view through downtown's towers: Transamerica, and its soaring white deco spires, its strange mysticism, a pyramid in a city. I walked to it. The temperature dropped the deeper I got between skyscrapers, streets the sun never seemed to touch.

Office workers streamed along the sidewalk's arteries into their chambers, in suits and blazers, trailing the smell of coffee. They stepped over homeless men and women sleeping near vents, swerved around a dirt-encrusted blonde woman squatting against a building, rocking, patting her chest with one hand. I believed in that moment that the chances of me ending up like her were very, very high.

I felt held in a thick cloud of indescribable sadness. The way people treated me on the streets didn't help. With panhandling, there was no bottom to people's cruelty when they decide you're not a human being. They watched movies and TV we couldn't, and worried about the world ending. Kids like me came from the place after that. We'd been plucked from our childhoods and dropped into the future. Into the madness of adult fears. Those who blinked when we asked for change saw for a moment through the veil into what we were going through, saw that we were their worst adult fears, articulated. It made them angry. How dare we remind them of their worst fears, of entitlement's inevitable catastrophe?

Most ignored me. I was used to being regarded as invisible by now. Their occasional eye contact was blinked away as a mistake. Now that I had nothing left, I finally understood why they wouldn't look at me.

At the base of the pyramid, I hopped up to sit on a row of metal newspaper boxes emblazoned in script, *The San Francisco Chronicle*. I let my eyes slowly travel up the pyramid's ethereal white spires, its crushed quartz exterior making the obelisk glow like it possessed ancient magics -- even though the skyscraper was built in 1972. I'd heard that thousands of dollars in spare change were thrown into the pit when they poured its concrete foundation, and that sunken shipwrecks had to be cleared from underneath before construction began. Somewhere near me, under the pavement, was the famous Gold Rush fortune-seeker ship The Niantic, which was run aground, burned, buried, found, lost, found again, and then lost yet again.

America's deteriorating middle class flowed around me. Pointedly ignoring me. They paid their rent on time, they ate branded cereal, they believed everyone's circumstances were deserved.

They had everything I didn't; they came from homes, they attended college, they swallowed Reaganomics and the war on drugs. I was an orphan from that war; a child from a war fought on home turf. I watched the workers pretend not to see me; they worshipped good school districts for their children, they sought retirement and the best quality of life, and they were so thoroughly extinguished on their feet that they could not look at me starving in front of them. Absolute cadavers in bespoke suits and brand-name jackets, casualties of the nostalgia industry. Maybe there was nothing about them I envied after all.

The Transamerica Pyramid was beautiful from every angle. Looking up at its strange angles reminded me I now spent my life looking at the ground. Every one of us, children finding the best garbage cans to eat from, we'd been robbed. We could not hope to have things. All I could think was that I was always losing things that were never mine in the first place. I imagined a shiny aluminum scar where my heart should be, reflecting light like sun hitting office windows in buildings around me.

The steel newsstand was ice cold through my jeans, felt almost like it was burning my skin through the fabric. More and more people scurried by me on their way to work. I watched their faces, so many studiously avoiding me, and tried to think of something, anything in my life that made sense.

My memories had come back since my accident, but as a malevolent atavistic shadow. Then I made it out of my mother's world, running away because I figured out that you can't heal in the same environment that made you sick. But in the movies, after you beat the bad guy, the monster goes away, and all the injuries heal up. That's not what happened to me.

And now I was being punished for daring to think I might not have to be alone. I was always going to wind up alone. Pain never turns its back on you.

I made sure no other homeless people were panhandling nearby, a professional courtesy, and started asking the suits for spare change. By the end of the morning, I had enough for a coffee and bagel, and bus fare to the city's far edge, the Pacific Ocean.

The latest book in my bag was *Zen and the Art of Archery*, and I read bits of it on the ride across San Francisco. Downtown gave way to Victorians and hills, in turn becoming wide-paved avenues next to thick green forestry. Golden Gate Park stretched her tendrils to reach sand dunes spilling onto the Great Highway.

I wanted to understand the book's philosophies about the power of release. The art is in how you let go of things, I thought. But what about when you have nothing left to let go of? I'd had to give up on school and I knew it meant I'd never be considered an equal by anyone, I would never be respected in any profession. I gave up on ever having a home and all the opportunities people got when they had stability. I'd given up on having family, a father, a mother. Half my friends were dead or missing. Mark was taken away from me, and I knew we'd never find each other again. I didn't understand why I clearly wasn't supposed to have any of these things.

Ocean Beach was empty. Its wide sand shelf swept from

an eldritch rock face under the jinxed Cliff House to curve away, growing small, headed south on Highway one. Gulls wheeled far off by the Bay's mouth like little gnats following a container ship stacked heavy with colorful Legos sailing to the Pacific Ocean's horizon. Another day for the Port of San Francisco.

It was bright out. Even though I had sunglasses, my post-concussion sensitivity to light was still acute. It still felt good to be on the chilly beach. The air smelled clean, cool and salty, and the waves were calm, their soundtrack a rhythmic crash followed by sand sucking at foam. I plodded my way across glittering sand to the shoreline.

I reached the line between wet and dry sand and couldn't believe what I saw. Hundreds and hundreds of perfect sand dollars speckled dark sand where the waves receded. They were everywhere. In every size. Their occult petal pattern on little white disks had washed ashore as far as the eye could see. I picked one up, smiling, rubbed drying sand off its edge with my thumb, and walked down the beach, stepping carefully, bemusedly picking my way around the delicate shells. It was some kind of mass die-off. Rare, but I remembered from a fourth grade field trip to Moss Beach that this was a natural cycle for these earthbound aliens. It sometimes happened from too much freshwater in their environment, and was part of the sea's aqueous flux in which darkly beautiful events occurred to keep things in balance.

I felt somehow honored.

Maybe the release I needed to get better at wasn't all about loss, trauma, and grief. I wasn't entirely sold on the idea of letting go of pain and anger. I refused to let all the threads that had bizarrely, inexplicably intertwined to make me who I am dissolve and recede like smoke. Everything I went through must be mined to serve a purpose. I decided I would never look back and let bad experiences own me. I would only look back to learn, to understand.

I knew we were biologically programmed to seek patterns, that our wiring constantly pressed us to find explanations. Some people chose fictional narratives, myths, or outright lies to ourselves and people around us. Yet even when we think we've got it, there's always a deeper truth we only see with time and distance. Maybe, I thought as I walked on the beach, I was just going to have to let go of needing to understand why life pushed me in the directions it did. And appreciate whatever it was making me good at, for myself and the people I cared about.

There's a world you're born into. And then there is the world you choose.

I still felt sad, angry, and lonely when I caught a bus back to the Haight. Mark was gone, Rogue was missing, Zeke was dead, and Jimmy tried to punch me. I was hungry and exhausted. My feet and back were killing me. I decided to stay in Upper Haight to panhandle and beg for food scraps while working on my role-playing game adventure for my remaining friends. I called it "The Banishing Ritual."

Sleep deprivation and hunger were a normal state on the streets, but led to dark outcomes in large amounts. It probably contributed to the terrible luck I had that day -- and into the night -- asking for food and money. I thought about just snatching a wallet or shoplifting some food. I'd gotten really good at stealing, but I had rules about that, too. Steal from Safeway, not your neighborhood shops. And never do crime when you're tired.

I was still stuck out on the sidewalk at one am. My life ached. I nearly got in a fist fight on Haight Street when two punk-turning-skinhead girls tried to intimidate me away from my spot in front of the punk club, the I-Beam. Begging in front of the bar at closing time was supposed to be a 'sure thing' for panhandling; drunks were usually generous. Even though I was so tired I was wobbly on my feet. Hunger had dug a painful root deep into the center of my abdomen. Its throb gave way to nausea, and I knew if I got any food that night, I'd need to force myself to eat. Slowly.

Everyone coming out of the bar passed me by. Everyone. Except one guy.

He stumbled out of the club drunk and stopped, just staring at me when I said, "Spare some change?"

It was like he didn't understand the question. He was an attractive Asian man in a black Exploited t-shirt, so he had that going for him. But no one's actually hot when they're wasted, and I really didn't want to deal with anyone creeping on me.

He fished a crumpled dollar out of this pocket. He handed it to me and turned to leave, swaying, then turned back.

"Hey," he said.

"Yeah?" I kept my face emotionless, calculated the distance from him to me.

He said, "Look, uhhh ..."

I watched a weird storm of confusion move across his face.

"Hey," he said again. "I live on Stanyan."

That was two blocks away. I said, "Huh."

"I've seen you around," he told me. "I don't do this ... but if you want to crash, you can."

"I don't do this either," I warned him. "Or that."

"No, no it's not ... not what I ... I mean, it's safe." He leaned in, too far, and I took a step back. "I'm sorry! I'm sorry,

I'm so sorry," he backpedaled. "I just thought ... you want a place to crash ..."

A war raged in me. Fuck, I was so, so bone tired. Weary. Worn-down. I was emotionally all over the place from exhaustion. And I could easily take this guy, probably, if he tried anything. But the past couple of hours I'd fought self-destructive impulses inside, the kind that try to tell you nothing matters anyway. And it was horrible how tired and sad I was. Doing this would break my rules. Going home with a strange dude on the street, now that's how you get raped and killed, I thought. God, where was Rogue?

But I was so fucking desperate.

I told him, "I'm not going to fuck you."

He said, "No! I don't want that, I swear."

I got up, and we started walking down Haight Street. I maintained a cautious distance between us.

"My name's Kenny," he said.

I said, "If you touch me, I'll kill you."

"Okay," he said.

Kenny's apartment was a tiny, second-floor one-bedroom in an Edwardian facing the shuttered Golden Gate Park police station. The city had closed it, we thought, to let the abandoned Haight neighborhood devour itself. Kenny's kitchen and living room were the same room. Even the fridge was little. He drunkenly fumbled with everything he touched, put his keys in an overflowing dish of pennies by the door, kick-shoved off his Converse, sloppily got each of us a glass of water. I perched on his weathered futon couch, watching him.

From across the room he asked, "Wanna sandwich? You can make one, I have turkey. And pickles. I think."

I said, "That'd be awesome." I felt a wave of relief about

getting some food in me, but this whole situation was freaky. I wondered what he would want in return. Or if I'd wake up on his couch during the night with him climbing on top of me. I tried to act normal while he went in the bedroom and turned my back to make a sandwich, noting where his keys were, the kitchen knives, the window to a fire escape overlooking the street.

"Here's a pillow and some blankets," he said, walking into the room with an armload of bedding. "You can fold out the futon, err not, whatever you want. I gotta go to sleep now, I'm sorry."

"Thank you," I said. He closed his bedroom door.

I thought, *okay.* This is really weird. I'm keeping my boots on.

But then I was asleep the minute my head hit the pillow.

I woke up from the sound of Kenny talking to me from his apartment's mini kitchen. It was morning and he was sober; he spoke quickly. He was dressed completely different than the night before. He was wearing a lot of white. "I have to go to work," he said.

I bolted up. "Okay." This was my signal to get out.

"You can sleep in if you want," he said. The rest came out in a rush. "I put a towel in the bathroom if you want to shower, and help yourself to food. Just make sure both locks are locked when you leave."

I was thinking *what the hell* but all I said was, "What?"

Kenny smiled. "Really. Also, in my bedroom there's a bunch of change on top of my dresser. You can have all of it." I think my mouth was open. "And ... here," he added, scribbling on a piece of note paper. He tore it off and handed it to me. "When you're hungry, call me the night before. Then show up at this address in the morning, at eight am, right at eight, and you can work for a couple hours. Free lunch."

"Oh my god," I was floored. I stammered, "I'd ... yes. Wait, what is it?"

"Oh, my parents' restaurant in Little Saigon. Can you chop vegetables?"

"Oh, uh ... "

"You'll learn," he said, and smiled. "Chill out here as long as you want."

"Okay," I shook my head in seconds-late disbelief. "Thank you, thank you so ..."

"Bye!" Kenny was already out the door.

31

BY THE TIME San Francisco designated a section in one of its poorest districts as "Little Saigon" and posted two guardian statue chimera atop pillars to demarcate its gateway, the neighborhood had been calling itself that for decades. The restaurants, tailors, dentists, jewelry stores, dive bars, and massage parlors with signs in English, Vietnamese, Cambodian, and Chinese were mostly closed when I walked to Kenny's restaurant at eight am. But Little Saigon was well into beginning its day. Parents hustled kids to school. Merchants swept and hosed off stained Tenderloin sidewalks. Delivery trucks blocked streets packed tight by parallel-parked cars, each filling the air with the mechanical hiss of lift gates lowering to deliver dry goods and vegetables.

I passed the tiny restaurant's grimy front window and went around to the back entrance, like Kenny told me when I called him the night before. I followed trash cans and puddled muck to a back door, which seemed to be guarded by an unfriendly-looking old man in an apron and kitchen whites sitting on a turned-over five-gallon bucket, smoking a cigarette. I stopped and we stared at each other for an uncomfortable minute. I started to panic that I was at the wrong restaurant. The old man narrowed his eyes, stood and flicked his cigarette into a puddle, and went in without saying a word.

I leaned to peek into a small, busy little kitchen full of more white aprons. Old men hefted boxes, washed dishes, and an old woman pushed her way through them with a giant bowl of some green vegetable I didn't recognize. A flood of relief hit me when Kenny's face appeared around a corner. He smiled when he saw me. "Hey! Perfect, you're on time," he said, motioning me inside. He was the only young person in the place. Well, aside from me.

"Here, here," he showed me where to put my jacket and bag, where to find clean aprons and the bin for dirty ones. "When you come in, just get suited up and come find me."

Kenny was going so fast. "Thank you so much for this," I blurted, feeling awkward and wary that I was going to screw up and today would be the only time I ever did this. I asked him, "Are you sure it's cool?"

He laughed. "Are you kidding? Free slave labor!" He saw my face and the rest came out in a rush. "No, it's my parents' restaurant, it's totally cool. I run it. You just need to be cool with working under the table. For now, anyway, but I mean, don't worry. We help each other out around here."

The tension in Little Saigon was something known about in San Francisco, but rarely acknowledged. It was a tight-knit community. Many of its residents fled Vietnam's brutal Communist regime in the seventies, and there were still militant factions in the US who murdered anyone sympathetic to the country's government. Those factions shook down local businesses for "donations" while SFPD wrote off the neighborhood's shootings in broad daylight as anything but political. Our cops didn't even care to have anyone on staff who could translate Vietnamese until 1984, when they put out a public call for a translator. It had all been in the papers. I didn't tell Kenny I read a subtext into what he was saying. I figured he was kind of living on the edge here, running the place, being responsible for everyone.

I said, "Wow. Your parents gave you a restaurant?"

Kenny laughed, his smile was like the sun coming out. "God, no. I wish! They're pretty stoked though. I'm the only kid who's interested in the family business. I did a year at CCA and my fate was sealed, ha-ha."

CCA was the culinary school on Polk Street nearby. I smiled, "Oh so you're the sucker who went to cooking school."

"Oh my god," he said it like a Valley Girl. "You'll fit right in." Then he toured me through the kitchen, showed me the walk-in refrigerator, and I caught a glimpse of the small dining area in front.

Kenny parked me at a small station and showed me how to wash vegetables, chop them with a giant knife, put them in containers, and repeat the process. Mountains of vegetables. Totally, completely amazing otherworldly vegetables I'd never seen before in my life. Leaving me, he said: "At eleven you're done, then you can pick whatever you want from the menu."

Two more older women arrived, and I quickly felt like a clueless baby elephant in the tiny space. Everyone knew what they were doing and no one talked to me, only to each other, and then only in Vietnamese. People shoved me to grab things around my little spot without saying anything, but I saw they did it to each other, too.

I noticed that smoke breaks on the bucket outside were a regular thing. They tried to keep it on the down-low when Kenny was around. The old man from the alley was on his second break when I noticed him abruptly stand and then shout something into the kitchen.

Someone tapped my arm. Another grumpy old man stood next to me, motioned to the doorway. He said, "Ripper."

"What?" Did I need to put down my knife and run?

The man in the doorway made a quick "come on" motion to me with his hands. I set my knife down and panic pushed me to the door.

Outside the door was a scruffy, short-hair, black-and-white dog, sort of prancing from foot to foot. His tail wagged so hard his whole back end shifted from side-to-side. The white parts of him were really dirty.

The old smoker smiled around his menthol, pointing at the dog. He repeated, "Ripper." The man who tapped my arm held meat scraps in his other hand. He threw them. Ripper jumped up and caught the leavings like an expert.

"Ripper!" I grinned. I asked the smoking man, "Is he your dog?" Both men shook their heads; no. "Whose dog is it?"

The smoking man shrugged while the other one waved his hand toward the street. He said, "Everyone."

"Wow," I said while smiling at Ripper, who wolfed down his scraps while his tail waved nonstop.

"He come at the same time, every day," said the smoking man. "Goes to all the restaurants. Smart."

Ripper finished his scraps and trotted off to his next appointment. We all went back to doing our tasks and gruffly not talking to each other. I liked it.

Kenny put his hand on my shoulder at eleven. "Time flies, huh? You know what you wanna eat?" He handed me a paper menu. I really didn't know, at all. Vietnamese food was completely new to me.

By 11:30 I sat with my coat and bag at one of the larger tables in the restaurant's dining area flanked by two of the ladies snapping apart vegetables. A giant, steaming bowl of noodles in a rich broth fragrant with mint and basil landed in front of me, and it became a comfort food for the rest of my life. I spotted the smoking man smile at me from the kitchen.

I still felt hollow inside on my walk to Cafe Mimic, wishing I could tell Rogue, Zeke, and Mark about what I hoped would be my new gig. But there was a new thing there, too. I was excited. At the cafe I told Frank about Kenny's kitchen, and he soaked up every word. Maybe he was just being polite, but he seemed genuinely happy that I was already talking about going back. Joey buzzed by with a grey tub of dirty cups and bowls.

"Be careful or he'll put you to work washing dishes," Frank said.

"Are you kidding? When do I start," I said. I hoped I wasn't pushing it.

Joey shook his head. Frank looked at him and said, "Well we are short staffed around here now."

I didn't want to get between them, so I left it at that, got a coffee from David, and joined Spider and Alex at their table. I sat down ready to tell the story of my adventures.

Spider said to Alex, "Does she know?" Her face was serious. A sinking feeling hit me, fast. I cursed myself for walking right by them to tell Frank and Joey about learning to chop vegetables.

"Do I know what?"

"Bad shit," said Alex. "Bad shit and some really weird shit." The bounce and smile drained from her face. I'd never seen that. She told Spider, "You tell her the weird shit first."

Spider said, "I don't drink anymore, but man, if I did-"

"No-" Alex shook her head.

"Okay, okay." Spider looked at me and said, "The skinheads are gone."

I couldn't even speak.

"Like, gone!" Alex's eyes were wide.

"What do you mean, they're gone?" I thought they were playing a joke on me.

"They're just ... gone," Spider said. She was plugged into everything on the streets. "They're just not around, or maybe they've gone somewhere, I dunno."

"Spider," Alex urged, "tell her what you told me."

I looked from Alex to Spider, who said "Okay, I heard a story. The Hell's Angels told them to fuck off."

"Oh, shit," I exhaled. If this was true ... well, I thought, this could be true. The Hell's Angels had a huge, strong presence in San Francisco and the Bay Area. I knew of at least one clubhouse of theirs in the Dogpatch neighborhood. It was well-documented that in the 1960s and 70s they were the Haight's unofficial police force. The Haight-Ashbury Free Clinic called them when the clinic had problems with tweakers, and there were rumors that the biker gang thought of the neighborhood as their business turf. I never saw them around, but who was I to complain about racist-on-racist violence?

"That's not exactly bad news," I said.

Spider gave a nod to Alex who said, "I've got the bad news. Joe is sick."

She was so matter of fact about it. "He's ..." I felt lightheaded. "Is he okay?" I didn't know what to ask.

"We talked after he got his results," Alex said. "I'm not even supposed to tell anyone, but I think he needs friends right now. I mean, if he sticks around."

"What do you mean?" I asked.

She said, "He doesn't want to deal with it. He knows what some of his options are for now. He's not like, sick-sick yet. He talked about going to live with his mom in San Jose. Denial, you know?"

My brain was reeling. What did he think he was going to do? Oh god, Joe, you have HIV, I thought. How ... why ... Joe. Joe the friend who cared about me, the guy who made sure I met the right people to stay alive on the streets. Joe the asshole who became a skinhead. Joe, the guy we all rejected, ostracized, I thought guiltily. Joe who was a history and World War II buff, and had gay and lesbian and trans and Black friends who loved him but who became a modern Nazi.

His awareness of history was what snapped my mind, and I thought that some people must learn about atrocities and then find themselves standing at an abyss of having to really face what these things meant, personally, and that's when the screaming inside starts, when they know that these things must never, ever happen to people they love, and that some things in history must never, ever be repeated, and we have to be vigilant about the signs, hold on with bloody fingernails to the people we love, and somehow find a way through it. Some people choose to look away. Some who want to die, embrace it. But how could you not try, struggle, and fight to be aware of what you're going through?

It was like losing Joe twice.

Right when I was feeling in control of something, I was helpless again.

Then I remembered. My blood went cold. I was due to get my AIDS test results. I'd never had sex without a condom but the terror I felt was paralyzing.

"Is there anything we can do?" I asked. There had to be something. I needed to call Ashley.

Alex's eyes held a soft challenge. "Well, you could come volunteer with me," she said. "Needle exchange, condom outreach, safer sex education, testing outreach. There's stuff you can do. And I've seen you. You can talk to anyone."

I thought, maybe my mother taught me something useful after all.

Spider said, "It feels better to fight."

I looked in Spider's eyes and said, "That's something I know how to do."

32

AIDEN'S VOICE on the back of my neck made my eyes snap open. "I know you're awake," he said. "I can feel you fidgeting."

I felt terrible. "I'm sorry," I said. "Is it too early?"

He shifted in the station wagon's cramped cargo area, and yeah, I felt every bit of it. "No," Aiden sighed, "it's okay. Don't be stressed."

He was talking about my AIDS test results, which I was going to get that afternoon. The night before, we sat together on the steps of a nearby Victorian on Broderick Street and drank a small bottle of whiskey. He asked if I wanted to talk about it, and I said no, and when he said he understood I believed him. I was too scared to ask Aiden what his status was. I know the whiskey was to calm me down, not just as a friend, but also because you can't really "toss and turn" when you're sleeping illegally with another person in the tiny back of a station wagon on Oak Street.

Nonetheless, I woke up before Aiden did. Not knowing what time it was, I stressed and tried to stay still in the hard, square compartment padded with our coats, under a tarp. I was thinking about how I was now able to guess time of day by the air and the sounds. It gets colder right before the sun comes up, and the air feels wetter, and I could hear that morning commute traffic hadn't quite begun. I felt wired from stress. Aiden would be cranky and tired, but I would at least be on time to the restaurant. I had a perfect record so far.

We tumbled out of the station wagon, limbs stiff from the

car's hard floor. From outside myself I saw how obvious we were, trying to be covert about it. I giggled, "Mmm, graceful."

Aiden smiled and hugged me. I hugged him a little too long, but I couldn't help it. I was learning to get used to the fact that out here in the wasteland of homeless kids, sometimes people just disappeared. But I'd never be able to accept it. You never knew if it was the last time you'd see someone.

I worked as hard as I could at the restaurant that day; the cool burn of fear kept me buzzing along like I'd done a line of coke. I noticed new details in my surroundings as if my brain was trying to record the most vivid memories. Like this was some kind of "time before." Lines on the brick-colored kitchen floor where the black rubber mats had skidded out of place. How the rows of stainless steel bowls and pots on shelves made the wall more silver than any other color. The pungent, earthy smell of the grease trap. My careful pull of plastic wrap over a bowl of cut greens, and the swift hand that swooped in to crumple my perfect setup; my surprised face caught the old man's smile and wink as he continued around the corner. Smoking man got me.

I put in three hours of hard work at Kenny's restaurant, my hands continually soggy from washing and chopping vegetables whose names I was learning in both English and Vietnamese. I felt like I finally knew how to look at a bunch of tasks and sort them by time, expectation, space in the kitchen. I also got my first turn at tossing meat scraps to Ripper. I think I was growing on the kitchen's grumpy codgers.

Kenny slid me a ten dollar bill with my noodles. He said, "I hope it helps."

I was blown away. Actual, regular money. I thanked

Kenny, but the relief still didn't do much to calm my nerves. What if I was HIV-positive? I could never lie to Kenny. I'd probably lose this job.

I forced myself to eat over the clamor in my chest. There was a war of dread and panic in my stomach. Arguments raged in my head; a voice tried to convince me to skip getting my test results. If you're sick you won't make it, the voice said. There's no one to help you and nowhere to go.

I knew the voice was right. This was why no one I knew on the streets wanted to get tested. For anything. We were already doomed, dead, hopeless in our folly of scrambling for leftovers and quarters just to make it to the next day, surrounded by people we joked were only moving toward death a bit more comfortably and slower than we were. Most of us believed the ones who had homes and normalcy and vented abuse on us for our predicaments, those people were already dead. They just didn't know it yet.

Another voice told me it was my responsibility to know. Like some kind of duty to the people around me, so I could do the right thing ... and tell them I had one of the most deadly, incurable viruses on earth. So they could stay away from me.

I thought about the outreach training I did with Alex and her needle exchange crew. I was through the looking glass with AIDS in San Francisco now; I knew all the facts we had, facts that people had fought and died for. I forced myself to chew noodles and had to think about swallowing, which made it harder, because I couldn't tell if knowing more facts made it better or worse.

So many things in my life had made me ready for this. Part of it surprised me. Not waiting for my life to fall apart again; if that was some cosmic "lesson" then I really needed someone to know I learned it already. No, the surprising thing was feeling equipped to be part of the AIDS fight, because everything about it was so wrong. Fighting AIDS involved things that were illegal and dangerous, like needle exchange. Turns out, I was raised to do dangerous and illegal things really well.

Alex did collection and rarely carried needles because it was an arrest risk. Successful outreach depended on people like Alex to go out and find intravenous drug users across the city, in all the sketchy places they go. Then, talk to them. Give them materials like condoms, bleach, and flyers explaining how to clean used needles, and about safer sex. And tell them that week's location for trading old needles for new ones (called "sharps").

Outreach in the Haight was partly in conjunction with the Haight-Ashbury Free Clinic, which had been among the first in San Francisco to give IV drug users bleach and wipes. Alex's group did the actual needle exchanges in the Tenderloin and other outdoor locations by word of mouth, sometimes hiding clean, new sharps for exchange in a baby stroller.

The government's stance was that drugs were bad, and that was it. But people were dying, and AIDS was spreading. I had plenty of memories of my mother hoovering white lines with DEA agents, and clearly remember knowing as a little kid that the war on drugs was a sham. Homeless, I'd stood around in comic shops reading graphic novels like *Brought to Light*, and there was no question in my mind that Oliver North had done war crimes working with coke traffickers to arm terrorists. I directly understood what had been done to people like my mother and I by "just say no" and the "war on drugs" lies.

But one thing caught me like a deer in headlights with the AIDS crisis. It was like genocide by way of a "war on sex." It seemed to me that both "wars" served some of the same agendas and came from the same factions, though the war on sex seemed far more insidious, oppressive, and deadly to me.

By telling people how HIV was spread, and giving people tools to keep from catching or spreading the disease, the outreach team could hopefully reduce its transmission, even if just by one person. That meant talking openly and non-judgmentally about drug use and sex. Handing out flyers on safer sex, asking questions about what kind of sex people were having, and telling people what no one else would -- namely, how AIDS was spread. It wasn't all brand-new to me because I'd devoured safe sex pamphlets handed out in the Castro by the Sisters and the STOP AIDS Project. But learning about harm reduction, and how to talk to people about sex, was completely new. It felt like occult knowledge.

I learned a lot. Condoms could really save lives, but their use was culturally steeped in mountains of bullshit and baggage. I imagined trying to tell Taylee to use condoms, that she needed to care about what went into the vagina she dried with a separate towel out of shame and disgust, and the repressed feminine anger she'd surely unleash on me. I thought my mother should get an AIDS test, and I could almost hear her mocking me in response, saying it was a "gay disease." I felt sad and eerily aware.

Alex's team told me I needed to "meet people where they are" in terms of their comfort around talking about sex and drug use. That meant just getting the facts and telling people what their risks and options were. This was "harm reduction," giving people the tools they needed to make the right decisions to reduce harm to themselves and the people around them.

My appetite for noodles decamped for brighter horizons while I thought about this, and how absolutely awful shooting up sounded. At training, Alex's group prepared me as best as they could. They drilled into my brain the importance of reminding people to rinse their needles with water after cleaning them with bleach. To encourage people to get fresh needles, to try and avoid the infections and vein bludgeoning that came from dull needles. Specially to keep people from sharing needles, which was the same as sharing blood, and was common because users were afraid to get caught by the cops with a needle on them. It blew my mind that helping people not die from shooting up was itself an illegal act. I thought about the people who scowled at me when I asked for spare change, and what a different world I lived in. I would never be one of their tribe.

Walking through Little Saigon, I finally felt like I understood the anger of groups like Act Up. The urgency of city officials who had come around to the epidemic, though too slowly. The avoidable loss of my friends and loved ones. I knew I had a duty to see my test results through, no matter the results. Even if it meant I would find out for certain that I would die alone. That I could fall up, and disappear. I was supposed to run my D&D game at the cafe later that afternoon. I hoped I would still be able to. My "Banishing Ritual" role-playing campaign was going really well.

I sat in the clinic's outer room knowing I would never forget that moment for the rest of my life. In there, I understood why Little Joe did what he did, leaping out a Tenderloin window. I wrote a panicked verse in my journal while I waited. On the page, I was trapped in a room with a yellowjacket frenetically, loudly trying to land on my lips.

I was called into a little office where I sat alone. A nurse came in with an unopened manilla envelope. She got right down to business, opened it, and ran her finger down the page to my results. I realized this moment of truth was carefully planned so we would read it together. My results were negative.

I felt like I had just missed being hit by a truck while crossing the street, yanked back at the last minute by intuition or chance.

* * *

WHEN I GOT to the cafe there was a "life drawing" session underway in the back room. Through two sets of double-wide kitchen doors I made out a small stage set up in the middle, surrounded by easels and people standing, drawing, and painting. A nude man posed on the center dais; sunlight filtered softly onto him through murky panes in the warehouse's high grid of glass windows. The only sound was charcoal on paper, pencil hiss across giant newsprint pads, a brush tinkling in a water jar before finding its color.

Out front, the cafe was another matter. Teacups clanked, a coffee machine coughed, men jostled behind the counter for space. Coins made reassuring clatter into a tip jar that read "Send Duchess to charm school!" with a little drawing of the cafe's mascot dog. Terry moved like a pro behind the coffee counter, though to me he looked a little flustered, thinner, kind of tired. He lined up everyone's orders like a machine. Seeing me, a smile broke his tense features. He said, "Usual hon?"

"Yes, my dear," I smiled back. "How's your day?"

"Crazy, crazy," his hand swept the room. "We are oh-so-very double booked. Wilted Bouquet is doing a play tonight." It took me a second to remember the theatre group; Wilted Bouquet was a band of heavily-bearded actors who performed in their own plays, dressed in flowy costumes, and wore elaborate makeup that made their faces look like surrealist warrior masks. I didn't understand their plays at all. I loved those guys.

Joey buzzed around Terry and called a quick "hi sweetie" to me from the sandwich board. "Got a sec?"

I said, "Sure, what's cookin'?"

Joey clucked his tongue, curling a smile under his moustache. "Very funny. I'll find you in a bit."

I grabbed my backpack of gaming supplies from under the counter. Getting the dough for what was in that bag took me plenty of strategizing. I had cobbled together a survival rhythm with food vouchers from Larkin Street Youth, begging and dumpster diving, selling chapbooks, Kenny's generosity -- and by stepping up my thieving activities. Not from the game store, never from local businesses. I could get up to twenty dollars a day by lifting new clothes from chain stores, handing them to a Hippie/Trustafarian to sell at Buffalo Exchange or Wasteland, and splitting the cash. I didn't like it, but it worked. After food and necessities, I took my cash to the game store on Divisadero. I knew it wasn't the best use of my money. But lucky for me, I got an employee discount, I think, on the basis of being interesting.

The game store was its own sitcom. This was evident the moment I walked in and interrupted a heated argument about mis-priced lead figurines. The boys who worked there, and they were all boys, had that undefinable nerd look. They had odd body angles, uneven shapes, a palpable discomfort in their own clothing, and the angry sensitive skin of people who might've evolved on a different planet, in a different atmosphere. As if the magic forces in the books and games they sold had cursed them to live on earth. The store's name was Gamescape, but something was always broken or wrong, yet also like a curse, it was always, magically, no one's fault. So, everyone in its orbit called it Blamescape. Anyway, everyone working there wanted to talk to the punk girl about games, and I made new friends who would probably blame someone else for any pricing mistakes on whatever I bought. I was grateful.

At the cafe, I got set up for gaming on the front couches with John Gone, Jess, Bozie, his moody gas-siphoning goth friend Jay, and Paisley. She was infrequent due to cheerleading practice, so when she could make it, her character arrived at everyone's current location by teleportation. Lisa and Tamara sat at a nearby table and listened. Tamara had a deck of tarot cards spread out for Lisa, an ashtray, and teacups on saucers at their table's edge.

My players began making their disastrous way through a rotting, dark cliffside pleasure garden that appeared deserted. They were about to find out it was actually haunted by capricious and bitter Victorian ghosts, and was the territory of stink wolves. Eventually, I hoped, they would realize this was an alternate version of Sutro Heights Park, near San Francisco's Cliff House. Paisley's teleportation arrival roll was really good. She didn't fall from a tree or materialize in stink-wolf poop. That meant I could make it pretty.

I paused for everyone's attention. "The hacked and pockmarked marble statues of gods and goddesses seem to glow in moonlight and fog. In their center, the mist swirls and becomes opaque."

Lisa interrupted. "What does opaque mean?" Her question reminded me that Little Shaun teased me about using big words "all the time." Now I felt worried. I hadn't seen him in a while. The last time I saw him, he and Big Shaun were hanging out with Scooter, who shot up. Maybe I'd see him when Alex and I did AIDS outreach. There were lots of things in this world that shouldn't happen, but they did.

Jay said, "Opaque means see-through."

Jess said, "No it doesn't."

"Does too."

"Does not."

"The swirly mist hardens," I said, "and suddenly you see Swamp Witch Kitaka."

"Yaaaaay," Jess trailed off softly.

Paisley looked smug. "See now that's how I'm supposed to arrive."

I liked Jay, but guys who were wrong and corrected girls anyway had an air about them that made me think they wouldn't survive in the wild. But he'd probably never need to. In the corner of my eye I saw Joey at the cafe's counter, waving me over. "Everyone hang on a sec. I'll be right back."

I was still walking over to Joey when he said, "Frank and I have been talking. And if you want to chip in around here, we could use the help."

"I'd love to." This was amazing.

"It's not glamorous, it's just dishes one day a week. But we can pay you a little bit and if you need to, you can sleep in the big room the night before your shift. It's on the floor though, I'm sorry, that's all we have."

"No, I mean, that's great," I stammered. "I'd love to," I repeated like an idiot. "Can I ask for one thing?" I worried I was pushing it but I had to try.

He took a drag off his cigarette. "Depends."

"Can I have something mailed here? Just one thing, and only once, I promise."

Joey was the only man I knew who could look surprised and judgey at the same time. He said, "Maybe. What is it?"

"I don't have any ID," I knew my mouth was open and words were just running out of it. "And I can't do anything without ID. I can't make money orders, I can't get a place to live, I can't open a bank account, and when I'm sixteen I won't be able to apply for a job. I'm like, not even a person, and I can't get ID unless I have a mailing address, which I'd need to have ID to get even if I wanted a PO box-"

"I get it, I get it already." Joey gave me a long, hard, unsmiling look. I worried people might think we were arguing. Joey looked back at Frank in the kitchen, in his big glasses and extra-wide apron. I knew Frank couldn't hear us, but he smiled at us anyway. Joey sighed. "Okay, but I mean it: That's it. If anything else comes here, you're in trouble."

I couldn't believe it. Once I got a bank account, I'd have a safe place to put money instead of in my bra, my pockets, in my socks... "I promise! I promise nothing else, thank you, I promise not to do anything else, you won't regret it, thank you so mu-"

"Okay already," I saw a smile creeping under his mustache again. "Just don't tell anyone."

"I won't."

He fanned his hand at me, "Go, go on, your game's getting cold."

33

ALEX and I ran as fast as we could, our boots clomping and splashing each step as we jumped the curb and plunged into the darkness of Buena Vista Park's forest. The rain came down in waves I could see in halos around the streetlights. Their spindly necks swayed slightly in the wind. The rain had turned the steep streets around Buena Vista Park into rushing brown rivers. It hit my face like little needles, funneled down my neck, onto my chest and back beneath my clothing; the icy water felt like shocks against the body heat I'd built up from running.

I started laughing. Alex looked at me like I was crazy, a big grin spread over her face, and we slowed to a jog. Nearly breathless, she panted: "Try to stay on the pavement so you don't slip."

"Duh," I joked. "But we're gonna have to do some off-roading."

She giggled. Her cheeky grin practically glowed in the dark. My backpack's already-heavy weight felt doubled now that it was wet. I could enjoy this because it wasn't my backpack, and it wasn't my stuff inside. Alex and I were loaded down with plastic packs full of brand-new shower curtains.

We were running them to homeless people sleeping in the park during the rain. The outreach crew had warmed us up with Styrofoam cups of coffee that we loaded up with dry chocolate milk mix for an extra kick. I looked forward to more when I got back.

Water ran down paths to meet us, small floods fanning up over the toes of our boots, overflowing from the park's tombstone-lined gutters. We trotted to the end of one path where we knew to find a blue tarp and someone under it.

"Hellooo-" called Alex in a flouncy tone. "We come bearing gifts!"

A raspy male growl returned Alex's call, unintelligible words in the grating cadence of a voice harsh from hard living, smoking, and street machismo. "Arrrhhaayy!"

Alex wiggled wet eyebrows at me. "Arrr," she said. "There be pirates here!"

It was my turn to giggle, blinking away water running into my eyes. I shouted, "Ahoy, matey! Wanna shower curtain?"

"Fuck yeah," said the voice under the tarp. It struck me then, he was curled up in it like a big blue taco, on a slant against the hillside. The tarp flapped up with a grimy, outstretched hand. Taking the shower curtain, he told us: "God bless." In the dark, no one saw me shrug.

We left to find the next encampment, and Alex called back over her shoulder: "Aye aye, Captain!" The cold might've made me laugh a little harder than I meant to.

I had been off the streets for one week. It happened one day in the cafe, when I wasn't working. I sat at a table alone, reading and writing in my journal. Tamara came in the cafe, saw me, and pulled up a chair.

Her eyes were a beautiful, piercing blue, rimmed in hot pink eyeliner that finished in delicate curls at her temples. The contrast with her silvery-blue hair was ethereal. I blinked and said, "'Sup Tamara?"

She said, "I'm leavin'."

My first response, inside, was that I was glad I didn't get

too attached to her. It surprised me, and I felt bad. I didn't want her to leave. She was one of the last close friends Rogue had. Intangibly, she kept that connection for me. And now that was going away, too.

"My boyfriend... Eh, my ex..." she sighed, searching for words. I knew her boyfriend was in a band called Fang. They were a big deal in the punk scene. She continued. "I'm moving back to New York. Anyway, I want you to have my room."

"Your room?" I realized I didn't know anything about her.

"It's alright," she said. "I mean it's not nice or anything. It's $142.66 a month. Can you handle it?"

"I ... yes," I stuttered. I'd saved a lot, nearly $200, working for Kenny, at the cafe, panhandling, and the sale of clothes I lifted from The Gap. I still didn't have a bank account. My ID had come to the cafe, no problem. But in the senseless chicken-and-egg bureaucracy of keeping homeless people homeless, I needed an address to get a bank account to get a place, and vice-versa. Tamara's offer meant I could skip the line on all this, and avoid lying about my age to find a room to rent.

She seemed glad in a lukewarm way that felt like she was trying to finish a to-do list. "Okay," she told me. "Get it in a money order. You can get one from the corner store by the house. Don't pay the rent in cash."

This caution went through my mind later that day when I met her at a crumbling Victorian in the Western Addition that was so neglected, I couldn't tell what color it had once been. Its layout and upkeep were strikingly similar to the Lower Haight squat shuttered after Jenn's death. It had a giant, dark, wilting parlor downstairs littered with threadbare street couches and thrown-away stuffed chairs.

Upstairs where the four bedrooms were, Tamara introduced me to two roommates. One was an unsmiling butch dyke named Jill, and the other was apparently our landlord, Joel. Dressed in a button-down shirt, he had short dark hair and a mustache, all of which seemed out of place in a punk pad. But it wasn't totally surprising considering the kinds of fratty guys that liked to hook up with punk girls, an aura he fairly oozed.

Joel said he was from Connecticut, and I made a mental note not to hang out with him. On the streets, we talked about how people from the East Coast seemed to compete with people from Los Angeles for how badly they treated SF and its people -- they treated us like we were disposable, and SF was just a trashy stop on their journey. (To us, East Coasters were different from New Yorkers, whom we felt understood us.) It was just another red flag on my always-running tally of flags my head kept on people around me, a list I always hoped I evaluated correctly.

He seemed nice enough though, and handed me keys on the spot. Joel seemed glad to have the room filled.

Tamara took me into her old room. She'd already moved out but left me a thin mattress on the floor. She said, "Keep your door locked. Don't want no one to rip you off. You get your own sink," she walked over to an alcove with a single bare lightbulb on a pull chain over an old basin. Pointing at the sink, she said: "We think this building used to be a mortuary, or a doctor's office or something."

I looked at the room around me. Its carpet was an atlas of stains and cigarette burns. Situated at the front of the house, the room's one window was intact, though I could see the street outside through holes in the walls. The house's interior woodwork looked like dark ribs inside the holes.

Tamara said, "The bathroom only has a tub, and don't step in the saggy part of the kitchen." She shrugged, a wry smile on her face. "Just clean up after yourself and you're all good."

I was excited, and strangely conflicted. It had happened so fast, but so had everything anyone had ever done to help me. It always just came down to someone being willing to take a chance on me.

"Oh," Tamara said, "I wanted to give you these." She dug into her purse and pulled out her Tarot cards. She took my hand, and pressed them into my palm; this made the back of my neck tingle, like when someone plays with my hair. She said, "I wanted to give you a reading before I left but I don't have enough time left. There's an instruction book in the box." She hugged me goodbye. At the window I watched her walk away from the house, the back of her black leather jacket declaring "FANG" in white paint to everyone she was leaving behind her.

I sat on the bare mattress, alone in a strange room. I thought, *I'm going to need ... everything.* I didn't know where to start. I was more used to eating with my hands than having a place to eat food, let alone know what sizes sheets came in, or where I'd get a pillow. What if this place was haunted? I opened the Tarot pack and randomly pulled out a card. It was the Five of Swords. I looked it up. It was a bad card. Well, that's just fucking great. I felt flighty. I'm not good at this, I thought. I'm good at running from cops, telling frilly stories, making loud Kung Fu noises during serious fist fights, palming black eyeliner, falling on my face when I run up stairs, and insulting people in Spanish. I was only good at being anywhere than here.

I went out for reinforcements. I could stay present as long

as I was helping someone. I found Jess and brought her back to the room.

"Dude!" she exclaimed when she saw the empty parlor. "We can roll dice all motherfucking night in here!" She was making me feel better about this. When we got to my room, she put her arms out and spun in a slow circle. "Bitch, this is a palace! I'm gonna wash my twat in your sink!"

I was laughing. "When you get your Barbie Dream Twat my sink is all yours."

That moment was when I noticed how much Jess had grown since we met. She was still tiny and younger than me, but had been taking hormones, gods bless the trans underground, and while she'd gotten a little taller, she'd also filled out in the hips and butt. To me, she looked like a million-dollar platinum punk doll.

I put a hand on my abdomen, it was aching. Maybe that was why nothing felt right. I told her, "Just be glad you don't get periods."

She went from silly to caring and present in a blink. "Oh sweetie. Are you hurting?"

I liked silly better. "Yeah, it's fucking medieval down there."

She laughed. "Blood, pain, horses dying."

I said, "Well, no... "

She cut in. "But sometimes a brave knight, right?"

"You been reading a lot of fantasy?" She laughed at that, and I saw she was unpacking her makeup bag in the room's creepy sink. I said, "You can stay here whenever you want."

"Yes! Depends on the night, though." Jess had sugar daddies, she'd told me earlier. Older men who took care of her, but who she kept at arm's length, on rotation. She still worked at 17th and Capp. She pulled a brush and a small can of Aqua Net out of her bag. She said, "Let's put on makeup and go get you some shit for this room."

We did makeup and hair and went out. San Francisco's streets were a perennial, randomized treasure hunt for furniture, books, and whatever odds and ends people put out on the streets. We stole as many milk crates as we could grab from sidewalks and alleys. These would be tables, shelves, a stackable dresser. Then we rounded up as many in our gaming crew as we could find. By nightfall, Jess and I were in the parlor setting up for a D&D game with Paisley, Bozie, and Jay.

Around eleven there was a knock on the door, followed by the door flying open -- and there stood John Gone. "Am I late?" he smiled. In one arm was a huge greasy bag of unsold pizza slices from the place in Upper Haight that gave us the "punk discount" for saving their tip jar. In the other was liquid gold: two six-packs of highly caffeinated Jolt Cola. We yelled and cheered like he'd slain a dragon for treasure.

And so, while the world went crazy around us on repeat, my friend's characters were playing, battling, bonding, and adventuring their way through the story I'd written -- and they really liked it.

Perhaps it helped that the land and people mirrored their own. Everyone quickly figured out the characters' world map corresponded to San Francisco. My version of D&D was very home-brew. But it worked.

Their characters had started out as hard-up, homeless individuals with unknown pasts in a brutal city of extremes. The City was an occult jewel, a wonder of the world on the edge of a continent. Its technologies and automations were glittering and unparalleled. Its promises became a prison for those who came to the City seeking fortune, equality, and freedom. The City, once harmonic and vibrant, was now a contrast of violent wealth and brutal squalor. Where once were dance halls and music, now were shanties and rats, above which the rich lived on hills in guarded compounds of splendor -- and caste systems.

The City's history books had been burned. My characters thought they knew who they were, but they didn't, not really.

The characters -- my friends as players -- all met in the game during a burglary gone wrong. Jess, as wood elf ranger Hella, and Nikolas the pirate (Bozie) were hired by two different wealthy factions to steal a book of spells from the City's Grand Library. The book of magics literally held the city together, structurally and technologically, with spells. Spells that seemed to be breaking, because buildings were cracking and things were failing in odd and dangerous ways.

Paisely, as swamp witch Kitaka, was initially out to get the book for herself. This had her breaking into one of the most heavily guarded libraries on the planet. John's human barbarian Bob, and Jay's gigantic character Sigmund were two of the library's guards. Everyone met when the various robberies intersected, and they figured out they'd all been set up.

Alarms blared while they stared at (and then fought over) a busted-open case with insets for a missing book -- and five missing keys. The book's absence might explain why all the City's magic seemed poisoned -- and people lived in misery. The group's quest was to find the keys, see what they opened, and hopefully, find the missing book.

John found the first key at a military fort by the bridge. It had a "voice" which could only be heard by John. The key whispered secrets about family he'd never known, generations of sentry slaves.

Paisley's key said her people were forced to work in the radioactive wastelands of the military ships, where they starved and lived in desperation. Jay's key revealed propaganda wars that his kinfolk had been forced to fabricate, tales and images of terror to frighten and control the citizens. Jess's key showed that her tribe were once powerful warriors, but were run down, hunted into hiding.

When last we played at the cafe, they'd finally found Bozie's key on the waterfront after being chased by city police. His key explained that his character was not just human, but also half-elf. Drow elf, to be specific. The Drow had come to the city to escape persecution but became enslaved.

That's where everyone started that night; the characters were trapped under a pier that was a lot like San Francisco's Pier 33. We rolled dice and adventured until morning light crept through the Victorian's dirty windows. No one in the house was around to care. Joel came through once and offered us coke (I declined) and then twitched his way off to somewhere else.

The next day I saw my other roommate Jill come in and go out, and heard crying coming from her room. I knocked, and met Jill's very, very femme girlfriend Blossom. Jill told me later that Blossom was really depressed, a state Jill attributed to Blossom having done too much Ecstasy. It didn't make sense to me, but I said I'd help with anything if Jill needed it. Blossom was unbelievably sweet, and incredibly beautiful. But yeah, she was very, very sad.

I wasn't sad, but I didn't know how to trust being happy. One of the problems that comes with clawing your way out of hell is that you think about all the people who didn't. And that feels really bad. I often thought of the line from

Slaughterhouse Five, where Billy Pilgrim is asked what it's like to be the only one who witnesses a slaughter and survive. He answers, "Everything was beautiful and nothing hurt."

I still didn't think I was off the streets; I couldn't let myself believe it. I kept my belongings ready to go at a moment's notice. I felt like I needed to do the normal thing, which was to go on like this wasn't going to fall apart in the middle of the night. I was hideously compelled to plan for the immediate end of any happiness I might snatch out of thin air. There is also a part of you that knows it has to stay sharp to survive for when it happens again. When you survive trauma, you could never let yourself become inured to its agenda.

At the same time, I didn't want to be one of those people who are so convinced things will turn out terrible that I ended up making the worst outcome happen, through accident or intent. As Rogue would've said, *No self-sabo.* I decided to plan for both, but to act like the better outcome was the real one. And hope that acting like things would turn out okay would just turn into things being okay after all.

If not, I would always be ready.

It was hard to be in one place. For anything. For anyone. I had one guy over, but I didn't want him to stay after sex. The sex wasn't bad. It was exactly what was on the label, but he didn't know me, and I didn't particularly want him to. There was another, a really cute boy who worked at a store in Upper Haight, all the girls on the street wanted him. We became lovers. I could never let myself stay at his Page Street apartment after sex. I never had him over. When he said he wanted to meet my friends, I ghosted him. I felt terrible about it.

Imagine telling a beautiful skater boy with good

intentions that you want to talk about having just read Dante's *Divine Comedy*, that you never back down to a fistfight, you believed in needle exchange, you have a warrant for your arrest, and your life is the result of failed witness protection wasted on a brilliant Stanford-engineer drug addict. The last part leading to the fact that cartels might be looking for your mother, to kill her. Maybe kill you, too.

I began having a recurring dream where I'd be in school and have no idea what was going on in class and begin to suffocate in panic. I wanted to run. Which was why in the next few days, when I applied for my first real job and got it, I didn't feel like celebrating. The job was at a chain of delis that had two locations in the city, and more throughout the East Bay, all down the peninsula. I lied about having a high school diploma. They didn't care or bother to check anything I put on the application. It was embittering to have confirmation that the diploma I nearly killed myself to try and get never really mattered.

I started the next day. The shift began at five am and consisted of slicing meats for hours, then making sandwiches and coffee for the rest of the day along an assembly line. There was no Ripper to toss meat scraps to. The manager was a mean little man who cautioned me not to "get bitchy about the guys." They charged us full price for our food. My male coworkers hit on me relentlessly. I would have to wait an extra week for my paycheck because I was a new hire.

This all contributed to why, when I had a shitty closing shift, I stole a big, foodservice-size bag of coffee. I had an idea.

One of my days off coincided with a day Cafe Mimic was closed. I decided to have a mini-cafe in my new pad. I centered it around a main event; spoken word performances and readings, and the Victorian's front parlor easily made a makeshift stage. I went by Kinko's and Upper Haight's comic store to invite all the 'zine people and writers I could find. I put out a tip jar and started making coffee at around four in the afternoon.

So many people came that I needed help to keep the coffee flowing. Jess and Alex pitched in. Some of the artists brought food and coffee they stole from work as contributions. It got so crowded that finding a spot to stand and hear the readings was almost impossible.

My main rule was that I had the final say about who could be there, and that if anyone was made uncomfortable by another person, they just needed to tell me and I'd throw them out. Simple. Right?

And then Alex came to me with this very problem. "There's someone outside," she said. "They want to come in, but I said to wait for you."

"Who is it?"

"It's a skinhead girl."

"What!? You're kidding." We hadn't seen a skinhead since ... well since whatever had happened to make them leave. Though many of us noticed they hadn't exactly left. It seemed like a significant number of skins had just changed their stripes and became rockabilly. They were easy to spot in the Haight where many still hung out. They were the ones at Club Deluxe who traded their boots and braces for bowling shirts and vintage slacks or blouses and capri pants, exchanging songs by The Mentors and 4Skinz for Sinatra.

I went out through the parlor. The house was so full, people were smoking and hanging out on the front porch and along the sidewalk. Alex pointed me to a girl with her back to me, and yep, she was dressed very obviously as a skin. She turned around and I recognized her. It was Taylee Cutler.

A flood of memories and anger washed over me when I saw her frosty blue, witchy eyes. I got nervous. I started to shake. I thought, I can't be scared. This girl is an idiot. I'm among all my friends. This is my house! But I remembered her smirking as my mother lied, and called me a liar, and how Taylee's father humiliated me, said I was beyond anyone's help.

Taylee smiled at me.

I said, "You can't be here."

"Oh yeah? Why not? It's a free country."

I remembered Jenn pulling the same shit line and getting walked out of the Cafe by Joey. "It's my house." I steeled myself. "And you're not welcome in it."

She came up close, inches from my face and said, "Huh." Taylee had changed. All her repressed anger and body horror had found an outlet. Now she had a group that gave her the approval and validation she was denied at home. Two beefy-looking rockabilly girls stood off to the side, watching us.

Without warning, Taylee grabbed my arms. Her eyes were wild, too bright. She grinned. Time slowed and I thought, there are a few things I could do. But I had to act fast. So, I tried something new. I headbutted her as hard as I could.

"Aaaah!" Taylee let go and stumbled backward. She put her hands to her head. "Owwww," she howled.

I looked at the rockabilly girls, who stood there, unsure of what to do.

Taylee whined, "That really hurt!"

I said, "Didn't hurt me." It was weird, but true. Maybe the person who does the butting gets less of the impact, I wondered.

"Ow ow!" she continued.

I asked her, "Do you want to do more of this? Or do you just want to go?"

"Fine," she said. "Asshole."

I tried not to laugh.

Things got worse at the deli. The manager said my paycheck would be delayed another week. One of the sandwich makers decided I was a bitch for not flirting back, and started sabotaging my end of day numbers, losing my inventory charts, dumping out my drinks when I wasn't looking. I became very careful about everything I did, tried to have as many witnesses around me as I could at all times. But I knew witnesses wouldn't really help me. I knew exactly who these men were. Once you have been taught to dismiss your own emotions, it is a simple step to dismiss those of others.

So, I'd had a rough week when I came home soaked from doing outreach with Alex in the rain. I flopped down on one of the ratty couches downstairs and worried about what I was going to do about the deli when there was a knock on the door.

I opened it. Two San Francisco sheriffs stood on the porch. I was too scared to think of what to do and stood there, saying nothing. They had paperwork in their hands. One asked me, "Is Joel Foley at home?"

"No," I said. "I haven't seen him in a few days." That was true.

"Well, this is formal notice of eviction," he said handing me papers. "Everyone on the premises has 24 hours to leave."

Shock rolled across my skin like electric current. "What! Why?"

"Rent hasn't been paid on this building in six months,"

the officer said. "We've delivered three notices in the past ninety days. The last notice one week ago."

"Oh my god," I said. "I didn't get any notices ... No one did! What do I do?"

"Sorry, miss. I recommend you get your belongings out immediately. You won't be able to get back in tomorrow. We'll be back to padlock it."

I closed the door, numb. I thought, *that fucker*. That cokehead fucker has been taking all our rent.

And then: Ah yes. Hello worst fear. I can't miss you if you never leave.

The screwed up thing was that I was already packed.

34

OUR HEROES HAD COME to the end of their journey.

We sat around a makeshift steel table comprised of a giant, stolen piece of road plate. The kind city workers place over gaping holes in the street so cars can drive over it. The sheet of steel sat on a heavy, homemade metal frame the warehouse's artists had welded together. Jess and Paisley sat together at one corner. Both characters (and players) had bonded through the course of the game. To my right and left were John Gone, then Bozie and Jay.

The warehouse took me in after I returned to homelessness. The first thing I asked them about was that huge piece of road plate. I wanted to know how they stole something so big and impossibly heavy from a nearby construction site.

I got a ridiculous story of art school kids in black casing a work site, their robbery setup using two trucks and a small, finicky electric forklift, and a moment of panic after they got it in the pickup truck and the weight nearly pinned their vehicle. Then another freakout, when the driver slammed on his brakes and they thought they'd be decapitated when the inch-thick steel rectangle slammed into the truck's cab. The artists laughed when they told the story. They said I should come with them for their next run because I could fit into small spaces. It sounded fun.

I'd gone from eviction back to the streets of Haight and Castro, then found this SOMA warehouse of art students. Part of me wondered if that brief break from homelessness had actually occurred. The guys were artist friends of Bozie's who made bizarre metal sculptures. They were inspired by an art trend of anthropomorphized machines, led by San Francisco's art collective Survival Research Laboratories (who I would later work with for over a decade).

There was a painter living in the warehouse, too. Leo's huge found-plywood paintings were everywhere in the space; colorful abstract riots hung, stacked, leaned against walls and propped up on shelves all over the warehouse's central space. It was like we were playing D&D in the middle of a motor oil-scented art vault, with a warren of bedrooms above us built into the building's upper ribcage of exposed wood.

It was too hot for anyone to make art that day, and nearly all the housemates were at Zeitgeist, a Mission biker bar with an outside garden. Leo didn't go with them; he wanted to watch a baseball game in the warehouse's TV area. It was a perfect afternoon for gaming, and we were getting to the final confrontations for my campaign, "The Banishing Ritual." I was thrilled. The group was about to enter the map's hidden dimension, to begin the ritual. To expel the villain who had poisoned the city's magic, put its people in bondage and erased their memories, kept magic in the hands of the powerful, and whose power fed off the people's misery.

Everything was in place.

We had the table covered in paper maps, character sheets, notes, drawings of characters, dice, and highly caffeinated colas sweating and becoming instantly warm in the late-summer heatwave. The steel table radiated a chill that confused my skin into thinking it was burning when I put my elbows on it.

The players had made it to the center of the map, led the

last little bit by a non-player character who was half robot, half human. I'll admit the android character was shamelessly modeled on Necron-99 from the film *Wizards*. It was one of my favorite movies as a child, watched on VHS with the Silicon Valley hippies my mother used to leave me with for weeks at a time.

The android followed our heroes from the shadows for a while until they discovered him. After a grilling made ridiculous by abysmally low perception dice-rolls, the characters got Necron to confess that he once worked for the villain, the man who set them all up to take the fall for the burglary, their starting point for the campaign.

Which is how everyone ended up standing in front of a giant oak tree in the middle of the city's oldest forested park, each giving Necron shit for not telling them what they should do next.

It was so hot in the warehouse I'd uncharacteristically removed my boots and socks. I was in cutoff Ben Davis work pants and Mark's old Social Distortion t-shirt, which I'd cut the sleeves off of. I figured he wouldn't mind. I liked to imagine that he'd kiss my forehead when I told him about it. Everyone else wore the punk version of summer clothes, with the exception of John, who kept his entire body covered (remember, he is covered in self-inflicted scars), and Paisley, who had on a white wifebeater she'd inked the words PUBLIC ENEMY and a crosshairs onto.

Bozie said, "Necron, where are you taking us?"

Jay asked, "Can I lull Necron into compliance with a song?"

Paisely asked, "Can I cast an influence spell over him?"

Jess said, "Can I just punch him."

I took a gulp of warm Jolt, then said, "Everybody roll again for perception."

John said, "Uh-oh," and scooped up his dice.

Everyone rolled and calculated their results against character sheets. "Okay," I said. "Jess, I mean Hella, you notice something weird about the oak tree. The bark in one spot looks ... different."

Jess said, "I go over to the tree. Slowly."

"When you get closer to the tree, your key starts whispering. But you can barely hear it."

Jess said, "I take out my key and -" I interrupted her. "When the key makes contact with your skin, you can hear it. It's as loud as a real voice. It's asking you, over and over: What is oak? What is oak?"

Paisley said, "What the hell." The players looked at each other in confusion.

Jess had an idea. "Hey guys, everyone come over here and pull out your keys."

I told them, "You all go to where Hella is standing and take out your keys. You can all hear it now, your keys are saying the same thing. It's like a chorus, saying, What is oak? What is oak?"

John said, "Oak is ... a tree?"

Leo walked through the room. "Hey, do you guys want some beer?" He came over to our table. "The game's about to start and I've got a six-pack in my room."

"Not yet but thanks," I told him. To the players I said, "The keys are still asking you."

Leo said, "Whoops, sorry. I'll bring some downstairs anyway."

The gamers tried a variety of different approaches to solve the puzzle. They pressed the keys to the tree, to each other's keys, Paisley tried a spell. Bozie said, "No, this has to be about the tree itself. It's about oak trees. Like a riddle. What do we know about oak trees?"

Jay said, "Their roots are the same above and below ground."

Paisley said, "So, they're strong."

I told everyone, "Your keys just went silent."

"Holy fuck," Jess said. "Oak is strong."

I tell them, "The bark on the tree in that spot Hella noticed begins to glow in a pattern that looks like the outside of a compass, or maybe a clock. You can all see it."

John repeated the phrase, "Oak is strong."

Everyone focused on me. "Another ring within the compass emerges, glowing gold light. For a second, just a second, you all see the air around the tree shimmer, and in that second you see a giant, enormous black Victorian where it shouldn't be. And then it disappears, but the second ring on the tree remains."

Eyes glittering with triumph, Paisley said: "Oak is strong."

And then, sitting at that table, it felt like a heavy door slammed shut in a small, airless room. The entire interior of the warehouse went into motion with the sound of creaks and pops coming from the walls around us, then increasing; soda cans fell over, dice bounced and went up, hanging lights jerked in the air, paintings jumped forward and off the walls as our chairs shoved us out of them. We were California kids, so we instantly hurled ourselves in two directions: Jess, Paisley, and John went under the table. Bozie, Jay, and I made a run for the warehouse's open front door.

Twenty-three seconds is a long time. I was the last one to leave the table. On my second step the first of the earthquake's whipcracks threw me into a stumble. I came down on my hands and knees as a trio of Leo's stacked paintings landed on my calves. The floor bucked under my hands and knees as I scrambled for purchase, as if the earth was rising to meet me as I clawed the floor toward the door. I got halfway up and saw Bozie hanging onto the doorframe, reaching for me. I made it two more steps before the floor came at me again and I heard more paintings crash to the floor behind me, glass shattering. I slammed back onto my hands and knees, up and down again, desperate, when Bozie suddenly grabbed my arm and hauled me into the doorway.

And then it was over.

We stood there, breathing hard, looking at each other's faces raw with terror. The silence was immense, it was wrong. I heard a loud gurgle, followed by a strange sucking noise behind me; it came from the ground. Rather, it came from a SOMA storm drain at the curb just outside the doorway. We turned to look at it, and then saw all the parked cars had been moved as if by some giant, frustrated toddler. Two cars were crushed and buried under bricks and wood that had fallen from a warehouse facade nearby. I saw people help each other get up off the sidewalk.

Bozie said, "Are you okay?"

"Thank you for ... I ... I think so." I was speeding on adrenaline. My fingernails were split and bloody. My knees throbbed. I looked down and saw bruising, swelling from kneecap to mid-shin, and blood oozed from where the skin split on my knees. The tops of my feet were scratched and bleeding. I tried a few steps, and it hurt a little, but I could walk. I didn't want to leave the doorway.

I looked back into the room and saw that the bookshelves had hurled their contents out across the room, like they'd projectile-vomited books, magazines, knick-knacks and sculptures outward in an arc. Every bit of glass, every dish in the kitchen was broken, a covering of shards across the floor.

"Is everyone okay!" It was Paisley, still under the table. The trio had stayed under the steel plate and tried to move with it during the quake, though they'd bounced around pretty hard, like I had. They were scraped up, but no major injuries.

Jay called out, "Leo?" I had forgotten about him.

"I'm here," he said, emerging from an area by the stairs. "I was coming downstairs and I ... I just kept getting thrown back *up* the stairs."

John went over to him, stopped, dug around the rubble that had been the warehouse's interior artwork, appointments, furnishings. John's smoker's cough laugh startled me. Holding up a mangled six-pack he said, "Well, the beer made it."

Jess aid, "Actual fuckin' miracle."

I said, "Gimme one."

We all looked at each other for a few minutes, shaking with the comedown of fear and our eyes a bit wider -- and wiser -- than an hour ago. The chairs where we'd sat had been tossed wildly, were covered with the books, paintings, random bits and pieces of the warehouse's interior. Things that used to be on shelves.

The silence outside was replaced by sirens. The power was out. Paisley tried to call her parents, but the line only emitted a rapid busy signal. "I have to get home," she said, her voice sounding panicked.

"Me too," said John, and Jay echoed him. Jess said, "I gotta find Lisa. She's in Upper Haight."

Bozie said, "If I can get my car out, I'll drive everyone, if the roads are ... clear I guess."

I pulled my boots on and went with them. I told Leo I'd be back to help clean up. Bozie's Oldsmobile was at an odd angle to where it had been parked, but had escaped the cave-ins covering other cars along the street. We talked to everyone we saw. Every stranger asked if each other were okay, if there was power, if anyone's phone worked, if we thought the water was safe to drink. One man told us, "The corner store is in bad shape. But they're giving out water to whoever needs it."

We carefully piled into Bozie's Oldsmobile and paused in silence again. Dazed. Five punk kids sitting in a car, sipping beer, being perfectly quiet.

"Seriously though," John broke the silence. I heard his Zippo open to light a cigarette, and the crackling puff of his first drag. He smiled. "That was fucking weird, right?"

I said, "Yeah." I had no idea what else to say.

Jess said, "Like, 'oak is -'"

"Don't say it!" Paisley cut her off. We froze. Paisley said, "I'm sorry."

Jess said, "It's okay."

My mind was a jumble. I told everyone, "I really don't understand what just happened. It's too weird."

Jay said, "Hey, at any part of the game it would've been weird."

"No one, like, fucking no one is going to believe us," Paisley added. I couldn't see her face, but I swear I could hear her smiling when she said it.

John surprised us by laughing, a chuckle that sounded like a cough at any moment. He said, "What are the fucking chances!"

We all let out what I later looked back on as a group stress laugh.

Bozie drove us slowly through South of Market. San Francisco's streets were an obstacle course of broken glass and brick. We could tell from sirens and trucks racing past that fires were breaking out. On one corner a group of people moved wreckage out of a residence hotel: there were people trapped inside. Most everything brick either crumbled or looked like it would crumble; many buildings we drove past were scabbed with enormous cracks spiderwebbing up their sides. Sections of sidewalks had split, some roads had frightening fissures across them. All the stoplights were out. To my surprise, people still stopped, took turns at the intersections.

We stopped for people at the side of the road who held their thumbs out trying to get home. One man in a business suit said he'd go as far as we could take him. He eyed our open beers in the car. I asked him, "Wanna sip?"

"Yes please. Thank you."

He told us that all underground trains were frozen in place, commuters were being evacuated by the thousands through the dark tunnels. I'd forgotten it was rush hour. Everyone was scared that the BART tunnel had flooded, or would. MUNI buses were continuing service as far as they could.

From what we learned, the city was cavalier in what she chose to spare. Some neighborhoods were untouched. Places in Chinatown, while without power, were largely fine. The Tenderloin was in bad shape. City Hall had flooded. The Marina was on fire and it was out of control. The Oakland Bay Bridge had collapsed and people were dead; the city was cut off. We were told that an entire section of Oakland's freeway had come down on top of rush-hour commuters on its lower level, crushing everyone in their cars.

We could only drop John and Jay off at the edge of the Mission; there was a huge gas leak. Families stood together on sidewalks and at street corners clutching what belongings they could carry. Waiting. One elderly Latina woman stood alone in a fur coat, holding a lamp, staring. Some just sat on curbs or in doorways and cried. At least one row of the Mission's dollhouse Victorians had cracked apart and slid from their foundations in a bunch, like stacks of books pushed over by a huge invisible hand.

We'd underestimated how hard it was to get across the city. Bozie, Jess, and Paisley dropped me off on Van Ness; they were headed back toward the Haight. I told them I'd go check on Cafe Mimic.

I was walking past Leo's warehouse to the cafe when the first big aftershock hit. All around me on streets and in buildings, people screamed.

Corner stores I passed were mazes of toppled shelving, their floors knee-deep from tsunamis of flung bottles, cans, boxes of pasta, chip bags, and it smelled rankly of warm wine and busted open booze bottles. Inside, strangers helped shopkeepers pick up the pieces.

On Sixth Street, a genuinely apocalyptic, large dark crack had torn open the street for blocks, stretching a long tendril toward the Golden Gate Theater at Market. We'd find out later that the quake's epicenter was somewhere near Santa Cruz, but this raw, rumpled, black tear down the street's fabric looked like it was the very spot where the tectonic plates had moved. An attempt to rip the city in two left unfinished. I had the strange thought that if this were a horror film, the people nervously glancing at the gigantic crack would've crossed themselves after doing so.

I turned down the alley and saw a crowd in front of the cafe, causing my stomach to lurch. I tried to run a few steps, but my painful legs wouldn't let me. My legs had become solid bruises from the knees down, an underskin waterfall of trapped blood in deep red and purple. I could feel the blood on top of my feet had dried stuck to my socks, and I pushed that out of my head to deal with later.

The sidewalk in front of the cafe, our cafe, was piled with chairs, books, crates of clothing, and a slow parade of belongings was coming out of the building.

"Honey!" Frank called out to me. "Oh baby, your legs, come here, come here." He was crying. Joey carried a box, cigarette in his mouth. He shouted back into the building, "Don't go near the stage!"

Frank pulled me tight over his aproned belly and I asked, "What happened?"

"If you walk over there," he nodded toward an adjacent street corner, "you can see it. The building behind us came down. Bricks came through our windows. The back roof is coming in."

From what I could suss, no one seemed to be injured. Frank said they knew the fire department, or some department, would come by and tell them they couldn't go in the building anymore. So, they were trying to get everything they could out, now. I was speechless. Every face I saw came for a hug; David, Alex, and Terry, after which Alex and I insisted that Terry and Frank sit, rest. We eased the older men into salvaged cafe chairs on the sidewalk.

We worked to get out a minimum of belongings. Difficult decisions were made. Aftershocks became so common that people would just pause to see if it got worse, then resume their task at hand with a little more haste, a quickened step. We moved the men and as much as everyone could carry to a nearby warehouse of friends offering temporary shelter.

I made my way back to Leo's warehouse while a deep kind of darkness settled over the city. Night descending on a metropolis mostly without power. It was on in a few places, but not in most. The warehouse had two new faces, Leo's girlfriend Melissa, and her roommate Beth.

The women had decamped to Leo's warehouse because they were afraid to sleep alone. Everyone was. Beth had been dying her hair black when the quake hit and water was cut off to their building. She'd quickly rinsed her hair in the only remaining water, the toilet. Melissa told me Bozie's roommate was in the Outer Richmond when it hit, in a pet store buying rats for Medusa, their snake. When she ran out of the shop, fish tanks sloshed their smelly contents onto her and toppled behind her. When she got outside, a brick building facade had come down on parked cars on the street, dusting her with red grit. We all moaned, knowing it might be a while until anyone could take a shower.

The sound of sirens never ceased that night. It was an agitating background din that held frayed nerves in a limbo of believing something awful was getting worse, while you tried to calm yourself thinking the nonstop sirens meant that people who needed help were getting it. The Transamerica Pyramid was dark and it made me wonder how many people had died to build this beautiful city.

Without power in SOMA, a sky full of stars shimmered in the warm air above me. Buffeted by constant aftershocks, I sat on the sidewalk looking at a sky that seemed like it was from when San Francisco was young. Before it was a cracked temple of storytellers, concrete, lost children, and technology. None of it mattered to the sky or earth. Everywhere was evidence of the folly built into every wish that had been made to force the will of fortune-seekers onto a mercurial peninsula that was always going to turn every weakness they planted into dust.

The wreckage around me was where foundation ejected dreams; where greed lost purchase in brick atop landfill that was once shoreline and sand; where luck met fate. Over the next few days many people in San Francisco and Oakland would now come to know the smell of death.

The city was without power for nearly a week. Residents regularly checked on one another to make sure everyone had food and water, or anything else. Fires broke out in the dozens during that time, many from candles and barbecues. The Marina, our little "LA by the Bay," suffered the worst in its heartbreaking destruction from the quake and fire. At one point, people carried water person by person. We were surrounded by water and there wasn't enough. Homes and lives were lost. The Marina, after all, is built on landfill, locals would muse with a knowing look in their eyes. It turns to Jello in earthquakes, we would always say to one another in school, like we were holders of occult knowledge, invisible swords hanging over neighborhoods that only we could see.

The Transamerica Pyramid suffered no damage in the earthquake.

Neighbors helped store owners board up shops over broken plate-glass windows. I saw a human chain form of residents, homeless, city workers, methadone clinic clients, all removing splintered wood and tossed furniture from a residence hotel near Howard Street to free people who were trapped inside. When the trapped people emerged, blinking and crying, covered in dust and streaked in filth, they were met with applause, hugs from strangers. Project Open Hand was a group of locals who delivered "meals with love" to AIDS victims too weak or impoverished to feed themselves. They knew what to do, and delivered food to earthquake survivors around the city.

You see it now. We have always taken care of each other.

This is what the city had always told its occupants from the first blood-soaked gold rush hundreds of years ago to the shattered survivors of each earthquake, and those who remained. It was as it had always been in this melting pot, taking in everyone no matter race or belief, gender or orientation, age or lineage, every immigrant no matter how poor or full of hope, every unwanted child and bastard and broken thing, every dreamer and fortune-seeker, no matter how wild or impossible the dream.

That's the thing about this city. You can't just be in it. No one just moves to San Francisco, though lots of people have, and they think it's just a spit of land to carve up or live on, but they're wrong. San Francisco is its own universe with its own rules. Outside rules are suspended. You can try to fight it or take it personally, but rules are rules. What this city asks is that you break out of other people's rules. To imagine yourself free. The rest is dream logic, the rules of a sleeping cat's subconscious wheeling between extremes.

The city became your story, part of your truth. If your heart of hearts depended on concealed weaknesses, untruths about your strength, she would shake you to your foundations and force you to come back strong and true.

The city knew that the future was born not in London or New York or Shanghai. It was born in San Francisco. Not through the birth of fantastical technologies, which we had, but through the soul-cracking labor of survival and our indelible web of compassion, united against everything that would prefer us erased.

I sat outside in darkness looking up at that younger sky, and understood what my traumas and this city had been trying to show me all along. That for some people, the city would only ever be loneliness and grey, but if you took the time to consider why all these different people had come here, the city would open up to you. No matter how cold it could be, you could think of the people who'd snuck into AIDS wards where even doctors feared, just to bring magazines to the dying; of immigrants who fled genocide to this sanctuary city; of homeless gutter punks who reach for the stars -- look in their eyes and this city will open up to you. Show you all her joys and oddities, rich and poor, tasteful and offensive, hidden gems and paper lanterns on crooked foggy streets, like an old friend. A mosaic of technologies and peoples that should never be together, but are.

I was still homeless, but I had a home.

35

I DIDN'T EXPECT that writing about being a homeless kid in San Francisco would turn into a true-crime investigation about myself -- one involving cocaine cartels and witness protection. I figured I'd have plenty to cover from experiencing my city's multi-decade homeless crisis firsthand; the AIDS epidemic when it was the number one cause of death for American males; and one of the most destructive earthquakes ever to hit a populated area of the United States. This book has been as capricious a storyteller as San Francisco herself.

Not everyone's stories ended here. Sadly, some did -- for me, at least.

Kenny's restaurant was closed from earthquake damage and we lost touch. Frank and Joey's cafe never reopened, and Frank's health worsened.

The couple eventually moved to a small apartment near City Hall and, for a few years, was the place to go for Thanksgiving.

We lost Terry during that time. It wouldn't be until 1996 that AIDS drugs breakthroughs meant diagnosis wasn't a death sentence. It was too late for so many. Those breakthroughs wouldn't have happened if it were not for the aggressive activism of ACT UP, the Stop AIDS Project, and other groups. I am grateful for my friends alive today, living (and in some cases, thriving) with HIV.

On the first Thanksgiving without Terry, I stayed late

knowing it would be my last for a while. I was in a lot of pain. Frank and I sat in a big chair together thumbing through their incredible collection of vintage LIFE magazines. I slipped him a $20 bill to contribute. It seemed like a fortune to me at the time. Jimmy was there, but we didn't talk.

I had to get out of town. I went back to Santa Cruz for a while thinking I might be able to stabilize in that creepy little beach town, where everything was so cheap. I didn't know where else to go. I lost touch with many people when I did that, and I regret it.

I was homeless on and off in Santa Cruz. I eventually found a cheap room to rent. Starting at five in the morning, I rode a bicycle several miles to and from work in a cafe every day. I ran an underground cafe out of my house on Sundays, much like I'd tried to do once before. It was popular, with lots of artists and writers coming by to drink too much stolen coffee and do spoken word performances in the evening.

One Sunday, Taylee showed up, surprising the hell out of me. No longer a skinhead, she was pregnant and said she was making her way back to Christ, along with the father of her baby who was also an ex-skinhead. Taylee asked if she could sleep on our couch. (I lived in yet another should-be-condemned house with nine housemates, and we had four ratty couches, each dragged in off the sidewalk.)

I let Taylee stay. After the cafe emptied out and we were alone that night, Taylee apologized to me for everything. I told her it was okay. She needed forgiveness and I gave it to her, because I believe what happened was not her fault. I never saw her again.

Working in a cafe for the rest of my life looked bleak, so I applied for financial aid to attend community college. With no high school diploma (and having not graduated ninth grade, twice) I was forced to take equivalency tests. Remedial math classes were required. I was denied financial aid because I had no proof of family. I remember trying to argue my case, telling the poor woman declining me that she should try to find my parents, because "I sure can't." It was the same thing I'd told Child Protective Services.

It didn't matter because everything quickly fell apart. A boyfriend convinced me to try and track down my mother, which, amazingly, I managed to do through the Yang family. My boyfriend was convinced mom and I could work it out.

She drove to meet me one afternoon. She was living in East Oakland, she said, running speed for a well-known group whose name I am omitting here. Her extra cash came from finding viable items in dumpsters and selling them at the Alameda Flea Market. She gave me her new phone number and a vintage Fisher Price toy she'd salvaged from the trash. She surprised me by giving me a phone number for her mother -- my maternal grandmother. Then she convinced me to loan her money to keep her phone line running. She promised she would pay me back.

I tried calling her phone number that night, and again over the next few days. It was bogus. I had stupidly "loaned" her all the money I'd saved for schoolbooks. I was forced to drop out.

According to what Striker Pierce Investigations discovered through research on this book, my mother's trail went cold in Oakland. Through SPI, I learned I am not legally related to my mother, and lack information such as her then-current identity's birth date. I have no "next of kin." I feel certain she is no longer alive, and I am okay with that.

Thanks to SPI and my journalism skill set, I finally understood what happened to me as a child. I knew the events of my mother's trips to South America, the DEA agents, new identities, and then, life on the run after she ditched witness protection, but I didn't know what any of it meant. I was just a little kid. Until writing this book, I did not know what happens when the federal government scrubs an identity. It's why my mother remains missing to this day. You cannot find someone who no longer exists.

After I saw my mother that last time, I cold-called my grandmother. She was living with her husband, a Coppola. They ran a restaurant of some kind at the California-Nevada border. She confirmed a relation to Edith Head and claimed, like my mother, that I was also related somehow to Nicolas Cage. I asked if I could come see them; she said yes. The following week a letter arrived in the mail. Her one-page, handwritten note said that they had disowned my mother and didn't want anything to do with her, or her life. She told me never to contact them again. Research for this book showed them to be deceased.

The same month my mother stole my school money, a male roommate began stalking me. None of my roommates believed me. He was breaking into my room and stealing my panties, following me, harassing me at work. That was my introduction to being stalked and having no one believe me, because he 'seemed okay' to them.

Terrified, I left Santa Cruz in the middle of the night.

Back home in San Francisco, I was on and off homeless yet again. I got re-hired locally at the corporate deli. While bussing dirty plates, glasses, and trash from a table one afternoon, a girl said, "Um, excuse me!" It was Ashley, and we hugged, despite my dirty apron. She told me something that, strangely, I knew the moment I hugged her. She was pregnant. He was a football player, and we laughed at the stereotype. Ashley was going to keep the baby and do the thing she was supposed to according to her upbringing and her parents, and I was happy for her, because she seemed happy with the new course of her life.

I eventually landed in a cheap flat on Divisadero. It was next to an occult bookstore, where I was hired and then managed the shop for years, working six days a week under the table, cash, without insurance. After work I'd hang out a couple blocks away at a punk rock recording studio built into an old Victorian -- Anne Rice's former home, where she wrote *The Vampire Lestat*. It was really spooky inside, and that was satisfying. The recording studio was called Razor's Edge, and I have fond memories of being fed by NOFX, among other generous people who worked and recorded there.

Managing Curious and Candles on Divisadero Street was my favorite job. The 28-year-old store was famous for many things. The dusty, ancient bookstore was packed with candles, hundreds of glass canisters of herbs, frogs in formaldehyde, forgotten spellbooks, jars of incense and oils, and a museum's worth of occult collectibles. It was the location scouted for the Magic Box in the TV series *Buffy The Vampire Slayer*. Jimmy Page came in and bought obscure Aleister Crowley books from us; Beastie Boy Adam Yauch bought Buddhist paraphernalia from me. Erotic dancers from Mitchell Brothers came in for money candles and tarot readings.

I loved it there. The store's packed bookshelves were floor to ceiling with dusty tomes on occultism, mysticism, religions of all kinds -- and I devoured them all. I could fill another book with the things I learned, the often-bizarre experiences I had there.

One very rainy night when I was in the shop alone, a barefoot and very dirty homeless man came in. He put a handful of wet change on the counter and asked if he had enough to get a frog. I decided he did, but I cautioned him that our frogs were both dead and in formaldehyde (reader: I was worried he would eat it). He said he knew, he knew. He didn't want a bag. I deposited the desiccated animal in his upturned palms, and he carefully carried it out into the rain, holding it aloft, smiling as he walked away.

San Francisco was home to a significant number of people who practiced New Orleans-style (and Haitian) voodoo, and Santeria. Our main customers were the many wonderful little old Black ladies who would come in and get their candles "dressed" (symbolically decorated) for various spells. OJ Simpson's mother came in and bought a case of "Just Judge" candles from me, dressed with symbols, powders, and oils. The candles were for her to burn for her son.

One afternoon two young Black women came in. I recognized her immediately.

It took everything I had not to rush to Rogue and hug her, cry. But I have grown cautious about former homeless kids and our need to cut off the past, so I held back, respectfully. Rogue looked beautiful; her hair was in a perfect relaxed bob. She asked if I remembered her, and I cried yes, and we hugged, and hugged some more. Rogue said that I'd apparently been dressing candles for her mother. I wondered how long Rogue knew I was here, but that was okay. The street teaches you that boundaries are what keep people whole, alive. And that respecting boundaries is one of the purest acts of love.

Rogue said she had a job doing stock at a "big box" store in the East Bay. She was living with her mother in the Lower Haight housing projects, but they had to move -- everyone there was being forcibly relocated, Rogue told me. She asked if I would make her a candle to help her and her mother to end up in a good place to live, because the authorities were moving them out of the city.

She came to Curious and Candles for one more candle after they moved. Rogue brought me a box of coffee cups she'd stolen from work as a present -- for my Sunday cafe. We talked about the housing projects she and her mother were evicted from. The entire city block along Haight Street went under quarantine after the residents were forced out. I saw they'd surrounded it with chain link fencing. Rogue said the rat problem was so bad inside the housing projects that demolition was a health risk to the rest of the neighborhood until they could exterminate them all.

I never saw Rogue after that, but she seemed happy in her new place with her mom. I keep that with me.

While working at the candle shop, my life changed again. It's where I was when my life intersected with technology (again); I began to work with industrial machine artists around the world, as well as becoming a sex educator, an author, and my involvement with the popular internet's beginnings, leading to hacking and security journalism. But that's another strange story, for another time.

In writing this book I put significant research and resources in fact-checking the past, and tried to find everyone. That includes my father. I was able to order my father's military records. He is dead; he died working as a desert park ranger who lived alone with a tabby cat. I could not find any living relatives on his side. It pained me to discover that his father also died alone, in a walk-up above a bar in Oakland (which was razed to make way for a Greyhound station). My Irish, Ireland-born grandfather died in that apartment of cirrhosis of the liver.

My father was a nuclear engineer for the US Navy, stationed in San Francisco, where he was born. He married my mother during Christmas when he was on leave. While he was overseas on a submarine, before I was born, he was notified by the military that his marriage to my mother was void, annulled. She didn't tell him she was already married to someone else. His records also revealed yet a different name used by my mother. My father had been receiving extra pay for his wife and child, and had to return the money. I was shocked to learn about my mother's other marriage and other name, and reader, I still have so many questions.

Writing this book made me miss my friends so much. I don't know what happened to Bozie, Jay, Aiden, John Gone, Joe, Lisa, or Jess, though I have looked everywhere for them, and still do. I never found Mark again.

The thing about being homeless is that it is very difficult to stop being homeless no matter how hard you want it. Getting off the streets is gradual, but you never stop feeling it. Looking back, it was when I worked at Curios and Candles that I first felt like I wasn't half a step away from homelessness all the time.

I often still feel like I'm pretending not to be a homeless person who's "faking it" so I can "pass" among normal people. My life is still marked by it in odd ways. At first, I couldn't sleep with my shoes off. Now I can't sleep with anything on my feet. I can't fall asleep unless I have a t-shirt over my face, and I sleep most comfortably when I'm completely buried, hidden under blankets, pillows, cloth on my face. I occasionally strip my life of unnecessary belongings "just in case."

Feeling like I "passed" took a period of adjustment. I hid my past and experiences on the streets for a very long time. I was mostly just worried about freaking people out, but I also found that people tended to treat me badly. When I do open up to someone close, it usually does freak them out. It's why I don't get too close to people.

This has gotten much more difficult in the past decade in San Francisco. The new friends I've made during the recent technology boom come from comfortable backgrounds, and have become very wealthy in a short amount of time. It has not made them better people. Let's just say that when you tell a newly-minted millionaire you'd love to get that new phone, or join them for dinner, but it's not in your budget, and they treat you like it's your fault, you know you have one less friend. I'm good with boundaries like that.

A few years ago, the publisher of one of my sexuality books talked me into doing a book signing. It was in Upper Haight, at The Booksmith. While sitting at a table signing books, I glanced at the doorway and commented to a shop employee that it was so weird to be sitting inside, doing this. She asked me what I meant. I took a risk and told her I used to sit outside the store and ask for spare change. It turned out I was confessing to one of the bookstore's owners. She asked if I would come back and attend an in-store event they were doing; it was for outreach between homeless services for teens, and the neighborhood's residents and merchants. To build bridges, to engender understanding. I said yes.

The event was packed. In the front of the room sat outreach workers from Larkin Street Youth Services, and others. I sat in the audience and watched the outreach workers come under fire from the neighborhood's residents, facing wave after wave of anger, disgust, and hate for homeless kids. Repudiating the very people trying to help youth in need. It was everything I'd had directed at me on the streets as a kid. The workers kept their cool while being interrupted and shouted at, and patiently tried to explain what the kids were going through, how on-the-ground services helped them, and the basics of harm reduction.

It reached an unbearable point for me. I began to raise my hand, speak up, then jump in. I spoke from my experiences, and explained how harm reduction services, like Larkin Street's, likely saved my life. I spoke to the residents from a compassionate place and made myself open to their questions.

After the event, the outreach workers surrounded me and peppered me with questions. One said, "We thought you ... we thought someone sent you to help us." No, I said, I'm just evidence that your work is real. An older women with silver hair said, "Oh," and smiled. "I remember you now." We hugged.

I went back for another event at The Booksmith. This time, I'd be 'onstage' with a young homeless girl who lived outside on Haight Street and had been invited to participate. Up there with us was an older man who said he was a formerly homeless, hippie beatnik in North Beach. The girl was visibly nervous, scared, as the room filled up. I told her, "I won't let them be shitty to you. If they fuck with you, let me deal with them." She relaxed a little.

She was right to be worried. The neighborhood's older residents seemed to romanticize the man's story of "bumming around" in Little Italy, yet directed rage at the girl. Well, let's just say they tried.

I remained calm but firm. I took the brunt of all of it. I saw their anger as opportunities to tell them things they didn't know, like the limited beds for homeless and the wait to get one night in them. The immense roadblocks posed by the simple fact there was no safe place to use a shower. That you can't get tampons with food stamps. We ended up having a giant group discussion, and because of The Booksmith, I think people left that night changed in positive ways. The homeless girl told me "thank you" and then said she was sorry for not saying very much. I hugged her and told her she was perfect.

San Francisco still has a homeless calamity on its hands. The United Nations recently declared San Francisco's homeless crisis a "violation of human rights." Sleeping in Buena Vista Park all those years ago, circled by mansions and soaring views of the Golden Gate, I wondered how it could be possible we starved in the dirt while the most fantastic technologies fueled the heart of a shining future being made all around us. Now I wonder how it can be so much worse. And how we can be reliving pandemic history like a recurring nightmare, where the federal government abandons us to a horrific virus, yet again.

When I hit my head, the world I was in cracked open, threatened to swallow me in a morass of dark memories, abandonment, betrayal, loss, pain, and loneliness. Instead, I chose to become something else. Maybe I would never know my family. Yet others had found me, chose me, and loved me truly, deeply, loyally, in ways the real strangers, my relatives, could not. Would not. Adults who were entrusted to protect me had betrayed that trust, but others had emerged to bring me to my knees with their generosity and kindness, nullifying the power that pain once held over me. Punk, 'zines, and art had extended an invitation for me to be a citizen of a larger world, to question the powerful, and when possible, to fight for those who could not. Even when that person who needed someone to stand up for them was me, for myself. Especially then.

REFERENCES

SAN FRANCISCO

- "Article 10 Landmark District | Duboce Park Landmark District," SF Planning Commission, December 5, 2012, http://commissions. sfplanning.org/hpcpackets/2011.0683L.pdf
- "Western Addition: A Basic History," Gary Kamiya, excerpt: "Cool Gray City of Love", 2013, http://www.foundsf.org/index. php?title=Western_Addition%3A_A_Basic_History
- "African American Segregation in San Francisco," Roz Murray, 2015, http://www.foundsf.org/index.php?title= African_American_Segregation_in_San_Francisco
- "Fillmore Redevelopment" Found SF, photographs 1959-1961, http://www.foundsf.org/index.php? title=Fillmore_Redevelopmen
- "Public Housing," Josh Alperin, 2008, http://www.foundsf.org/ index.php?title=PUBLIC_HOUSING
- "Fillmore Revisited — How Redevelopment Tore Through the Western Addition," Rachel Brahinsky, Sep 23, 2019, https:// sfpublicpress.org/news/2019-09/fillmore-revisited-how-redevelopment-tore-through-the-western-addition
- "Is desegregation dead?" Heather Knight, Nov 24, 2017, https:// www.sfchronicle.com/schools-desegregation/
- "School Desegregation: The San Francisco Unified School District and the Consent Decree of 1983," Carnegie Mellon University Computer Club, 2005 http://www.club.cc.cmu.edu/~scu/8202/desegregation_sfusd.htm

- "As Courts Flip-Flopped on School Integration, Diversity Has Remained Elusive," Sanne Bergh and Paul Lorgerie, Feb 5, 2015, https://sfpublicpress.org/news/2015-02/as-courts-flip-flopped-on-school-integration-diversity-has-remained-elusive

- "ALHS Oral History Project Interview Transcription," Abraham Lincoln High School, Bill Mustanich, May 9, 2012, http://www.alhsoralhistoryproject.org/word_press/home/lincoln-alumni-oral-histories/bill-mustanich/

- "San Francisco's Sunset District Experiences an Architectural Renaissance," Dara Kerr, Dec 10, 2012, http://www.californiahomedesign.com/gallery/san-francisco-s-sunset-district-experiences-architectural-renaissance

- "Your Neighborhood SLA Bank Robbery," Alex Bevk, Aug 27, 2012, https://sf.curbed.com/2012/8/27/10335478/your-neighborhood-sla-bank-robbery

- "Terror in Little Saigon, A. C. Thompson, November 3, 2013, https://www.pbs.org/wgbh/frontline/article/terror-in-little-saigon-2/

- "Little Saigon district thrives in San Francisco," Ken McLaughlin, January 25, 2009, https://www.eastbaytimes.com/2009/01/25/little-saigon-district-thrives-in-san-francisco/

- "1989 Online Earthquake Exhibit," Oral histories, http://www.sfmuseum.org/1906/89.html

- "San Francisco is Burning," Jon Ronson, June 22, 2017, https://www.gq.com/story/san-francisco-is-burning

- "San Francisco in the 1980s," KRON-TV video series, 1997, https://diva.sfsu.edu/collections/sfbatv/bundles/227153

PUNK

- "From Disco To Punk, Remembering The I-Beam," Camden Avery, August 3, 2014, http://hoodline.com/2014/08/flashback-remembering-the-i-beam

- "7 Modern Day Zine Makers on Empowerment, Resistance, and the Post-Internet Zine Renaissance," Alex Wong, February 05, 2018, https://thehundreds.com/blogs/content/7-modern-day-zine-makers-on-empowerment-resistance-post-internet-zine-renaissance

- "Review: Turn It Around: The Story of East Bay Punk," Ken Korman, Sep 8, 2017, https://www.bestofneworleans.com/thelatest/archives/2017/09/08/review-turn-it-around-the-story-of-east-bay-punk

- "The List: A Low-Budget Newsletter Keeping Punx Connected Since 1990," Jessica Lipsky, Apr 26, 2018, https://www.kqed.org/arts/13830408/going-strong-since-1990-this-low-budget-newsletter-is-a-punk-institution

- "Powell Street Punks," Oral Histories: "Gimme Something Better", 2010, http://gimmesomethingbetter.com/excerpts/powell-street-punks

- "Skate and Destroy," Oral Histories: "Gimme Something Better", 2010, http://gimmesomethingbetter.com/excerpts/skate-and-destroy

- "Shred of Dignity," Oral Histories: "Gimme Something Better", 2010, http://gimmesomethingbetter.com/excerpts/shred-of-dignity

- "Peace Punks," Oral Histories: "Gimme Something Better", 2010, http://gimmesomethingbetter.com/excerpts/peace-punks

LGBTQ

- "The gayest cook in the Castro," Jonathan Kauffman, October 16, 2017, https://www.sfchronicle.com/food/article/The-gayest-cook-in-the-Castro-12281983.php

- "Today Is Reagan's Birthday! His Administration Laughed Off Thousands of AIDS Deaths," R. S. Benedict, February 6, 2016, https://hornetapp.com/stories/ronald-reagan-birthday/

- "San Francisco closes homosexual clubs because of AIDS," Robert Strand, Oct. 9, 1984, https://www.upi.com/Archives/1984/10/09/San-Francisco-closes-homosexual-clubs-because-of-AIDS/3788466142400/

- "Bay Area Reporter," Internet Archive scans, Volume 19, Number 41, October 12, 1989

- "Bay Area Reporter," Internet Archive scans, Volume 19, Number 42, October 19, 1989

- "Bay Area Reporter," Internet Archive scans, Volume 19, Number 46, November 16, 1989

- "Bay Area Reporter," Internet Archive scans, Volume 19, Number 48, November 30, 1989

- "At the Height of AIDS, San Francisco's Queer Nightlife Became a Refuge," , Marke B., February 15, 2019, https://www.them.us/story/san-francisco-queer-nightlife-80s-90s

COCAINE

- "The Fall and Rise of Cocaine," Mike Vigil, April 22, 2016, https://www.thecipherbrief.com/the-fall-and-rise-of-cocaine
- "Cocaine, the Military and Shining Path 1980-1995," Pablo G. Dreyfus, September 1998, https://pdfs.semanticscholar.org/244f/63843e0b0331a49fb60b506d4553cc3d1ef9.pdf
- "The "War on Coca" in Peru: An Examination of the 1980s and 1990s U.S. "Supply Side" Policies," Kelsey Hutchinson, Spring 2009, http://www.wou.edu/history/files/2015/08/Kelsey-Hutchinson-HST-499.pdf
- "Peruvian Cocaine and the Boomerang of History," Paul Gootenberg, June 17, 2014, https://nacla.org/article/peruvian-cocaine-and-boomerang-history

HOMELESSNESS

- "Did Reagan's Crazy Mental Health Policies Cause Today's Homelessness?", Joel John Roberts, Oct 14, 2013, http://www.povertyinsights.org/2013/10/14/did-reagans-crazy-mental-health-policies-cause-todays-homelessness/
- "Polytechnic High School's Gynmasiums Still Standing Strong", Alex Bevk, Jan 11, 2013, https://sf.curbed.com/2013/1/11/10286362/polytechnic-high-schools-gynmasiums-still-standing-strong
- "Larkin Street Youth Services The First 25 Years,"Text by William F. Campbe, 2009, https://larkinstreetyouth.org/larkin-street-youth-services-the-first-25-years/
- "Ronald Reagan's shameful legacy: Violence, the homeless, mental illness," Dr. E. Fuller Torrey, Sept 29, 2013, https://www.salon.com/2013/09/29/

ronald_reagans_shameful_legacy_violence_the_homeless_mental_illness/

- "Trump Says Homeless Californians Are Ruining Cities' 'Prestige'," Sarah Ruiz-Grossman, 09/17/2019, https://www.huffpost.com/entry/trump-california-homeless-prestige_n_5d813ef4e4b05f8fb6eef4de

- "UN expert: San Francisco's homelessness crisis is a human rights violation and suggests 'a cruelty that is unsurpassed'," Aria Bendix, Nov 12, 2018, https://www.businessinsider.com/un-expert-san-francisco-homeless-cruelty-2018-11

- "San Francisco Tech Billionaires Go to War over Homelessness," Adam Rogers, Nitasha Tiku October 29, 2018, https://www.wired.com/story/san-francisco-tech-billionaires-war-over-homelessness/

- "Alice's life on the sidewalk ends with a dignified death," Heather Knight, Feb 27, 2018, https://www.sfchronicle.com/news/article/Alice-s-life-on-the-sidewalk-ends-with-a-12710768.php

- "After Homelessness: One Former Haight Street Kid's Story," Jennie Butler, April 28, 2015, https://hoodline.com/2015/04/after-homelessness-one-former-haight-street-kid-s-story

OTHER

- "In the Footsteps of a Killer," Michelle McNamara, February 27, 2013, http://www.lamag.com/longform/in-the-footsteps-of-a-killer/2/

- "San Francisco Child Abuse Prevention Center: History," https://safeandsound.org/about-us/history/

- "Diary of a concussion," Elizabeth Lopatto, Sep 27, 2017, https://www.theverge.com/2017/9/27/16086018/concussion-diary-brain-injury-recovery-symptoms
- "Postconcussive Syndrome Psychiatric Care: Background, Pathophysiology, Epidemiology," Roy H Lubit, MD, PhD; Chief Editor: David Bienenfeld, MD, Jul 25, 2019, https://emedicine.medscape.com/article/292326-overview
- "Atari's Hard-Partying Origin Story: An Oral History," Adam Fisher, July 6, 2018, https://medium.com/s/story/ataris-hard-partying-origin-story-an-oral-history-c438b0ce9440
- "State agency blasts San Jose foster care provider Unity Care for failures with high-risk youth," Julia Prodis Sulek, March 23, 2019, https://www.eastbaytimes.com/2019/03/23/san-jose-state-moves-to-revoke-licenses-of-unity-care-foster-homes-citing-poor-care/

BOOKS

- *Talbot, David. Season of the Witch*
- *Asbury, Herbert. The Barbary Coast*
- *Riggin, Lisa. San Francisco's Queen of Vice*
- *Coyote, Peter. Sleeping Where I Fall*
- Toobin, Jeffrey. *American Heiress*
- *Dr. Weirde's Guide to Mysterious San Francisco by Dr. Weirde*
- *Evans, Galbraith, Law. Tales from the San Francisco Cacophony Society*
- *San Francisco's Castro by Strange de Jim*
- *Mau Dicker, Laverne. The Chinese in San Francisco*

ACKNOWLEDGMENTS

I owe a debt of deepest gratitude and enduring admiration to Striker Pierce Investigations who dedicated their time, ingenuity, research expertise, and personal sensitivity to doing everything possible to find what pieces of my childhood and family history were left to be found, and for the patience and emotional sensitivity shared when we did (or did not) find answers. Thank you for your work to help homeless kids. And especially: Thank you Brian O'Shea.

This book was only possible because every community that intersects my life showed up for me when I needed them most.

The blood, sweat, and tears of its creation were possible with the encouragement, willingness to test read, and generosity of Patreon supporters who kept the lights on in my apartment while reading every word and never giving up on me -- 76 in total. I would especially like to thank Bernard Lyons, Preston Rittenhouse, Lisa C., M. Wild, Charles Lewis III, Kris Jones, Rob Funk, Spiffy Voxel, David Stanley, Scott Simmons, Andrew Minkof, Chris K, Steven, Rudy, Mike, Geoff Campbell, Chris Willmore, Mike Bennett, and Geoffrey Meyers.

This book is in your eyes, hands, and heart now thanks to the kindness, belief, and support of its 513 Kickstarter backers. My deep gratitude for bringing this project across the Kickstarter finish line and into the world goes to: Cecilia Tan, Patricia Elzie-Tuttle, Ariel Waldman, Kurt Collins (@TimeSync), Andrew, Addie Chernow, Deviant Ollam ツ,

Mike Bennett, Jon Callas, C.C. Chapman, Tod Beardsley, Andrew Pam, SteveD3, Gene Ha, Matt Harris, Karel P Kerezman, Rick Wagner, DLTQ, Leslie Rosenberg, GA and BKF Smith, Emily Dare, Kaos, Bill Weiss, Philip LaRose, Diana J. Brodie, Blake Barrett, Sarah Heile, Brendan, godzero, Oonagh, Tess Arnold, Kevin Sonney, Ashley Niblock, Eugen Neuber, JV Cake, Ello Skelling, Ben Hahl, David Banks & Family, Matthew Walker, Ev Maus, lcj in memory of aje, Ansi.sys(x86), MC, Sal Manzo, Rick Timkovich, Luke Yin, Angel Hall, J. Toffaletti, snark, joshing.skull, Neil James Reda, John Norman (in memoriam), Matt Harris, Jamie Gump, Phosphor Wulf, Johannes Ehrenthal, Moto Ashmore, Mark Johnston, Gustavo Felisberto, Pedro Rodrigues, malpertuis, Apurva Desai, Harvey Simmons, Vincenzo Lombardi, Elizabeth McClellan, Seb, Ben Romer, stakyman, Dan Ellingsen, and Paul Rogers.

My friends and chosen family held me up when the heartbreak of researching and writing this memoir was almost too heavy to bear, and without even trying, continue to remind me what it means to never be alone. I love you Scotland, Ariel, Phillip, Limor, Luna, Patricia, Nicole, JWZ, Richard Kadrey, Anneke, Sean, Richie Nakano, Midori, Eve Batey, Tim Ehalt, Tadd S., Andrew Blair Hawkins, Tom Tomorrow, and the incredible Mental Health and Horror community. Mikl, I wish you could've seen this.

Finally, I know they won't read this, but I wouldn't have made it through this book, the continuing pandemic, or anything else without the loyal and loving companionship of the cat who owns my heart, Max, a space shared by his sweet "little" brother, Sam.

ABOUT THE AUTHOR

Violet Blue® (violetblue.com) is an investigative journalist on hacking and cybercrime, as well as a prolific author and editor, and a five-time Independent Publisher Book Awards ("IPPY") winner. She is a noted columnist, having bylined for outlets including *O The Oprah Magazine, Financial Times, CNN, CBS News, CNET, The San Francisco Chronicle, Popular Science,* and many others. *Guardian UK* called Ms. Blue, "One of the leading figures in tech writing in the world." She is a member of the Internet Press Guild and an Advisor to online legal privacy resource Without My Consent.

Ms. Blue's most notable book appearance was on *The Oprah Winfrey Show* in an episode dedicated to the subject matter of her book about women and pornography, and was featured and praised by Ms. Winfrey on the show (as well as twice in *O Magazine*). Blue's books have been translated into French, German, Italian, Spanish, and Russian.

CPSIA information can be obtained
at www.ICGtesting.com
Printed in the USA
LVHW010806270723
753441LV00001B/6